When God Spoke Greek

WHEN GOD SPOKE GREEK

The Septuagint and the Making of the Christian Bible

TIMOTHY MICHAEL LAW

OXFORD
UNIVERSITY PRESS

OXFORD

UNIVERSITY PRESS

Oxford University Press is a department of the University of Oxford.
It furthers the University's objective of excellence in research, scholarship,
and education by publishing worldwide.

Oxford   New York

Auckland   Cape Town   Dar es Salaam   Hong Kong   Karachi
Kuala Lumpur   Madrid   Melbourne   Mexico City   Nairobi
New Delhi   Shanghai   Taipei   Toronto

With offices in

Argentina   Austria   Brazil   Chile   Czech Republic   France   Greece
Guatemala   Hungary   Italy   Japan   Poland   Portugal   Singapore
South Korea   Switzerland   Thailand   Turkey   Ukraine   Vietnam

Oxford is a registered trademark of Oxford University Press
in the UK and certain other countries.

Published in the United States of America by
Oxford University Press
198 Madison Avenue, New York, NY 10016

Library of Congress Cataloging-in-Publication Data
Law, T. M. (Timothy Michael), 1979–
When God spoke Greek : the Septuagint and the making of the Christian
Bible / Timothy Michael Law.
pages cm
Includes bibliographical references and index.
ISBN 978-0-19-978172-0 (pbk. : alk. paper) – ISBN 978-0-19-978171-3
(cloth : alk. paper)
1. Bible. O.T. Greek–Versions–Septuagint.   2. Bible. N.T.–Criticism,
interpretation, etc.   3. Bible. O.T. Greek–History.   4. Bible.
O.T.–Influence–Civilization, Western.   I. Title.
BS744.L39 2013
221.4'8–dc23
2012045781

5 7 9 8 6
Printed in the United States of America
on acid-free paper

To Elizabeth Rose,
whose life was just beginning
when I wrote the first word in this book

Contents

Acknowledgments

I AM INDEBTED to many colleagues and friends who encouraged me along the way, and in particular to Alison Salvesen and her family. Karen Jobes wrote an article for a confessional publication entitled "When God Spoke Greek," and I'm grateful she was happy I borrowed her title. I wake up each morning eager to work with the team at the *Marginalia Review of Books* family, the most creative and exciting people with whom I've ever partnered. Charles Halton, David Lincicum, and Angela Erisman are daily e-conversation partners. I am also in debt to Joel Watts, who efficiently prepared the index; to Christopher M. Hays for his advice on many points; and to Faimon Roberts and Kyle McDaniel, who for some reason care about what I write. Ed Gallagher and Michael Graves read substantial portions of the draft of this book and were good sports in debate. Michael in particular has had a big influence on my ideas of Jerome, particularly on the Jerome-Augustine correspondence. He has now posted on his faculty webpage some of his ideas from his seminars, so the ambitious reader can see where he and I converge and diverge. I am also thankful to the Alexander von Humboldt Foundation and to my first friends in Germany, where I finished this book. These first friends are special to me because they enthusiastically cheered me on to the finish line: Richard, Sana, Marrija, Svetlana, Kevin (ABBQB), Estefanía, Katarina, and Zyad. Finally, highest gratitude is reserved for my wife and daughter. They were proud of this book from the first day, and it is appropriately dedicated to my Elizabeth.

@TMichaelLaw
April 4, 2013
Göttingen

When God Spoke Greek

I

Why This Book?

YOU HAVE PROBABLY encountered the Septuagint already. You may never have heard of it, but the Septuagint will have made its way to you if you have read or so much as glanced at a Bible. The names of some of the books in the Old Testament come from titles given to these books in Septuagint manuscripts: *genesis* is the Greek word for beginning, *exodos* for going out, *leuitikon* notes the book contains material about the Levites, and *deuteronomion* comes from the Greek translator's interpretation of Deuteronomy 17:18, which in Hebrew reads "a copy of this teaching" but which the translator understood to mean a repetition of the Law. He thus translated this phrase "second Law," which is the meaning of Deuteronomion or, as we know it, Deuteronomy. The beloved children's story of Joseph's coat of many colors is also found in the Septuagint. In Genesis 37:3, the Hebrew Bible indicates that Joseph wore a coat that covered his arms and legs and was in some ways ornamented, but the Septuagint and later the Latin Vulgate describe the coat as "multicolored." Footnotes in modern English versions also mention the Greek Old Testament where the translation committee believed the Septuagint offered a better reading than the Hebrew Bible upon which the English is for the most part based. Neither have readers of the New Testament escaped the Septuagint's reach. Apart from the numerous quotations of the Old Testament in the New, which were almost entirely from the Greek, the language and theology of the New Testament writers are indebted far more to the Septuagint than to the Hebrew Bible. Consequently, the Septuagint plays a critical role in the history of Christian theology and exegesis.

Every week millions of the faithful around the world gather to teach, to read, and to hear the Bible. Although Christians have always found it difficult to know how the Jewish scriptures they call Old Testament are relevant, they are familiar with the famous stories of creation, flood, and wilderness sojourning; with characters like Noah, Moses, Abraham, and Ezekiel; and with events like the Golden Calf episode, Israel's conquest of the Promised Land, and David versus Goliath. Yet fewer will have reflected on how these stories came into being or how the biblical books as we know them were formed. At best, many readers of this tremendous book we now call "the Bible" assume that writers like Jeremiah sat down one sunny afternoon and jotted down his prophecy, dispatched it, and then went about his way. But the biblical books were formed after a long process of accumulation, combination, and reformulation of other sources. For a long time it was easy to discard these explanations as examples of navel-gazing in the academy or, worse, of the designs of unbelieving scholars to destroy the believer's confidence in the Bible. The theories of the prehistory of the biblical texts were based largely on the scholar's intuition from close reading, but there was no tangible proof in the form of textual artifacts in Hebrew. Only one manuscript tradition of the Hebrew scriptures existed, and it matched the Hebrew Bible of modern editions and therefore the modern English translations. In the absence of Hebrew sources to verify their hypotheses, scholars pointed to the ancient versions of the Hebrew Bible. The Greek translation known as the Septuagint was central to the discussion, since numerous passages stood at odds with the Hebrew. Commentators suggested that the Septuagint illuminates a lost part of the history of the formation of the Old Testament, that the Greek translation actually shows us different stages of the Hebrew text long before it reached its final form. Nonetheless, since the authoritative text for Protestant churches has been the Hebrew Bible for half a millennium, it was easy for many to dismiss these hypotheses and to imagine instead that the Hebrew Bible found in the medieval manuscripts, and now in a modern edition easily purchased in a bookshop, came from the pens of the biblical authors. The divergences noted in the Septuagint could be explained easily: the translators were creative or they didn't understand the Hebrew before them, but the Greek translation in no way provides evidence of another form of the Hebrew text in antiquity. There was only ever one.

And then suddenly everything changed. The discoveries in the Judean Desert in the middle of the twentieth century revolutionized our understanding of the Bible's history or, better, its prehistory (see Chapter 3). Out from the dark, dank caves around the Dead Sea, Hebrew biblical manuscripts were brought into the light. One of the first things researchers recognized was that many of these manuscripts were different from the received Hebrew Bible, and in some cases they even agreed with those divergent Septuagint passages. Perhaps the Septuagint translators were *not* responsible for the differences in the biblical text; maybe they were translating other Hebrew texts after all. For many who had insisted on the authority of the Hebrew Bible, the most uncomfortable realization was that these Hebrew manuscripts appeared to reflect earlier stages of the biblical books. The argument against scholarly reconstructions and hypotheses suddenly lost its breath. Here was real, hold-in-your-hands proof that some biblical books once existed in a different form.

Even so, the Septuagint remains foreign to most, including biblical scholars, indeed even Old Testament scholars. Those footnotes in English versions often treat the Septuagint as the stepchild of the received Hebrew Bible and reference the Greek only whenever something appears to have gone wrong in the transmission of the Hebrew text. Some continue to explain the radical divergences between the Septuagint and the Hebrew Bible as evidence that the Greek translators used nonstandard, or non-canonical, forms of the Hebrew, even though we know a canonical Hebrew Bible did not exist until several centuries after the Septuagint was translated. There are modern theological biases that keep the Septuagint at bay.

It is apparent how revolutionary the discovery of the Dead Sea Scrolls and the new appreciation for the Septuagint has been for scholars and students of the Hebrew Bible, or the Old Testament, but even the study of the New Testament and early Christianity has been affected. Many have never considered the Septuagint's role in the early years of the Church and in the formation of early Christian theology. The prejudice in the contemporary Church in favor of the rabbinic Hebrew Bible is startling, but not unexpected given that Christian educational institutions teach future scholars and clergy the Old Testament exclusively from the Hebrew Bible, relegating the Septuagint to the sidelines of an upper-level elective course. Students thus graduate from schools that teach Christian history and theology without ever considering that the scriptures used by the New Testament writers and the first Old Testament of the Church is not the Hebrew Bible they spent time and money to study.

Should You Continue Reading?

I am indebted throughout this book to the standard Septuagint introduction textbooks and the ones that have been most helpful to me through the years are mentioned in Further Reading. Jennifer Dines always had the right expression in her introductory text, and Natalio Fernández Marcos took the study of the Septuagint to new heights with his advanced level introduction. I am likewise indebted to the voluminous work on the

Septuagint that has appeared especially in the last couple of decades from the fields of Jewish studies, biblical studies, and early Christian studies and more particularly from the small field of Septuagint studies. This book contains my own insights and original ideas at many points, but I have also attempted to take what is already known and to explain it more clearly to those who are interested in the history of the Bible and in its use in the early centuries of the Christian Church but who may never have considered the Septuagint's role in that story. The study of the Septuagint is perhaps more exciting now at the beginning of the twenty-first century than it has been in a very long time, but we who call ourselves specialists in this field have not communicated very well to those outside of our societies. It is possible that the new interest in translating the Septuagint into modern languages—there are translations now in most of the European languages and even one in Japanese!—will go some way toward popularizing the Greek Scriptures. I have also discovered during the course of writing this book that it is much easier to continue talking to scholars in our private scholarly language (not quite the tongues of angels) than it is to take scholarly language and break it down for the benefit of even more readers. In short, I have written this book because my mother still asks what I do for a living, and my father knows but still gets tripped up on the final syllable of *Sep-tu-a-gint*.

Should you keep reading? There are at least four reasons why you may find what follows interesting. First, the Septuagint sheds light on the development of Jewish thought between the third century BCE and the first century CE. Others like Tessa Rajak (see Further Reading) have demonstrated the value of the Septuagint for our understanding of Hellenistic Judaism, but little reflection has been devoted to the importance of the Septuagint for understanding the New Testament and early Christianity. As we shall discover, the New Testament cannot be read apart from its context in Hellenistic Judaism, and one comes closer to understanding that context by reading the Septuagint. For these reasons, this book will not explore the exciting terrain covered by Rajak but will stay close to the Septuagint in the Christian story.

Second, the Old Testament translation of almost every modern English version of the Bible is based on the Hebrew Bible, but the form of scripture used by the New Testament authors and the early Church was most often the Septuagint. I devote several chapters to the use of the Septuagint in the New Testament and the early Church, and without complicating the issue I hope also to demonstrate that access to the scriptures in the first centuries CE was not as simple as we might expect. Nonetheless, the forms of scripture used by the New Testament authors is an important question, and Augustine and others throughout history argued that if the New Testament authors used the Septuagint, the Church ought to affirm its authority as well. Moreover, the creation of the concept of an "Old Testament" by the New Testament authors and early Christians depended almost entirely on the availability of these scriptures in Greek for a Mediterranean world that was predominantly Greek. In the first century, a religion's claim to antiquity could guarantee respect. The new Greek writings about the life and ministry of Jesus and of the early years of the Church—those soon collected and called the New Testament— needed to be seen as the continuation of a more ancient story. Christianity was not new on the scene, they wanted to say, but had roots in the days of the patriarchs. The Septuagint, the Greek Jewish scriptures, allowed early Christians to claim a historic heritage. To be sure, they could have told this message even if the Jewish scriptures had remained in Hebrew and Aramaic through their own ad hoc translations or commentaries on the text, but the potential for the Church's expansion increased exponentially when they had this ancient story of Israel available in the language of the Mediterranean world.

The third reason for the Septuagint's importance is that not only did most of the earliest Christians use the Septuagint but also their theology was explicitly shaped by it and not by the Hebrew Bible. Many of the most beloved teachings of the New Testament are shaped by and in some cases directly derived from the Septuagint, so one is justified to ask what would have filled their places had the Hebrew Bible been the basis for the New Testament writers. Matthew wrote about the prophecy of the virgin birth, which he found explicit in the Septuagint, not in the Hebrew Bible, and the most theologically important book in the history of Christianity, Paul's epistle to the Romans, has been influenced entirely by the Greek version of Isaiah, not by the Hebrew version. The use of the Greek scriptures continues after the first century, and the early Church developed its central doctrines through contact with the Septuagint. One cannot imagine the development of orthodoxy without it. So in the most formative period of Christian theology, when the early Church framed many of those beliefs now taken for granted by Christians worldwide, their thoughts were molded not by the Hebrew Bible that underlies our modern English Bibles but by the Greek Septuagint. None of this would be terribly significant if the Septuagint were *merely* a translation of the Hebrew, as some have taken pains to assert; as we shall see, however, the Septuagint in many places contains a spectacularly different message. This is not only because the translators of the Septuagint books created new meanings in their translation but also for another more shocking reason altogether. And that's the fourth reason that the Septuagint is significant.

The Septuagint often preserves a witness to an *alternative*, sometimes *older*, form of the Hebrew text. When the Reformers and their predecessors talked about returning to the original Hebrew (*ad fontes!*), and when modern Christians talk about studying the Hebrew because it is the "original text," they are perpetuating in those statements several mistaken assumptions. The Hebrew Bible in the editions we now use is often *not* the oldest form of the Hebrew text, and in fact it is not a singular text at all but an amalgamation of similar though not identical sources. In many cases the Septuagint provides the only access we have to the oldest form. Our modern editions of the Hebrew Bible contain a text that was more or less established in the second century CE, and while textual traditions for some of the books go back to the third and possibly even the fifth century BCE, their text is from only one of the traditions known and used by readers of scripture in ancient times. It is now indisputable that the Hebrew Bible is part of a different tradition from the biblical texts known in other sources. The Septuagint has truly upended the simple picture with which we have become acquainted.

There is more in the following pages. I begin by explaining the ancient contexts of the Bible and of the translation of the Hebrew Bible into Greek. I then attempt to clarify the bewildering story of the diversity of biblical texts found among the famous Dead Sea Scrolls. The story is more interesting when the books of the Septuagint are surveyed, and we discover that the Greek Bible continues this trend of diversity and that many of the books we know so well through the Hebrew Bible's translation into English are different in Greek. The Apocrypha is an important part of our story, not only because it is a collection of books known to more than one billion Christians outside of the Protestant tradition but also because it was influential to the New Testament writers and the early Church.

It is at this point that many readers will discover for the first time how Christianity is indebted to the Septuagint. The New Testament authors almost always used the Septuagint to access the Jewish scriptures they so often quote. Examples from the Gospels, from the apostle Paul, and from the writer of Hebrews demonstrate that the Greek Septuagint had a profound impact on the development of New Testament thought. Whether or not they were aware of the divergences between the Septuagint and the Hebrew Bible is irrelevant, as is whether or not they thought that the Septuagint's authority was based on the Hebrew. Whether consciously or not, they were transmitting a message based on a theological reading of the Jewish scriptures that was often different from the Hebrew Bible's message. We can also see that the New Testament authors sometimes use Septuagint readings we know to be mistranslations of the Hebrew, an unsettling reality but a reality nonetheless. I then try to demonstrate how the Septuagint lies at the foundations of Christianity, even though two later branches of Christianity, Catholicism and Protestantism, left it behind. In light of the proven diversity of the Hebrew and Greek forms of scripture in the ancient period, in the time of the New Testament, and in the Patristic age, we may ask in the Postscript why the role of the Septuagint has been diminished in modern Christian thought.

Some Definitions and Notes on Use

It is important in a book like this to define some key concepts from the outset. I refer often to the *scriptures*, or *scriptural text(s)*, which are authoritative texts in a religious community. Their appearance in individual scrolls and manuscripts and the diversity of the forms of the individual books is different from what is usually assumed by the term *Bible*. For most contemporary readers, the Bible implies a closed collection of books, each with a fixed form, and neither the form of the books nor the contents of the Bible can be changed. We often refer to this as the *canon*. The term *Hebrew Bible* will refer to the canonical form of the Hebrew scriptures more or less established by the second century CE. It is sometimes called the "rabbinic Hebrew Bible" since scholars date its formation and imagine its sociological context to be that of the time of the budding rabbinic movement after the fall of Jerusalem and the destruction of the Temple in 70 CE. Often in the scholarly literature the actual text of the Hebrew Bible is called the *Masoretic Text*, but the Masoretic Text is a group of similar manuscripts, not a single text. The Tiberian Masoretes were medieval editors who finalized the Hebrew text found in all modern editions of the Hebrew Bible. They transmitted an ancient type of text, but its final form is indeed very late, about a millennium after the time of Jesus. In this book, however, I will refer to the Masoretic Text as the Hebrew Bible, asking scholars for the permission to simplify. In only a few cases where it was absolutely necessary did I have to use "Masoretic Text," and these mainly appear in

Chapter 3. The most important term in this book is *Septuagint*, which is an unsatisfactory name as well. Like "Bible," Septuagint is usually taken to mean a closed collection of Greek biblical books, but our earliest complete Greek Bible manuscripts are dated to the fourth century. So when I say, for example, that the New Testament authors used the Septuagint, I am fully aware of the complexities of identifying the original Septuagint and its revisions and of the fact that before the fourth century Jews and Christians would not have been carrying to their debates two calf-skin leather Bibles with their name engraved on the front. Having mentioned these nuances, I have chosen in this book to use the term Septuagint to refer to the original Greek and its revisions, making note of the distinctions when necessary.

Unless otherwise noted, verse numbers are given according to the English Bibles, which often follow the Hebrew, and where divergent the Greek numbers are in parentheses. I have used the New Revised Standard Version (NRSV) for the Hebrew Bible and New Testament, unless otherwise noted, and to cite the Septuagint I have used, with some minor modifications, the New English Translation of the Septuagint (NETS). This is a new version of the Bible translated from the Septuagint, but it is still for the most part a scholarly edition. The editors and translators admirably attempted to replicate the methodology of the Septuagint translators vis-à-vis the Hebrew text, as understood by the NETS project, but the result is that this version of the Bible will be enigmatic to many, especially to those outside of scholarship. Although NETS has usefully been published in a single volume and is now indispensible for the scholarly study of the Septuagint (and is therefore highly recommended for students and academics), we must continue to wait for a translation of the Septuagint that would appeal to nonspecialist readers of the Bible.

2

When the World Became Greek

Those who were vanquished by Alexander are happier than those who escaped his hand; for these had no one to put an end to the wretchedness of their existence, while the victor compelled those others to lead a happy life...Alexander's new subjects would not have been civilized, had they not been vanquished; Egypt would not have its Alexandria, nor Mesopotamia its Seleuceia, nor Sogdiana its Prophthasia, nor India its Bucephalia, nor the Caucasus a Greek city hard by; for by the founding of cities in these places savagery was extinguished and the worse element, gaining familiarity with the better, changed under its influence.

PLUTARCH, *On the Fortunes of Alexander* 1.5

AS SOON AS the sun had set on the seventh century BCE, Nebuchadnezzar marched on Jerusalem and brought with him the darkest night in the relatively short history of ancient Judah.[1] Only 125 years after the Assyrians had destroyed the northern kingdom of Israel and captured Samaria, Nebuchadnezzar's Babylonian soldiers took Jerusalem in the southern kingdom of Judah, humiliating both Yahweh and his people by exiling a number of the elites. This began the so-called Babylonian Exile. There were two or three different deportations (2 Kings 24–25; Jeremiah 39–43, 52). The capture of Jerusalem and exile of 597 is related also in the Babylonian Chronicles and included only King Jehoiachin and some members of the Judean nobility (cf. Jeremiah 52:28) because the Babylonians exiled only the literate, upper classes, and left many behind.[2] In Jehoiachin's stead, Nebuchadnezzar appointed Mattaniah and renamed him Zedekiah; after his new proxy revolted by allying with the Egyptians about a decade later, Nebuchadnezzar returned to exile even more elites along with his appointed king, but not before gouging out Zedekiah's eyes and forcing him to watch the slaughter of his sons (Jeremiah 52:10–11). In 582, a final deportation may have happened, but some Judeans, including Jeremiah, also went to Egypt (cf. Jeremiah 52:29–30).

About two generations after the attack on Jerusalem, the king of Persia, Cyrus II ("the Great"), put an end to the Babylonian Empire in 539 BCE. In the preceding decade Cyrus had taken the Median Empire and, shortly thereafter, the Lydian. With the exception of one major conflict in which the Babylonians were routed at Opis, a city on the Tigris just north of modern Baghdad, Cyrus marched into Babylon almost untouched. It was the final, decisive battle that allowed Cyrus to declare himself, preserved on what is known as the Cyrus Cylinder, "great king, mighty king, king of Babylon, king of Sumer and Akkad, king of the four quarters."[3] Before his death in 530, Cyrus's Achaemenid Empire, so named after its eponymous founder Achaemenes (Old Persian: Hakhâmaniš), stretched from Asia Minor (modern day Turkey) in the West all the way to India and only a few years later would be home to between fifty and eighty million people.[4]

The rise of the Persian Empire introduced the period historians call the post-exilic, or the Second Temple period. The latter name implicitly affirms the biblical narrative's claim that during this time the temple Ezra built was a rebuilding of an original Solomonic Temple. It is perhaps the most decisive period in Jewish history: the exile was over, according to the Bible the exiles were permitted to return to the homeland, most of the Hebrew Bible was written, and Judaism developed into a formal religion. During the early years under Persian rule the old pre-exilic Judean religion was transformed; even though aspects could be traced to more ancient times, in this period the religion took on new dimensions and began to reflect more organization and to cohere with much of the Pentateuchal material that was simultaneously being organized into a more coherent literature. The biblical material directly related to the early phase of the Persian post-exilic period is found for the most part in Ezra-Nehemiah (one book in the Hebrew Bible), Haggai, and Zechariah 1–8. According to these accounts, one year after his ascension Cyrus issued a decree that the Jerusalem Temple should be rebuilt in Jerusalem and all Judeans who wished to leave Babylonia could return to their homeland. Ezra 1:2–4 records:

> Thus says King Cyrus of Persia: "The Lord, the God of heaven, has given me all the kingdoms of the earth, and he has charged me to build him a house at Jerusalem in Judah. Any of those among you

who are of his people—may their God be with them!—are now permitted to go up to Jerusalem in Judah, and rebuild the house of the
Lord, the God of Israel—he is the God who is in Jerusalem; and let
all survivors, in whatever place they reside, be assisted by the people
of their place with silver and gold, with goods and with animals,
besides freewill-offerings for the house of God in Jerusalem."

In the Hebrew text of Ezra 1:2, Cyrus claims that it was "Yahweh, the God
of heaven" who made him ruler of all the nations and commanded him
to build the Temple in Jerusalem. The writer of this text tells his readers
that Cyrus was acting at the bidding of their God. In contrast, the Cyrus
Cylinder praises Cyrus as victor over the Neo-Babylonian Empire, and
asserts that the Persian ruler acted at the instigation of the Babylonian
god Marduk who was unhappy with the Babylonian king Nabonidus. Jews
are not even mentioned. There is only a reference to Mesopotamian tem-
ples. Nonetheless, there is a second edict reported in Ezra 6:3–5, written in
Aramaic instead of Hebrew, which some scholars take to be authentic:

> In the first year of his reign, King Cyrus issued a decree: "Concerning
> the house of God at Jerusalem, let the house be rebuilt, the place
> where sacrifices are offered and burnt-offerings are brought; its
> height shall be sixty cubits and its width sixty cubits, with three
> courses of hewn stones and one course of timber; let the cost be
> paid from the royal treasury. Moreover, let the gold and silver vessels
> of the house of God, which Nebuchadnezzar took out of the temple
> in Jerusalem and brought to Babylon, be restored and brought back
> to the temple in Jerusalem, each to its place; you shall put them in
> the house of God."[5]

Whoever Cyrus believed inspired him to invade Babylon, once he became
king he decreed the rebuilding of the Jerusalem Temple.

According to the biblical view of the return, only a number actually took
Cyrus up on the offer of repatriation; many preferred to stay in the land
of their exile. The exiles that returned saw themselves as more divinely
favored than the many who had remained in the land, perhaps because
of their social status before the exile, but they discovered that the unex-
iled were less than eager to move out of the way for the homecoming.[6]
The returnees took a hard line, excluding everyone else from participat-
ing in the rebuilding efforts: "But Zerubbabel, Jeshua, and the rest of the

heads of families in Israel said to them, 'You shall have no part with us in building a house to our God; but we alone will build to the Lord, the God of Israel, as King Cyrus of Persia has commanded us'" (Ezra 4:3). The biblical accounts are written by and give the perspective of the returnees, and thus they depict the exiles as those who came back with the edict of Cyrus and the blessing of God. It is plausible that the returnees used the production of an edict of Cyrus to preempt any who would oppose their position. This bitter conflict continued, but the rebuilding of the Temple was finally completed in 515 BCE.

In addition to rebuilding the city and the Temple, they created a law book that would in time become the core of the Torah. In Judaism, "Torah" refers to the law of God; more specifically, when biblical scholars refer to Torah they mean the books tradition claims to have been written by Moses: Genesis through Deuteronomy. Another word that comes from Greek, Pentateuch (from Greek: *penta* "five" + *teuchos* "scroll"), is also used to refer these five books. The priestly compilers of the Torah gathered together strands of documentary materials and ancient stories that had been transmitted in oral and written form for many years and stitched them together into a continuous though not entirely uniform narrative. Even though the Torah includes narrative and other material unrelated to "law" in a strictly legal sense, the form of the Torah gives the appearance that it was to be read as the words of God to regulate Judean society. Furthermore, its possible Persian authorization also implies that it was seen as Law, as the Persians would have had no interest to involve themselves in the writing of any kind of narrative.[7] In this sense, the Torah was known early on as "Law," and even though the Hebrew word *torah* means "teaching" or "instruction," the Greek translators to whom we will soon be introduced use the Greek word *nomos*, "law," to translate the Hebrew word *torah* wherever it appeared. The end of the fifth or beginning of the fourth century BCE is the earliest date at which anything closely resembling the Torah may have appeared.

The political conditions under Persian rule support this assessment. The Persians were not interested in pummeling their subjects but patronized them instead and allowed them to regulate their own affairs. Administratively this created far less of a strain on the government, especially since the rapidity of the Persian rise to dominance meant that they had neither the manpower nor the organization to rule their new enormous territory. Even if Darius I (550–486 BCE) organized a committee of Egyptian priests to set down an Egyptian law code, the evidence is lacking to prove that Cyrus or his local administrators officially interfered in the production of the Judean legal constitution in any official capacity. Authorization, however, is a different matter, and we are on firmer ground to suppose that the Persians allowed the local Judean community to organize themselves according to their own law that they themselves were formulating.[8] During this same period, scribes whom modern scholars call the Deuteronomists edited Joshua, Judges, Samuel, and Kings in the light of Deuteronomy. The basic theme in the "Deuteronomistic History" is the editors' interpretation that all the good in Israel's history since the conquest of the land was a demonstration of God's pleasure with the people for their obedience to the Torah. Conversely, negative events were divine punishments for disobedience. The narrative in the Deuteronomistic History has the appearance of antiquity, but much of it was finished after the exile. Among the prophets, Hosea, Amos, and Isaiah were active in the eighth century, although Isaiah's work is limited to material throughout the first thirty-nine chapters of the prophetic masterpiece attributed to his name. These three prophets' oracles were transmitted from the eighth on down to the sixth century when they, along with more material attributed to the prophet Isaiah, the prophecies of Jeremiah, Ezekiel, and the so-called Twelve Minor Prophets, were finally worked into the forms approaching what we have today. Some of the books in the Hebrew Bible's Writings section, often called "Poetic" and "Wisdom" books in the Christian Old Testament, had roots in earlier times, but they were all finished in the late Persian and early Hellenistic periods, between the fifth and third centuries BCE. The oldest of these containing pre-exilic material are some of Psalms and some portions of Proverbs. The biblical books of Ezra-Nehemiah and Chronicles are the end of the biblical "historians."

The apparently peaceful period in Judea first under Persian and then under Hellenistic rule, in which we have no record of Jews engaging in military conflict, lasted until about 170 BCE before it all came undone. To understand the reasons for the end to the peace, we must understand what resulted from the transfer of power from Persian to Greek hands.

Transformation

The result of Alexander the Great's victory over Darius in 330 BCE not only shifted the balance of power in the ancient world to the Macedonian general but also instigated a political and cultural transformation that has shaped the course of Western history down to the present day. Although

the fall of Constantinople in 1453 brought an end to Greek cultural dominance in the Mediterranean world, the legacy of Greek thought never met
the same end.[9] As we shall come to see, it was this singular event in world
history that led to the translation of the Hebrew scriptures into Greek,
which paved the way for the creation and expansion of Christianity. For
many centuries, the fortunes of the church would be tied intimately to
those of Greek culture, and the direction of Western history would be
closely related to that of the church.

The Hellenistic Age begins with Alexander the Great's victory in 330
and lasts exactly three hundred years until the triumph of Octavian at the
Battle of Actium and the consequent establishment of the Roman Empire
in 30 BCE. The megalomaniacal Macedonian general left no plan to
ensure a smooth transfer of power after him; chaos erupted with his death
in 323. His generals carved up the territorial spoils of his wars, and the
empire was divided into four main regions, the two most important of
which were established in Egypt by Ptolemy I Soter (reigned 305–282
BCE) and in the eastern part of the empire by Seleucus after his victory
at Babylon in 311. Of these, the Ptolemaic would rise to become the most
powerful kingdom in the ancient world for three centuries.

The Greek term from which the adjective "Hellenistic" was invented
is *hellenismos*, used in the Septuagint book of 2 Maccabees (4:13) to refer
to the adoption of Greek customs and language. Since then, the term
has referred generally to the Mediterranean world's immersion in Greek
language and culture. Even though Greek culture had made inroads in
the East long before Alexander took up his shield and spear, the cultural
deluge after Alexander flooded this part of the world with a new intensity
but affected inhabitants in its path to different degrees. On one end of the
spectrum stood a native Egyptian or Syrian who either rejected Greek culture outright or simply did not encounter it in the countryside; at the other
end stood an urban elite seeking and then procuring Greek citizenship. In
between were many options for natives, and evidences of enculturation
range from rather innocuous examples such as the use of Greek vases in
a Mesopotamian house to the more conspicuous participation in Greek
theatre or speaking fluent Greek.[10] Immersion in Greek culture became an
acute issue for Jews of the Mediterranean world, as we shall soon see, but
even they demonstrate a range of cultural absorption.[11]

There has never been such a widespread adoption of culture in history.
If the closest analogy is the spread of Arabic language and Islamic culture
in the wake of Mohammed's victories, even this wasn't as widespread or

rapid as the Hellenization of the world from Greece to India between the fourth and first centuries BCE. Hellenism, it is often assumed, began with Alexander: the Macedonian general brought with his campaigns the fascinations of the Greek world, and local cultures couldn't help but gobble it up. The sentiment is not all wrong, but there was already a dispersion of Greek culture much earlier, and quite significantly in the fifth century after the victory at Thermopylae in the Greco-Persian wars. During this period, the moneyed citizens of the Syro-Palestinian coast could avail themselves of the extravagances of Athenian manufacturers, and by the fourth century coins modeled after Athenian types were circulating even within Persian Judea.[12] The role of Greek material goods in the spread of Athenian fame is certain, but the diffusion of the Greek language after Alexander was the primary catalyst for the transformation of the Mediterranean world. Traders who spoke the *koine* ("common") Greek dialect could communicate in Carthage and Kabul, in Rome and Persepolis. If the Greeks didn't force their language and culture on the newly conquered, they certainly expected them to adopt it. Alexander is said to have arranged lessons for captive Persians, and the Greeks began using their own myths to explain the histories of the people they conquered.[13] Many others never required coercion, but readily welcomed and embraced the mysterious, alluring language. *Koine* became the bridge from ancient to Modern Greek. It was the language of the great works of the Hellenistic age, of the translators of the Septuagint, of the authors of the New Testament, of many early Christian writers, and of the Byzantine world. In the West, a common Latin eventually replaced it; however, even in the first century the apostle Paul could write a letter in Greek to the church in Rome, and the author of the book of Hebrews produced his work in that same city or somewhere else in Italy without a nod to Latin. Alexander was not the first to spread Greek culture. But he did douse the world with a fuel that caused a Greek fire quickly to engulf the entire Mediterranean and beyond.

The Hellenistic period in the Mediterranean world lasted culturally until the fall of Constantinople in 1453, even if politically the Romans brought an end to Greek dominance in the first century BCE when the Seleucid and Ptolemaic kingdoms fell. The fortunes of the Jews would soon face a rapid deterioration under Roman rule; during the Ptolemaic period, however, they would experience their cultural apogee.

Jews had been dispersed all over the Mediterranean world since the Babylonian captivity of the sixth century BCE but perhaps even as early as the seventh. The word used now in English to describe the movements of migrant populations outside of their homeland, "diaspora," is the Greek term used first in the Septuagint to refer to forced migrations by exiling masters.[14] Evidence of Jewish settlements has turned up in North Africa, Syria, Asia Minor, Mesopotamia, and elsewhere, but the place for which we have the most information about life in the Diaspora is Egypt. At least two factors may be responsible: the Egyptian sand and climate have proven useful conservators of documentary evidence, and the city of Alexandria was the cultural capital of the Hellenistic world under the Ptolemies.

A lax immigration policy under Ptolemy Soter followed Alexander's Egyptian conquest. Tens of thousands of Jews found a new home in Egypt, mostly having come as soldiers, slaves, and economic migrants.[15] Since the Ptolemies began raising up an army composed entirely of foreigners, many Jews found themselves employed under the new Hellenistic rulers in the same way their compatriots had several generations before under Persian leadership. Jews also fled from Judea to Egypt to escape the poor economic conditions of the homeland: the wealth of Egypt and the optimism of the new Ptolemaic leadership provided the incentive for many to make their journey south. They settled not only in the three major cities of early Hellenistic Egypt—Naucratis, Ptolemais, and Alexandria—but also in the countryside, where newly appointed soldiers, administrators, and craftsmen were posted. In the cities, Jews organized themselves in districts—not yet ghettos—presumably to preserve some of their heritage even as many wished to participate as fully as possible in Greek culture. While there is evidence of continued use of Hebrew and Aramaic during this period, most Jews will have fully adopted *koine* Greek. Evidence of prayer houses, probably the precursor to the synagogue that had yet to emerge, prove that while language was negotiable they were nevertheless able to continue their religious traditions, albeit in a new dress.[16]

Hellenism continued long after the Romans established a new imperial authority, and its perseverance was possible since Hellenists did not seek to erase entirely the native culture. Rather, Hellenism was about fusion, and inherently so: it was a Macedonian general who expanded the Greek empire and his Macedonian generals who became Hellenistic rulers in lands whose civilizations had reached back into the distant past. They were Macedonians in Egypt and Babylon, among other places, practicing a Greek way of life, amalgamating Greek culture to local traditions to create new possibilities altogether. If this picture represents the intention of the Hellenistic enterprise, Alexandria was the city in which these fusions of culture were most apparent.

In Alexandria between the third and first centuries BCE the Jews experienced all the attractions, and the trappings, of Hellenistic culture, and before long they were faced with the perennial question: how does an immigrant religious community that has been transplanted from another cultural universe retain its convictions and its distinctiveness? No evidence demonstrates the Hellenization of the Jews in the Mediterranean Diaspora, and how they responded to the dilemma of assimilation, more spectacularly than the Greek translation of the Hebrew scriptures. The Torah was translated first, in Alexandria in the third century BCE. Other books of the Septuagint were produced in Alexandria in the second century but some also in Palestine, since not even the Jewish homeland was immune to the pressure of Hellenism.

The traditional account claims that in 167 BCE the Seleucid king Antiochus IV unleashed a persecution against the Jews in the homeland.[7] In addition to repealing the rights that his father Antiochus III gave the Jews, Antiochus IV introduced idol worship and prostitution in the Temple, violated specific Jewish laws such as the Sabbath and festivals, made possession of the Torah a crime, banned circumcision, and prohibited dietary laws. A small band of Jews gathered together and rose up against the oppression and won back their city and Temple by 165–164. The celebration of Hanukkah ("rededication"), still celebrated annually, was instituted in 165 to remember this victory (1 Maccabees 4:59). Reading the account through the perspective of the writers of 1 and 2 Maccabees, it might appear that the sole cause of the war was Hellenization, against which a devoted group of traditionalists fought. The Maccabean brothers, however, spoke Greek and followed Greek political protocols, and Judah even had in his entourage Eupolemus, who was probably the author of the first Hellenistic Jewish history written in Palestine. That for the next century the Hasmoneans would be comfortably installed as the leaders of a Judea that had itself experienced the seductions of Hellenism and was increasingly enveloped in a Hellenistic Mediterranean world shows that even the Jewish homeland was a place in which the Greek way of life, and more especially the Greek language, could flourish.

A Greek Legacy

The Hebrew Bible begins with, "In the beginning," and its first chapters aim to give an account of the history of the world from creation to the call of Abraham. Along with other great world civilizations, scribes in the sixth century BCE put into writing their own account of the origins of the world that, according to form, has one of their own as the first human being. During a time of relative tranquility, the Temple and the Torah emerged as the centerpieces of the Judean worldview. Judaism was born. It was also during the Persian era that we have the first material evidence of a significant population of Jews in Egypt, who would soon become actors in the drama of the Bible's history. After Cyrus fell, a torrential flood of Greek art, architecture, customs, and language soaked the entire Mediterranean world: from Greece in the West to India in the East, the world had become Greek. During the early decades of the new Hellenistic age, it was already apparent that a radical cultural transformation was taking place, not only through the flow of material commodities and intellectual sciences but also, more importantly, through that of language. Soon after Alexander died, inhabitants in faraway lands were able to communicate with one another. Like Aramaic in the Achaemenid Persian Empire before it or English today, *koine* Greek became the lingua franca from Berenice (modern-day Benghazi, Libya) to southwest Asia. Rulers would come and go. Even the great Hellenistic kings heard their own demise in the rhythmic thump of the sandals of the approaching Roman soldiers. But while the balance of power would shift from Greek to Roman hands, the legacies of Athens and of Alexander survived as the Mediterranean world continued to converse and write in Greek and to enjoy Greek ways of life. We should not overstate the case since local cultures continued to preserve their identities to various degrees, but the impact of Hellenization could hardly have been ignored, especially in the cities. The translation of the Hebrew Torah, the creation of the Septuagint, was unarguably one of the greatest cultural achievements of any people in the ancient world. It was followed by the translation of numerous other Hebrew texts, including those that became "canonical" and others that did not. But before we investigate further that initial translation, we must ask a more fundamental question often bypassed: in what form would the translators have found the Hebrew scriptures they sought to put into Greek?

3

Was There a Bible before the Bible?

*The first statement to make about the Bible at Qumran
is that we should probably not think of a "Bible" in the
first century BCE or the first century CE at Qumran, or
elsewhere.*

E. ULRICH

IT IS OFTEN taken for granted that a Bible existed in and before the time of
Jesus, the first century CE.[1] Scholars have recently begun using terminology more judiciously and now prefer to speak of "scriptures" or "scriptural
texts" prior to the second century CE. "Scriptures" allows for an open number of religiously authoritative texts whose individual forms may still be
evolving, but "Bible" implies a closed collection of authoritative scriptures
whose individual forms are fixed forever. To be candid: before the Bible,
there was no Bible. Before the beginning of the second century CE, there
were Jewish scriptures whose forms were still in flux and many scriptures
were excluded in the finalization of the Hebrew Bible. Prior to the second
century there was no way of knowing which scriptural books would be
included within the collection and which would be left out; nor was there
any way of knowing how the final version of the individual books would
appear. There are several important implications, some of which we shall
see unfold in the following chapters: Jesus and Paul did not have a Bible;
before the production of a "Bible," Jews and Christians used numerous
scriptural texts that never made it into the "canon"; and the forms that
later became biblical books were in an extraordinary state of fluctuation
between the third century BCE and the second CE.

We will soon encounter some remarkable differences between the
Hebrew and Greek scriptures. This should be stated very clearly right
away since the Septuagint translation is sometimes misjudged as merely
a translation when it is more than that. In many places the messages

contained in the Septuagint are different from what we have in the Hebrew Bible, a significance whose weight will be forced upon us when we see how New Testament authors and early Christian writers constructed their theological visions on the basis of the Septuagint. The divergent character of the Septuagint is not always a result of the ingenuity of its translators. Sometimes we see evidence that the Greek translation was produced from an alternative Hebrew text that has since been lost. The Septuagint and Hebrew Bible often reflect divergent traditions of scriptural texts in the same biblical books, and it is not always possible to discover if one was from an earlier time than another. Sometimes they are simply different, perhaps parallel traditions. Today most English Bible versions are based on a medieval edition of the Hebrew Bible. Until the last century many assumed the Hebrew scriptures existed only in this form preserved in the medieval edition, but most now recognize it reflects only one of several forms of the scriptures in circulation before the second century CE.[2]

The Multiple Forms of the Hebrew Scriptures

There are certain biblical books with two distinct literary versions in the Septuagint and in the Hebrew Bible—Exodus, Samuel, Kings, Jeremiah, Ezekiel, Esther, and Daniel have most often been cited as examples, but there are others. The current absence of evidence for distinct literary editions of other books does not mean they did not exist for those books. The preservation of evidence for only some of them is a matter of accident, and it is quite possible other variant literary editions perished without leaving a trace, especially since the textual tradition after the second century CE became almost entirely unified and would therefore have caused the loss of abundant divergent materials. Nevertheless, even these other books that appear to be identical in both Greek and Hebrew display characteristics that distinguish them one from the other.

Although some biblical exegetes had already argued that the Septuagint sometimes reflects an alternative Hebrew edition that has since been lost, until the middle of the twentieth century the accepted narrative in scholarship was that the Septuagint translators used a source identical to those reflected in the medieval Masoretic Text we now call "the Hebrew Bible." The Greek translators must have introduced the divergences with our Hebrew Bible. They may have had theological reasons, may have been confused by the obscurity or difficulty of the Hebrew text before them, or may have had motives we do not understand. These ancient Hebrew scriptures, according to this supposition, were eventually adopted by the early rabbinic movement and after that the medieval Hebrew scribes who handed down to us the edition of the Hebrew Bible we now possess. The single archetypal Hebrew text was transmitted with extreme accuracy since the scribes believed these words were the very words of God. Many scholars thus thought of the Septuagint only as a tool for reconstructing certain passages where the Hebrew text was obviously corrupted. For example, even the most conservative scholars have readily turned to the Septuagint translation of Samuel to clarify certain difficulties in the Hebrew tradition, and you can see how the English versions of the Bible supply footnotes to mark many of these selections.

We will soon see that the differences between the Greek and Hebrew Bible are often not only to do with small details. The new consensus, but one that some commentators have still not fully appreciated, is that the Septuagint is not merely a guide to understand the Hebrew Bible better, but it is sometimes is our only source preserving alternative versions of the Hebrew scriptures. In the twentieth century a revolution in biblical and early Jewish studies began when the manuscripts from the Judean Desert, popularly called the Dead Sea Scrolls, were discovered. The scrolls forever altered our understanding of the history of the Bible.[3]

The most striking impact the scrolls have had on our understanding of the history of the Bible is to provide us with Hebrew and Aramaic biblical manuscripts of far greater antiquity than any we had before. The Leningrad Codex—the oldest complete manuscript of the Hebrew Bible and the basis for most modern editions and consequently almost all modern English Bible translations—dates to the eleventh century CE. The Aleppo Codex dates to the tenth but is only partially preserved today. Prior to the Dead Sea Scrolls we could rely only on these biblical manuscripts produced around a millennium after the time of Jesus. Some never considered this a problem since they assumed that the earliest history of the biblical text was characterized not by textual variety but by homogeneity. Because they pointed to later rabbinic and medieval concepts of scribal diligence, they assumed that even though we had only medieval manuscripts these copies preserve the most ancient testimony. These ideas are not entirely mistaken. The medieval manuscripts indeed preserve very ancient texts and bear witness to the careful textual transmission through the rabbinic and early medieval eras. There is no question that the text of the Hebrew Bible we know today is very ancient. But the Dead Sea Scrolls, along with a renewed appreciation of the Septuagint, force us to adopt a new perspective: while the medieval Masoretic scribes preserved an ancient tradition, they transmitted *only one scriptural tradition* out of a number of divergent possibilities that existed before the second century CE. The earlier period was characterized by plurality, not uniformity. There is nothing at all mistaken in affirming that the Hebrew Bible in today's editions reflects a very ancient tradition reaching back at least to the third century BCE and perhaps even earlier. But this is only part of the story.

Before 1947 scholars usually explained the history of the Bible by referring to three main witnesses to, or "types" of, the Old Testament text: the Masoretic Text, the Samaritan Pentateuch, and the Septuagint.[4] The Masoretic Text actually refers not to a single text but to a group of manuscripts that have shared features. The text, or the text group, was edited between the seventh and eleventh centuries CE by a group of scholars known as Masoretes. Up to their time, all biblical Hebrew manuscripts contained only consonants, as Modern Hebrew does today. A tourist in Israel will notice the absence of vowels in road signs, menus, and many other printed materials. In both the modern and ancient contexts, native Hebrew speakers do not and did not need texts printed with vowels; however, in Late Antique Palestine Aramaic was the daily language of Jews, and Hebrew was transitioning to become the language of liturgy and poetry.[5] The ability to read Hebrew correctly might have posed challenges to some, and by the seventh or eighth century CE they might have needed help to read the ancient Hebrew text. One can imagine the difficulty of reading without vowels and the different interpretations that could arise from such a text, as in the following sentence of consonants. Note the increasingly ridiculous different possibilities that follow it:

> *Jn rn t th str t by brd.*
> *Jon ran to the store to buy bread.*
> *Jon, run to the store to buy bread!*
> *Jon ran to the store to buy a board.*
> *Jan ran to the stair, at a bay beard.*
> *Jane, I run to thee, a star to obey, a bride!*

These are laughable examples, but they show that, even if one is competent in the language, various interpretations can arise—some plausible, some absurd.[6] We see this at times in the Septuagint, where it appears the Greek translators were confused by the Hebrew before them and tried to guess the meaning. One of the contributions the Masoretes made to the history of the Hebrew Bible was the introduction of vowels into the consonantal text to clarify the reading tradition. This entails that in those places where various interpretations could arise the Masoretes determined the appropriate reading. In this first layer of vowels added into the text, modern readers are already subjected to the interpretations of medieval Tiberian scribes whose vowels dictate how we will interpret the ancient Hebrew biblical text.[7] In many cases, modern scholars disagree with the vowels given by the Masoretes and will propose alternative readings they believe make better sense of the text. Yet it is not as if all of these readings were invented by the Masoretes. While we do not know the extent of their own creative guesswork, we do know that many of the reading traditions of the Hebrew Bible are very ancient. When the Masoretes inserted vowels into the text, they were for the most part simply adding to the visible appearance of the text what was known in an ancient reading tradition. On the other hand, Hebrew manuscripts from other places like Yemen and Cairo indicate that the diversity we knew of in the earlier period had, even if to a minimal extent, continued right through the first millennium until it was intentionally eliminated.[8] Perhaps most importantly, we must recognize that the Hebrew Bible editions in our hands today, those based on the medieval Masoretic Text, do not represent the "original text" of the Bible. The greatest modern authority on the Hebrew textual tradition puts it bluntly: "One thing is clear, it should not be postulated that the Masoretic Text better or more frequently reflects the original text of the biblical books than any other text."[9] That this text became prominent in early Judaism and its proponents eventually stamped out all rivals does not mean it is the best or most original text. The selection of the Masoretic Text was perhaps not even a selection at all. It may have been employed from a certain moment simply because these types of manuscripts were the ones available.[10]

The Samaritan Pentateuch is different from the Septuagint in that it is not a translation but is instead a version of the Hebrew Torah, edited by Samaritans who were at odds with the centralized Jerusalem leadership. The most famously cited example of the sectarian rivalry is over the place where the people were to erect an altar after crossing the Jordan. In the Samaritan Pentateuch version of the Ten Commandments, God decrees that an altar is to be built on Mount Gerizim, but elsewhere in the Hebrew Bible God commands that the altar should be built on Mount

Ebal (Deuteronomy 27:4). Normally the Samaritans are held responsible for making a sectarian modification to the text. However, this same reading highlighting Mount Gerizim is also found in an Old Latin manuscript that preserves the oldest reading of the Septuagint, which more likely points us to a Hebrew text of greater antiquity. Perhaps this was not a sectarian reading of the Samaritans, and instead the editors of the Hebrew Bible changed the oldest reading.[11] Aside from these types of differences, the Samaritan Pentateuch is valuable because of its witness to the differences in Samaritan ideology and because it contains copious agreements with the Septuagint against the Masoretic Text. The New Testament also furnishes proof of the antiquity of some of the Samaritan Pentateuch's readings against the Masoretic Text. In Acts 7:4, Stephen says that Abraham left Haran for Canaan after his father died, agreeing with the Samaritan Pentateuch; the Masoretic Text claims that Abraham's father died sixty years after he had left (Genesis 11:32). The Dead Sea Scrolls demonstrated the antiquity of the Samaritan Pentateuch by revealing many manuscripts that shared agreements with these early readings.

To be sure, the scrolls also confirm the antiquity of the tradition of the Masoretic Text. Thus, in many places in the Hebrew Bible, the text we now have is exactly the same as that found in these very ancient manuscripts. Nonetheless, while some scholars are eager to point out the antiquity of the Hebrew Bible, occasionally for apologetic reasons they have allowed this to overshadow the more startling discovery of textual plurality in the ancient period. Most of the older biblical scholarship assumed a clean, tripartite division between the witnesses of the Hebrew Bible, the Samaritan Pentateuch, and the Septuagint, but the manuscripts from the Judean Desert showed that, even if there are three main branches of the Hebrew text tradition, there is great variety within the groups. Some scriptural texts resist classification altogether.[12] In light of the Dead Sea Scrolls, it would be more sensible to assume that we still have only a partial picture of the textual plurality and that the forms of the biblical text were probably even more numerous than our evidence indicates. As far as the Septuagint is concerned, the Judean Desert manuscripts forced a change of almost every assumption of the Septuagint's value as a witness to the earliest history of the Bible. They vindicated earlier speculations that the Septuagint was translated from alternative Hebrew texts. The strongest proof was in these newly discovered Hebrew sources that contained unmistakable agreements with the Septuagint, proving more than merely suggesting that the Septuagint translators sometimes used different Hebrew texts.

An alternative, hypothetical Hebrew text no longer had to be reconstructed from the Greek: for the first time there was evidence in Hebrew more than one thousand years older than the medieval Masoretic Text.

At Qumran, there were roughly thirty-six copies of some portion of Psalms (though not thirty-six copies of the entire Book of Psalms we now know); thirty-two of Deuteronomy; twenty-three or twenty-four of Genesis; twenty-one of Isaiah; sixteen of Exodus; fourteen of Leviticus; eight or nine of the Minor Prophets; eight of Daniel; six each of Numbers, Jeremiah, and Ezekiel; four of Samuel, Proverbs, Job, Canticles (Song of Songs), Ruth, and Lamentations; three of Judges and Kings; two of Joshua, Qoheleth (Ecclesiastes), and Ezra-Nehemiah; and one of Chronicles.[13] Esther is the only book that lacks manuscript evidence. Other books that were later called "Apocrypha" and "Pseudepigrapha" were also discovered in the Judean Desert in Hebrew and Aramaic forms (e.g., Tobit, Jubilees, Enoch, Sirach). These too were part of the textual milieu of Second Temple Judaism. The preponderance of Torah (ninety-one or ninety-two), Psalms (thirty-six), and Isaiah (twenty-one) manuscripts is expected. The Mosaic Law, and especially its expression in Deuteronomy, would have been prioritized, the psalms would have been used for worship or prayer, and Isaiah seems to have been considered the greatest of the prophets. Indeed, this same prioritization of texts is apparent in the New Testament authors' citations of the Jewish scriptures, which we shall soon see (Chapter 9). In addition to most of the finds at Qumran, there were other sites around the area that gave up treasures. Twenty-five biblical manuscripts were found at Masada, Wadi Murabba'at, Wadi Sdeir, Nahal Hever, Nahal Arugot, and Nahal Se'elim, and in these locations outside of Qumran the texts agree in almost every detail with the Masoretic tradition. The overwhelming agreement with the Hebrew Bible should not be overestimated, since the number of manuscripts—twenty-five!—is far too small to make any conclusive judgments. Within Qumran there is more variation. Manuscripts of the Torah reflect the Masoretic Text only 48 percent of the time, while the remaining books outside the Torah reflect the Masoretic Text only 44 percent of the time.[14] This is hardly the picture of textual uniformity to which we had been accustomed. What is more, some of these were found stored together in the same cave. That different editions of the same biblical books could coexist in the same community seems not to have caused any concern for ancient readers of scripture. We shall soon see that the New Testament authors are likewise unperturbed by the existence of multiple versions of the same biblical book. Again, these are not different versions in the way one might compare modern English translations of the Bible, where differences can be slight and are often related simply to the style of the English. Between the third century BCE and the second CE there was no real preoccupation with a fixed text and authoritative status was shared by different versions of the same books.

How Meaningful Are the Differences?

We mentioned already that for many years scholars conceived of the transmission of the Hebrew Torah—Genesis through Deuteronomy—as a monotonous history, since it was assumed that the forms of these books were never in flux.[15] The manuscripts of these most central books in the Jewish religion were guarded zealously and transmitted always in one singular form.[16] The few differences that might have appeared among the various traditions of the Pentateuchal books were regarded as insignificant. The Torah manuscripts among the Dead Sea Scrolls have been highlighted frequently, and due to the relatively stable transmission of the Torah any deviations from the norm were normally classified as non-scriptural texts. This view is no longer tenable.

While it is true that the shape of the Torah was for the most part finished by the fourth century BCE, not all alternative editions were completely eradicated until much later. It may be surprising to some that even the Torah manuscripts reveal that the books had not reached their final form just yet. For example, the chronological information found in Genesis 5, 8, and 11 vary greatly between the Masoretic Text, the Samaritan Pentateuch, and the Septuagint. One example that has raised questions is the number of Jacob's descendants. In the Septuagint and in the New Testament book of Acts (7:14), Jacob had seventy-five descendants rather than the seventy found in the Hebrew Bible. There is now a Hebrew manuscript that contains the seventy-five of the Septuagint and Acts. Another Qumran fragment of Exodus (100–25 BCE) ends at Exodus 37:16 but places the making of the Incense Altar between 26:35 and 26:36, in agreement with the Samaritan Pentateuch but in contrast to the order found in both the Hebrew Bible and the Septuagint, where it appears in 30:1–10.[17] In another case in Numbers 27:22–23, Moses lays his hands on Joshua to commission him to lead the people. The Hebrew Bible stops there, but in a fragment of Numbers found among the scrolls the commissioning is followed with a challenge to Joshua to be courageous, borrowed from Deuteronomy 3:21–22. This arrangement, along with other examples in

Numbers, is also shared with the Samaritan Pentateuch, indicating that the Torah was still open to reshaping in this period.

Through other recent investigations, we have learned of even more radical editorial practices. Some Torah fragments are so different from the Hebrew Bible's version that they have attracted the name "rewritten scripture." In rewritten works, there are additions of new material, omissions, and numerous types of alterations such as rearrangement of text, paraphrase, and replacement.[18] Formerly, because of the bias in favor of the Hebrew Bible, scholars assumed that the more the text was rewritten, the further away it stood from the authentic form of scripture. According to this view, rewritten scripture compositions were treated not as authoritative scripture but as some sort of commentary on the text. But scholars have now realized that the line between scripture and rewritten commentarial literature was not as sharp, if it could be noticed at all. The view of a continuum with "scripture" on one end and "rewritten" works on the other should be abandoned. Instead, we now realize that there are books that sit all along the virtual continuum, from those that are obviously commentaries on the biblical text to those that were extensive rewritings. Some in the latter category may have been produced to replace or to be read alongside of other forms of scripture. In one manuscript of Exodus, elements of Exodus 15 are combined with Exodus 6:3–8 so that the promise and fulfillment of the liberation from Egypt is brought together.[19] In another manuscript, perhaps more interesting to modern readers, there is evidence of a tradition in which God spoke only the first two commandments and the other eight were mediated through Moses.[20] Still other manuscripts arrange differently the order of the Ten Commandments, also called the Decalogue. The order in English Bibles may be fixed, but in this period there was fluctuation. These are not trivial details. We have in the manuscripts from the Judean Desert witnesses to alternative reports of the episode of the Ten Commandments that are dissimilar to almost two thousand years of an established tradition. Deciding which of these texts was more original and which represents rewritten material may not be important, but it unmistakably indicates that the plurality was there.[21] Compared with other books one could stress that the larger structures of the books of the Torah were fixed in the Persian period, but internally there is not an inconsequential amount of restructuring and rewriting. Even the Torah was not yet etched in stone.

The remains of Isaiah from the Dead Sea Scrolls are also important. The Great Isaiah Scroll (c. 125 BCE)—so named for its size, not for its perceived value—is the best known of all the manuscripts from the Judean Desert. It is the most extensively studied manuscript, but scholars have reached two different conclusions about its value. For some, the Great Isaiah Scroll is virtually identical to the Masoretic Text, and thus the later Hebrew Bible, so it is frequently discussed in apologetic and theological contexts. Some scholars working on the scroll, however, concluded that "the text displayed multifaceted disagreement" with the Masoretic Text.[22] While the scroll conforms to the Masoretic Text to a large degree, the two are not entirely the same. There are many cases where the Great Scroll diverges, but many of these have to do with issues particular to the scroll.[23] One small example of a divergent reading is in Isaiah 53:11. In the Masoretic Text, there is no mention of "the light" that is found in most modern English versions. The King James Version (KJV) follows the Hebrew Bible here: "He shall see of the travail of his soul," but others choose the reading from the Great Isaiah Scroll against the Hebrew Bible, such as the New Revised Standard Version (NRSV) ("Out of his anguish he shall see light") and the New International Version (NIV) ("After he has suffered, he will see the light of life"). The reading is also found in the Septuagint, which here again shows the older Hebrew tradition.

The Great Isaiah Scroll is not the only witness to Isaiah from the Judean Desert, but it is the most often discussed. There are many places in which the scroll confirms the antiquity of the Masoretic Text, and thus the Hebrew Bible, but these many agreements should not be taken to mean the texts were identical.

In the years since the discovery of the scrolls, it has become clear that, when combined with the evidence from the Septuagint, instead of the same editions of biblical books containing many minor differences, there were different literary editions of no less than thirteen but possibly as many as fifteen of the twenty-four books of the Hebrew Bible: Exodus, Numbers, Joshua, Judges, Samuel, Kings, Jeremiah, Ezekiel, Job, Psalms, Proverbs, Song of Songs, and Daniel.[24] The best examples of these different literary editions are found in Jeremiah and Samuel. The Septuagint version of Jeremiah is roughly one-sixth shorter than the Hebrew Bible, the order of the chapters in the latter half of the book are arranged differently, and there are also distinctive words or phrases used. Though other Qumran manuscripts of Jeremiah agree with the Hebrew Bible, it is now widely accepted that the Septuagint was translated from a Hebrew text like two of the Qumran manuscripts of Jeremiah (4Q Jer[b,d]) and that this was an earlier edition on which the editors in the tradition of the Hebrew Bible expanded.[25] Whole sections were added (e.g., 33:14–26 and 51:44b–49a), and other additions can be recognized by interruptions in an otherwise sensible text so that now the book of Jeremiah in our English Bibles is a larger text than that known to many earlier readers of the prophet's work. For instance, 27:19–22 has been enlarged.

Septuagint (NETS)	Hebrew Bible (NRSV)
[19]...Even some of the remaining vessels	[19]...and the rest of the vessels that are left in this city
[20]which the king of Babylon did not take when he exiled Jeconiah from Jerusalem, shall enter into Babylon, says the Lord.	[20]which King Nebuchadnezzar of Babylon did not take away when he took into exile from Jerusalem to Babylon King Jeconiah son of Jehoiakim of Judah, and all the nobles of Judah and Jerusalem—[21]thus says the Lord of hosts, the God of Israel, concerning the vessels left in the house of the Lord, in the house of the king of Judah, and in Jerusalem: [22]They shall be carried to Babylon, and there they shall stay, until the day when I give attention to them, says the Lord. Then I will bring them up and restore them to this place.

The arrangement of the text is also sometimes different in the older version: 23:7–8 of the later Hebrew Bible is found after verse 40 in the Septuagint, and the text in 10:1–11 contains omissions and differences in order. Entire chapters are also ordered differently, but there was probably a thematic reason for the most significant arrangement of the section known as the "Oracles against the Nations." In the Hebrew Bible these prophecies appear at the end in chapters 46–51, but in the alternative Hebrew text used by the translators of the Septuagint they are placed after 25:14. The reasons for this disturbance of order have to do with the intentions of the editors of the Hebrew Bible to magnify the prophet, and their decision to remove the Oracles against the Nations and place them at the end of the book might have to do with securing Jeremiah's reputation as a prophet of ancient Israel. Without these oracles at the end of the book, the role of Baruch (chapters 36–45) is the last word, because the final chapter 52 is a much later addition to the entire Hebrew tradition and comes from 2 Kings 25. Incidentally, Baruch himself may have added the Oracles after 25:14 in the original Hebrew edition.[26]

The book of Samuel was also a place of exciting discovery when the Dead Sea Scrolls were first analyzed and for the same reasons as Jeremiah, though it is also important to point out that a manuscript of Samuel that matches the Septuagint has *not* been found. As in Jeremiah, scholars knew that there were radical divergences between the Septuagint and Hebrew Bible, but Samuel is special because all scholars will admit that the Hebrew Bible contains a highly corrupted text. Modern English Bibles even give evidence in their footnotes where often the editor has been forced to resort to another ancient version to determine what the text says. The NRSV, for example, has at the end of 1 Samuel 10 the paragraph about King Nahash, which is absent from the Hebrew Bible and also from most other English translations. Some scholars propose that this paragraph was original to the text (as seen in the Qumran fragment) and was only later accidentally lost by a scribal error. The Hebrew Bible of Samuel displays numerous instances of scribal corruptions, but it is not always a loss of material that sets the Hebrew Bible apart. As we saw in Jeremiah, in Samuel often the Hebrew Bible is the expansionistic edition. An example that most clearly illustrates the character of the two literary editions of Samuel is the David and Goliath story in 1 Samuel 16–18. In the Hebrew Bible the story of David and Goliath takes up eighty-eight verses, but in the Septuagint the story spans only forty-nine. This is a shorter text by almost half, and some parts are missing altogether. Has the Hebrew Bible expanded upon a shorter story or has the Septuagint translator shortened a longer text? Unfortunately, there is no fragment from the Dead Sea Scrolls to provide tangible evidence of a divergent Hebrew source behind the Septuagint in this section. Nonetheless, the material from the Dead Sea Scrolls in other parts of Samuel shows a remarkable resemblance to the Greek tradition, making it more reasonable to begin with the assumption that the Greek is based on an alternative Hebrew tradition. The Greek translator's technique also indicates that he intended to produce a close translation of the Hebrew source, and the nature of the differences in the David and Goliath story means it unreasonable to suggest that a translator would have introduced such radical changes. We can be absolutely certain that the story in the Septuagint is based on a Hebrew edition that reflects an earlier stage in the development of the tradition of this story, and the Hebrew Bible is a later expansion of that tradition. In the process of enlarging the story disturbances were introduced into the text but were left unresolved. Conscientious readers of the English Bible may have already noticed certain confusing aspects of the David and Goliath story that are there because the Hebrew Bible is used as the basis for the English translations. For example, both the Septuagint and the Hebrew Bible tell how David is introduced to Saul in 16:17–23 as a harpist whom Saul loved so much that he made him his armor bearer. In 17:55–58, which is found only in the later Hebrew Bible, Saul oddly has no clue who David is. The famous story of the love shared between David and Jonathan (18:1–4) and Saul's attempt to kill David when an evil spirit came upon him (18:10–11) were also later additions not found in the earlier version.

The discovery of the Samuel Scrolls in Qumran and the study of the Septuagint translator's literal translation technique has made it clear that, like Jeremiah, the Greek translation was based on a Hebrew edition that differs from the Hebrew Bible.[27] Many of the divergences between the Septuagint and the Hebrew Bible can no longer be explained by the creativity of the Greek translator, or by any other process within the Greek tradition, but are the result of alternative Hebrew traditions. One of them was used by the Septuagint translator, and another became the Hebrew Bible. While the Qumran fragments of the book of Samuel offer plenty of examples of convergence between the Septuagint and this alternative Hebrew edition, the Septuagint was not translated from a text identical to the Qumran fragments of Samuel. Instead, all of this evidence again insists that before the second century CE the biblical text was still extraordinarily fluid and that there were multiple divergent textual traditions of many of the biblical books. It is unfortunate that these issues cause greater concern to modern readers for whom contradictions and inconsistencies pose problems, but in the world in which the Bible was shaping up these seem not to have been problematic at all. We could appreciate positively the growth of the biblical tradition witnessed through these texts rather than interpret negatively—or worse, ignore—the evidence that lies before us.

All of these texts from Qumran—biblical and otherwise—have been studied extensively for the past half-century, and we now understand more about the community to which they belonged. They were sectarians, probably priests in the Temple in Jerusalem, but, believing the Temple to have become defiled, they left to build another community in the desert.[28]

Nonetheless, after a close reading of the scrolls no cases of explicit sectarian interference have been detected. Ancient scribal habits in Qumran are the same as those found elsewhere, and in any case even texts kept in the Temple in Jerusalem were known to have been characterized by variety.[29] The Qumran manuscripts reveal nothing that would indicate their producers created sectarian texts that systematically deviated from authoritative originals. Rather, the evidence underscores that there was at this time no single text that had universal approval as "the" Bible. The variety attested in the Judean Desert reflects the variety known also from the Septuagint.[30]

Studying the Qumran biblical manuscripts alongside the Septuagint and the Hebrew Bible sheds light on a period of textual plurality between the third century BCE and the second CE. These manuscripts from the Judean Desert prove not only that indeed the Hebrew Bible is ancient but also that it is only one of the many traditions of scriptural texts used before the second century CE. We should be careful not to distort the evidence by looking back at this period through the lenses of our present knowledge of the authoritative status later gained by the Hebrew Bible. It is not the way one could have described the situation prior to the second century CE. There would have been no way to predict which Hebrew version of any given book would eventually become the standard, and to judge all others as variants of the authoritative tradition is to view the evidence with one's conclusions already shaped by that later tradition.

4

The First Bible Translators

For what was originally expressed in Hebrew does not have the same force when it is in fact rendered in another language. And not only in this case, but also in the case of the Law itself and the Prophets and the rest of the books the difference is not small when these are expressed in their own language.

PROLOGUE TO BEN SIRA

TRANSLATING IS BRIDGE building. Users of one language are able to cross a ravine of incomprehension to another: a translation decodes a speech or text so that it may be understood to others outside of the original target audience. Especially in an increasingly globally connected world, much of life depends on translations, between diplomats, public servants, teachers, and neighbors. If a translation is done accurately, the new audience can peer into the original; if it is done poorly, it could start wars. But even at its best, a translation can never capture the sense and sometimes not even the meaning of the original. In biblical translation, for example, the richness of Hebrew poetry cannot be communicated in ancient Greek or in modern English, so even when the meaning may not be too different, if at all, the color and depth usually is. Inevitably, however, the translator will be faced with an obscure expression in the source language; assuming she understands it she may nonetheless find no acceptable counterpart in her language. She is forced to devise some alternative and may attempt to stay close to what she thinks is the meaning of the obscurity, but she may also abandon it altogether and invent something else. She creates something new and, in a sense, rewrites the original.

The Greek translators of the Hebrew Torah did not invent the art and science of translation.[1] By the time the translators sat down at their tables and spread out their manuscripts, the ancient world had already become acquainted with the translation of texts from one language to another. Multilingual administrative documents were in use across the ancient Mediterranean world and possibly as far east as India. The earliest we know of came from the third millennium BCE and consists of Sumerian records translated into Akkadian. Bilingualism or multilingualism was, and still is, a prerequisite for any translation and was a skill possessed by a small number of highly educated scribes right through from the ancient Near East to the Greco-Roman world.[2] From the seventh century BCE, Aramaic had become the lingua franca of the Assyrian world, and we read in 2 Kings 18:26 that King Hezekiah of Judah spoke to Assyrian ambassadors in Aramaic. The Babylonians whom we met in connection with the biblical history outlined in the preceding chapter had also adopted Aramaic as the everyday spoken language but had tried to resurrect Akkadian as the language of government administration. Because of the geographical proximity of the two peoples, their languages had a significant impact on one another's development, in much the same way Spanish and Portuguese have shared similarities due to the interactions of their speakers. This linguistic shaping was also influenced by the translation of Sumerian names into Akkadian in some early tablets of the third millennium, and the translations continued with king lists and other sorts of documents for many years.[3] For kings, there was a personal interest in translation, and they often used them to boast of their exploits as widely as possible. We find a good example of this in the inscription on the side of Mount Bisitun (Behistun) in northwestern Iran, now a United Nations Educational, Scientific and Cultural Organization (UNESCO) World Heritage Site. Onto the face of the mountain, Darius I, king of the Achaemenid Empire from 522 to 486 BCE, had a proclamation to legitimize his rule engraved in Old Persian, Elamite, and Akkadian. The Bisitun Inscription was viewed with admiration throughout the medieval period, but it was not until the nineteenth century that scholars were able to use the inscription to decode the ancient cuneiform script.

Greeks and Romans were also acquainted with translations. Herodotus and Thucydides both referred to translators and translations.[4] In the same century in which our Septuagint was translated, in Rome Livius Andronicus gave Homer new life when he translated the Odyssey into Latin, and in Egypt in the third century bilingual and trilingual texts were produced.[5] Given the widespread multilingual scribal activity in the ancient world, the idea of translation itself would not have been novel in the third century in Alexandria. The subject of the undertaking, however, was indeed unique.

None of the previous translations in antiquity had to do with a formal religion, much less that of a small immigrant people. The size may also have been considered daunting. More than three hundred thousand letters divided among almost eighty thousand words make up the body of the Torah. The precise statistical details may vary depending on who is counting the words and with which manuscripts, but if the Torah was known in its entirety in the third century the general picture of the size of this body of literature was the same then as it is now.[6] It is one thing to translate lists of names or other administrative records as in the Ancient Near Eastern examples, but when the text to be translated purports to be the very words of God the translator's task takes on a new dimension.

The Letter of Aristeas to Philocrates

In Egypt for several generations and now in the cultural efflorescence of Alexandria, the Egyptian Jewish population in the third century BCE had enough learned men to accomplish the tremendous feat of translating the Hebrew Torah. The Septuagint, the translation of the Hebrew Torah into the lingua franca of the Hellenistic world, was "at once the greatest achievement of Hellenistic Jewry and its most important legacy to western mankind."[7] The ancient world already knew of translations, but no translation of a religious body of literature of this size into an entirely different language had ever been attempted. While one may wonder if the translation effectively represented the abandonment of one of the prized possessions of Judaism—the Hebrew language as the vehicle of Divine revelation—it was rather the very means of ensuring the survival of Judaism in a period in which it might have seemed nothing could resist being pressed into a Greek mold. To refuse translation and to hold stubbornly to the language of the homeland might have brought about the rapid demise of all forms of Judaism outside Judea. Translation was a matter of survival.[8]

The answer to the elusive question of the origins of the Septuagint should be stated modestly: in the late third or early second century BCE, Jewish scholars in Alexandria produced a translation of the Hebrew Torah. This unexceptional claim is based on circumstantial evidence because we have no contemporary historical account to explain its origins. It is about all we should attempt to say with conviction. That the Greek Pentateuch was produced at the very latest in the second century BCE is proven by the linguistic evidence of the translation, by the citations of the Greek Pentateuch in other Hellenistic authors and in later Septuagint books dated to the second century, and by manuscripts dating also to the second century. Other places of origin, such as the Egyptian cities of Leontopolis or Memphis or even parts of North Africa (e.g., Cyrene) and Asia Minor (e.g., Ephesus), have also been put forth as options but none are as convincing as the city of Alexandria.[9] The Greek Pentateuch contains enough hints of Egyptian origin to rule out non-Egyptian sites, and Alexandria is the most plausible given its status as the center of Greek culture during this period.

In the absence of direct sources we can paint only a very general picture of the origins of the translation from our knowledge of Hellenistic Egypt and from the evaluation of the translation itself. Whatever may be the reasons for the shortage of firsthand accounts, we do have one literary source from the second century BCE, the *Letter of Aristeas to Philocrates*, which is of great importance because it claims to be an eyewitness account. It is a legend written by a Jew, who pretends to be a courtier of Ptolemy to give the story credibility. The entire narrative is constructed to present two avenues to affirming the authority of the Septuagint—one via a Greek perspective and the other via a Jewish perspective—and the writer highlights two themes at the very start.[10] First, Aristeas requests that the Jewish High Priest Eleazar sends translators to Egypt to undertake the translation of the Hebrew Torah into Greek. Second, in exchange for their services Philadelphus was to release from Egypt thousands of Jewish slaves that had been held captive as prisoners of war. The *Letter of Aristeas* rewrites the Exodus. In the biblical story, the Jews went out from Egypt because God rescued them from an evil Pharaoh; here they are released from slavery by a willing liberator, Ptolemy II Philadelphus, but because of his benevolence they can remain in Egypt without fear. In the biblical account, they must flee so they can receive the Law at Sinai; in the *Letter of Aristeas* they can remain and receive the Law in Alexandria in Greek.[11] The Exodus motif in the *Letter of Aristeas* is thus used to bolster the authority of the Septuagint.

After this introduction the narrative reports that the king's librarian, Demetrius of Phalerum, set about collecting as many of the books of the world as he could. The plan was apparently the king's, but Demetrius successfully completed the task by purchasing these works and having others translated. The librarian claims that two hundred thousand books had been deposited in the library but that a goal of five hundred thousand lay before him, among which the "lawbooks of the Jews" should be included. The king insisted that nothing should stop Demetrius from obtaining these books, even the fact that they were written in a strange language (Hebrew). With the unfathomable finances of the kingdom at his disposal, Demetrius had all he needed to obtain translators for the project, and Philadelphus penned a letter to the High Priest in Jerusalem to make the formal request. Aristeas feels, however, that it would be unjust to authorize the translation of the Jewish Law while so many thousands of Jews are enslaved in the kingdom. Aristeas praises the Ptolemaic reputation of justice and appeals passionately for their release. The king grants the wish but does more by lavishing upon them a substantial amount of wealth (sections 9–27).

Demetrius conducts an investigation to discern which Jewish scrolls were available and concludes that a fresh translation with the very best scrolls would be necessary. The scrolls of the Law of the Jews were not only written in the Hebrew language and stood in need of translation. They were also full of mistakes due to careless copying since, as Demetrius reports, they had not been produced under royal patronage. If the Ptolemaic Library were to include the Jewish Law, an accurate version was necessary. This outstanding version was to be completed by seventy-two translators, six from each of the twelve tribes, and it is no accident that the feature of seventy-two translators is close to the number of the seventy elders who went with Moses to Sinai (sections 28–32; cf. Exodus 24:1, 9). The Septuagint, the *Letter of Aristeas* implies, is a new revelation.

Only at the very end of the letter do we come to the few concluding paragraphs on the matter of the translation, but we are still short on detail. We read how they edited their work in only two sentences: "They set to completing their several tasks, reaching agreement among themselves on each by comparing versions. The result of their agreement thus was made into a fair copy by Demetrius" (302). That is all that is said. The translators were divided up according to an unknown scheme but then compared with one another their different versions and came to an agreement on the correct translation of the whole. Does this mean that each of the seventy-two translators was given a certain section of text to translate, perhaps divided neatly into seventy-two sections? Did each translate the entire Torah and then compare with one another their results? Did smaller teams, perhaps six teams of twelve, or twelve teams of six, conduct the work and then compare with other groups? The *Letter of Aristeas* provides no answers, but the method is unimportant compared with the greater aim of the narrator to report that the translation happened. While Aristeas doesn't explicitly incorporate supernaturalism into his explanation of the translation, the author does wonder aloud: "The outcome was such that in seventy-two days the business of translation was completed, just as if such a result was achieved by some deliberate design" (307). The seeds are sown in this statement, and both Jews and Christians would reap their fruit later.

The narration continues with Demetrius making a copy of the agreed upon text, after which he read it aloud to the Alexandrian Jews and secured the approval not only of the translators but also of the community that had gathered to hear. Some have suggested that the gathering of the entire community hearkens back to the giving of the Hebrew Law at Sinai where the people of Israel waited at the foot of the mountain while Moses received the revelation, but others have rather likened the allusion to Ezra's read-ing of the Law after the exile (Nehemiah 8:1–6). It would seem that the Exodus motif in the *Letter of Aristeas* would support the former and that Demetrius is meant to be declaring the new Law, the Greek Septuagint, to be the very revelation of God.[12] Moreover, Demetrius warns them against any further interpolations and changes to the text as it now stood. When the translation was completed and the approval of the Jewish community was secured, Philadelphus himself read the text and was satisfied. The translators are then dismissed to Jerusalem bearing even more gifts for Eleazar (sections 301–322).

Some scholars suggest that the *Letter of Aristeas* was nothing more than a piece of propagandistic literature written as an apologetic tract for the Jewish religion in the face of challenges from the Greek world. Others propose that whether it was apologetic or not, it still lacks historical merit and is thus entirely useless on the question of Septuagint origins.[13] A more positive assessment takes into account the literary aims of the author, sep-arating history from myth and appreciating the *Letter of Aristeas* within the context of Hellenistic Jewish literature.[14] Even so, there remains pre-cious little to tell us about the origins of the Septuagint translation. At least one of the author's primary purposes could have been to provide the Alexandrian Jewish community with a "charter myth," a story of begin-nings intended to justify the use of the Septuagint as a sacred text in the present.[15]

The most important aim of the author of the *Letter of Aristeas* may never be determined with absolute certainty. There are elements of apolo-getic argument—like Eleazar's lengthy description of the reasonableness of the Jewish laws—which would seem to indicate that the author wished to make his account available primarily to Greeks. This may be true, but there is also an unambiguous appeal to the Jewish reader. The author may have hoped to convince his reader that the Greek translation was the very word of God for Alexandrian Jews. It is not clear if he intended to put this Greek Pentateuch above the celebrated Hebrew Bible of the Palestinian homeland. However, he certainly left the door open for later writers to do so and he implied that it was at least equal in status. The author's insistence on the translators' credentials serves to bolster the integrity of the Greek Pentateuch: the translators were not only on equal footing with the Greek philosophers (an appeal to the Hellenistic readership) but were also men specially selected by the High Priest Eleazar himself (an appeal to Jewish readers). Because such exemplary individuals rendered this translation, it stood to reason that it was just as suitable a vehicle of Divine revelation as was the Hebrew original. Moreover, the patronage of the king, the pristine original deposited in the library, and the reformulation of the motif of the Exodus and the giving of the Law at Sinai were used to validate the sacrosanctity of the translation. As we shall see, intentional modifications made in the earliest translation altered the meaning of the text for its new audience. What the translators had created was in effect a new Torah, and we did not need the *Letter of Aristeas* to tell us that. Some Jews and most Christians would soon come to believe it was indeed a new revelation from God himself.

Who Were the Translators?

Who were the translators of the Hebrew Torah? Were they transported from Palestine, as the *Letter of Aristeas* suggests, from elsewhere, or were they already in Egypt? Within the Pentateuch we do find hints that the translation was produced in Egypt. There may be traces in some books of a resistance to the Greek mysteries of Ptolemaic Egypt, such as in Deuteronomy 23:17, where there is an injunction prohibiting one from becoming an "initiate," which may refer to Dionysiac initiation.[16] There are also some Aramaic words (e.g., *sabbata* "Sabbath," *manna* "manna") that make their way into the Septuagint as loanwords, and these can be explained best as having been embedded into Egyptian Jewish linguistic usage earlier than the translation, at the time when Aramaic was giving way to Greek as the common language. Apart from Aramaic loanwords, there are others that reflect Egyptian connections, like *achei* "reeds," *thibis* "basket," and *oiphi* "epha," which are rare in Greek but found in Egyptian papyri of the third and second centuries BCE. These words are also in the Hebrew Bible as Egyptian loanwords in Hebrew, but the Greek transcriptions come straight from the Egyptian. The name of Moses is also Egyptian. In Greek, the translators gave the Hebrew *Moshe* the name *Mōūsēs*, probably based on the Egyptian word for water, *moou*.[17] None of these loanwords would have required that the translators knew the Egyptian language, but they do reflect the common vocabulary used in an Egyptian setting even by immigrants. An English speaker living in Mexico will refer to an enchilada as an enchilada even when speaking English at home; she doesn't invent a new word because the loanword has been fully appropriated in English. Cases of Egyptian language would seem to prove the Egyptian setting of the translation and its translators.

On occasion, the Septuagint evinces a concern to produce a translation with some panache, even if it would, by virtue of being a translation, fall short of the excellence of a contemporary like Polybius.[18] In the Pentateuch, the translators vary the words used to translate the same Hebrew word, alliterate in the absence of alliteration in the Hebrew source, and echo sound patterns, all of which are marks of style.[19] We have a clear example of the latter in Genesis 1:2. The Hebrew has a succession of poetic sounds for "a formless void" and "deep," and the translator has mimicked in Greek form the Hebrew assonances by using words beginning with a- and ending with -os/-ou: *ahoratos...akataskeuastos...abussou*. The English translation of the Greek with words beginning with un- preserves the same harmony of sound: "unseen...unsorted...unsounded." The style of the translation indicates that the translators had at least a basic education, but their training may have been no more than elementary.[20] All the evidence seems to point to moderately educated, Hellenized Jews in Alexandria. Unfortunately, certainty escapes us.

Why the Septuagint?

Why was the Septuagint produced? Scholars have pointed to several potential explanations. Even though the *Letter of Aristeas* is a fictional account, the royal patronage and deposit of the translation into the famous library is historically possible. If Ptolemy's instigation had nothing to do with inclusion in the library, he may still have allowed the Jews to have their own "native" law book to handle local disputes among themselves. As we saw in the previous chapter, this has historical precedent with Darius I allowing Egyptian priests to compile their own code and possible Persian support for the authorization of the Hebrew Torah after the exile. Even more relevant is the Greek translation of the Demotic Casebook produced probably under Philadelphus, but no evidence has proven the Demotic Casebook operated as local law.[21] The translation might have been produced for liturgical purposes to enable Hellenized Jews to continue their religious traditions even as their competence in Hebrew was diminishing.

Some scholars have very recently argued that the Septuagint is best understood when it is viewed "in a relation of dependence and subservience to its parent" and perhaps even that the Greek translation was produced in a school context, where students could use it with constant reference to the Hebrew.[22] Thus, the Septuagint at its initial point of creation was not an independent text, an autonomous document; it became such only in later reception. The view that has come to be called the Interlinear Paradigm guided the translators in the New English Translation of the Septuagint (NETS). NETS is a translation of the entire Septuagint, but even if the paradigm can explain the more literal translations, it is far less certain to be a useful way of thinking about the books whose translators had other stylistic concerns. While the theory has sometimes been caricatured, its theorists have perhaps gone too far to assert the inherent unintelligibility of the Septuagint.[23] Incomprehensibility may be a characteristic of *some* of the translations, but this is probably true only when the focus is on small translation units, usually only on individual words. It is less realistic to imagine that ancient readers could not have understood the text as a whole since one always reads a text in a context. Here too is a potential weakness of the paradigm. The theorists would argue for a sharp distinction between translation and reception; the ability of later users to make sense of it apart from the Hebrew poses no problem. But *later reception* does not mean the *original translation* was executed with the aim of readability.[24] Nevertheless, it is difficult to separate a translation from reception, or to hypothesize that the translation is unintelligible, since one is already a receiver of the text. Whatever its strengths, the Interlinear Paradigm has not convinced everyone. It is perhaps useful for some translated books but doubtful for all of them.

On balance, we struggle to find an explanation of the origins of the Septuagint. Jews in the third century BCE in Ptolemaic Alexandria had embraced the spirit of the culture around them to various degrees and almost universally through the linguistic medium. Alexandria was an exciting city of culture and learning, and translation and textual scholarship was in the air. In this environment these Jewish translators rendered their Hebrew scriptures into the language of the day. That may be all we can say about the origins of the Septuagint, even if the most attractive assumption is that a religious purpose motivated the project. We stand on firmer ground once we leave the hypothetical constructions of Septuagint origins and move into the early reception. There we find that whatever may explain the creation of the Septuagint, Hellenistic Jews soon began to use the texts as scripture. The Septuagint delivered to them the words they believed God gave to Moses, reformulated and communicated anew.

Once we move outside of these five books of Moses, which were unquestionably of unrivaled authority for Jews, it is more difficult to determine the contexts of the translations of the other books. Perhaps in the Maccabean period in the middle of the second century BCE processes were set in motion to begin finalizing the Hebrew Bible that we know today, and by the end of that century there would have been a Torah-Prophets collection, which probably also included Psalms.[25] Scholars have normally assumed that most of the other books in the Septuagint were translated in this same century and that the movement to establish Hebrew scriptural texts may have inspired the translation of other books near Jerusalem and in the Diaspora. But we cannot push this too far. Some are not at all persuaded to see a canonical motivation for the translation of the other books; the Greek books may rather be the result of a new literary consciousness.[26]

5

Gog and His Not-So-Merry Grasshoppers

This is what the Lord God showed me: he was forming
locusts at the time the latter growth began to sprout (it was
the latter growth after the king's mowings).

AMOS 7:1, Hebrew Bible

Thus the Lord showed me and behold, an early offspring
of grasshoppers coming, and behold, one locust larva, Gog
the king.

AMOS 7:1, Septuagint

HAD THE GREEK translators worked only a few centuries later—after the Hebrew Bible reached the end of its long process of growth (see Chapter 7)—we would have had a very different Septuagint. The various translations, however, were produced in a period of textual plurality, so we should expect the Septuagint to be a repository of textual artifacts that were otherwise lost once the Hebrew Bible was formed and all variety extinguished. We should also acknowledge that the Septuagint is unusual since it is composed of various translations created across different centuries and in different places. The translators would have had access to different Hebrew texts according to when and where they worked. As a collection both of translations of randomly chosen scriptural texts and of original Greek compositions, the Septuagint is an extraordinary monument to the textual plurality in early Judaism. When centuries later these manuscripts were brought together into collections, forerunners to our modern Bibles, the compilers accidently preserved the variety from the Bible's formative years. We shall see in the following chapters that the establishment of the Hebrew Bible had far-reaching effects, one of which was to give the impression that the text as it is now is the only one that ever was. Ever since the fulmination of Martin Luther's sixteenth-century conflict with the church many Protestants have never heard of the Septuagint and have never known that it played an integral part in the early church or that it remains the Bible of many other Christians to this day.

To gain a sense of how the Septuagint is unique, we must survey its books and highlight those places where differences emerge between the Hebrew and Greek forms. It should be clear by now that referring to the Septuagint as a Bible is anachronistic; the earliest evidence we have of a "Bible," in the modern sense of the term, is from the fourth century. At the time of the translations of these books, there were only loose collections of books with undefined borders. Nonetheless, very early in the Christian era the Septuagint was assumed to be the entire collection of the Greek Jewish Scriptures, even if it had not yet appeared in a single Bible. To avoid excessive confusion over these issues with which scholars continue to grapple, we will in this chapter focus only on those books translated from Hebrew texts that later made up the Hebrew Bible.

Exegetes often use the Septuagint only to discover which of the forms of scripture (whether Greek or Hebrew) represent the most "original" text, to which they also attribute the label "superior." We should not get distracted here by pursuing this question, especially since the Septuagint often transmits an alternative tradition that is neither earlier nor later but one that could have coexisted with the sources that made up the Hebrew Bible. Some of the differences in the Septuagint are related to the translators' use of divergent Hebrew texts but others are the translators' intentional changes and others still are their errors. An example of the latter is found in Numbers 16:15, where the translator read "desire" instead of "donkey" because the two words look almost identical in Hebrew script. We can usually detect that the translator had a different Hebrew base text if he utilizes a literal method of translation. Yet even as we observe how the Septuagint is a different form of scripture, we should refrain from exaggeration because much of the Septuagint is indeed very similar to the Hebrew Bible and thus to our English versions. So on one hand, nothing in the Septuagint will grab headlines for proving Solomon was celibate, that Elijah lived on a tract of land that would become Colorado, or that Adam and Eve were duped by a clever monkey instead of a serpent. On the other, the divergences are important enough and occur in enough places to demonstrate that before the second century CE the biblical text was characterized by variety and that the forms of scripture used by the New

Testament authors and early Christians in the church's formative stages (to be discussed later) undermine the impression of stability gained from reading modern Bibles.

Moses in Greek Dress

The translations of the five books traditionally attributed to Moses—Genesis to Deuteronomy—were produced sometime in the third or by the early second century BCE, and they may have provided the impetus if they were not the very source of the stream of Greek translations to follow. Some of the books that were to be translated in the following centuries appear to have drawn inspiration from the Pentateuch's vocabulary, leading some to suggest these books stood as a pilot version of the entire project. The various approaches to translation not only between the five books but also within individual books themselves might indicate a trial period in which the translators were grappling with the challenge of translating Hebrew to Greek, but nothing can tell us whether the translators intended eventually to translate the Hebrew scriptural texts outside the Torah. Whatever may have been the plan from the beginning, we know only that the Pentateuch came first and the others followed.

The Hebrew Torah is a composite of various materials gathered through centuries of oral and written tradition, finally compiled into an often disjointed but nevertheless beautiful narrative that tells the history of God's chosen people from creation to the death of Moses. In the previous chapter we discussed the mistaken assumption that the Torah was transmitted with more care than other books, ostensibly from a unique religious devotion to this portion of Hebrew scripture, but we saw from the examples among the Dead Sea Scrolls that the Torah was also undergoing transformations during this period. The Septuagint Pentateuch provides a glimpse of these developments in progress. There are harmonizations, places where two texts are slightly adjusted to cohere with one another. Some scholars point to the Septuagint translators as instigators of all harmonizing activity, but sometimes their Hebrew text contained harmonizations already. We find the tendency to eliminate contradictions more prevalent in the Septuagint of Genesis and Deuteronomy than in the other three books. When the harmonizations are found in both the Septuagint and the Samaritan Pentateuch, these suggest common Hebrew sources, or sources from a common origin in the distant past. There are doubtless features that may be attributed to the translator, but these are often exaggerated to support the myth of the textual stability of the Torah.

The translator of Genesis was, perhaps, "feeling his way step by step."[1] That this may have been the first translation is merely a guess, but it is not a bad one. Philo already assumes it in the first century CE (*On the Life of Moses* 2.37), and the translation style is inconsistent, oscillating between Greek elegance and clumsiness due to privileging the exact form of the Hebrew expression. There are interesting differences in the Septuagint. In Genesis 2:2, the New Standard Revised Version (NRSV), following the Hebrew Bible, reads: "And on the seventh day God finished the work that he had done..." It was on the sixth day, however, that God created his final work, the human being, and the Septuagint reflects a concern known elsewhere in Jewish traditions to resolve this apparent problem, recording in Genesis 2:2 that God finished his work on the sixth day. The seventh day is thus made a true Sabbath, since God was not finishing his work but resting completely. A very difficult issue in Genesis 4:7 has troubled exegetes. How could God condemn Cain for bringing an offering that is otherwise acceptable in the Mosaic Law?[2] The NRSV, on the basis of the Hebrew Bible, has God saying to Cain: "If you do well, will you not be accepted? And if you do not do well, sin is lurking at the door; its desire is for you, but you must master it." The Greek translator attempts to clarify: "If you offer correctly but do not divide correctly, have you not sinned? Be still; its recourse is to you, and you will rule over it." The rendition remains somewhat clumsy, but the Septuagint now suggests that Cain sinned because he did not divide the offering correctly.[3]

The Greek Exodus was produced by an "adventurous" translator.[4] He was versed in Jewish exegetical practices, as some of the renderings in chapters 12–23 are similar to those found in rabbinic writings much later. The Tabernacle accounts (chapters 25–31 and 35–40) have fascinated many exegetes because we can tell from the study of the translation technique that the Greek translator had before him an alternative Hebrew text.[5] In the second Tabernacle account, the Hebrew Bible and the Septuagint are at odds in their length and in their arrangement of the material, not an insignificant matter since these are meant to be God's precise regulations. Against the Hebrew Bible's ordering of chapters 36–39, the Septuagint's order in chapters 36–37 is not unlike the Temple Scroll found at Qumran (11QTᵃ).[6] The Hebrew Bible seems to be an expansion of an earlier, shorter Hebrew text that we can access now only through a careful reading of the Septuagint. This phenomenon of later expansion is seen again and again when reading the Septuagint and the Hebrew Bible in tandem.

In Numbers there are also indications that the Septuagint and the Hebrew Bible reflect two different literary stages of the book. In Numbers 27:15–23, for example, the two versions depart from one another in vocabulary and in the implementation of the command to appoint Joshua.[7] Likewise, in the Song of the Ark (Numbers 10:33–36) the order differs. In the Hebrew edition translated by the Septuagint, verse 34 followed 35 and 36, giving the more sensible order vv. 33–35–36–34.

Deuteronomy was translated by one well acquainted with Jewish law, who was not reluctant to update the text to address concerns in his own day. We saw already (Chapter 4) that in 23:17–18 we may have a reference to the Dionysiac mysteries of Ptolemaic Egypt. Whether or not the additional phrase refers to this specific cult, it is surely a modification intended to address temptations Jews were facing in the Hellenistic world. Other forms of Deuteronomy found at Qumran that are more expansionistic than the Hebrew Bible (e.g., 4QDeut[d]) help us to understand the Greek Deuteronomy's version of the *Shema*. In the Hebrew Bible the *Shema* is found at 6:4. However, by including a preface that is a recitation of a formula such as that found in Deuteronomy 4:45 the Septuagint reflects an ancient Jewish reading (whether the Septuagint translator himself created it or the reading was based on a Hebrew text that had the preface) that has tied the central confession of the Jewish faith inseparably to the Decalogue (the "Ten Commandments" are referred to as the "Decalogue"; once again, the word is Greek: *deka-* "ten" + *logos* "word," a translation of the Hebrew *asereth hadevarim* "ten words").[8]

Septuagint	Hebrew Bible
[4] And these are the statues and the judgments with the Lord commanded to the sons of Israel in the wilderness as they were coming out from the land of Egypt.	
Hear, O Israel: The Lord our God is one Lord.	[4]Hear, O Israel: The Lord is our God, the Lord alone.

Another prominent example is at the end of the Song of Moses, in 32:43 where the Greek is longer than the Hebrew.

Septuagint	Hebrew Bible = New International Version (NIV)
Be glad, O skies, with him, and let all the divine sons do obeisance to him.	
Be glad, O nations, with his people, and let all the angels of God prevail for him.	Rejoice, O nations, with his people,
For he will avenge the blood of his sons and take revenge and repay the enemies with a sentence, and he will repay those who hate,	for he will avenge the blood of his servants; he will take vengeance on his enemies
and the Lord shall cleanse the land of his people.	and make atonement for his land and people.

good example

The King James Version (KJV) and NIV mirror the Hebrew Bible, but the NRSV has made several modifications by taking some of the readings from the Septuagint. We can see that even for readers of the English Bible an acquaintance with the Septuagint would be useful:

> Praise, O heavens, his people, worship him, all you gods! For he will avenge the blood of his children, and take vengeance on his adversaries; he will repay those who hate him, and cleanse the land for his people. (NRSV)

The degree of correlation between the Septuagint Pentateuch and the Hebrew Bible is relatively high, but we already see here in the first translation that the text for Greek-speaking Jews is different to the tradition that soon became the Hebrew Bible. In the centuries following this translation we shall see how the legend of the *Letter of Aristeas* is reframed and reinterpreted by Jewish and Christian writers. The different meanings that flow from the Greek Pentateuch and stand in contrast to those from the Hebrew Torah required later interpreters to stress that God inspired the Greek translators. Although the writer of the *Letter of Aristeas* himself does not make this explicit, Philo and others eventually will; indeed, they had to justify the use of scriptures that led them down interpretative paths away from those of the Hebrew Torah.

After the Pentateuch

Most of the remaining books in the Septuagint were probably translated in the next two centuries after the completion of the Greek Pentateuch. Some scholars have proposed a rough sketch of estimated dates, which implies some order of importance to the books that were translated, but the dates are difficult and sometimes impossible to confirm, although many were probably finished by the end of the first century BCE. The order in which they were translated is also difficult to determine. One could deny the order of the translations was tied to the canonical process within Judaism, but it may also make sense that the growing authoritative status of the Prophets, which in early Jewish tradition included Joshua to 2 Kings, provided an impetus for their translation. It might also mean these books were more important in this period of Judaism: the translators may have moved from Torah to Psalms and Prophets and only then on to the remaining books. This sequence would have been the most natural, given that the so-called tripartite canon of the Hebrew Bible—Torah, Nevi'im, Ketuvim: Law, Prophets, Writings—was not known until second century BCE at the earliest, and the Ketuvim would have been a shifting collection until the Hebrew Bible was finalized in the second century CE. There was presumably less urgency to translate books like Ecclesiastes, whose canonical status was in any case debated quite vigorously for centuries to come.

Alternative Versions of Israel's History

The Septuagint versions of Joshua, Judges, Samuel, and Kings were translated no later than the first half of the second century BCE, confirmed by their use already in the second half of the second century by the Jewish Hellenistic historian Eupolemus.[9] Yet because the Hebrew Bible wasn't finalized until after the Greek translation, the Septuagint translation of the Deuteronomistic History (Joshua to 2 Kings) allows us to see an alternative version of the Hebrew text from the third and second centuries BCE. There are interesting cases in Joshua and Judges, but the most significant glimpses of alternative scriptural traditions are in the books of Samuel and Kings.[10]

The books of Samuel are not the most frequently discussed in Jewish and Christian exegetical traditions but many of their stories are familiar to the most casual reader of the Bible. Samuel and Kings are part of the same mini-narrative within the larger Deuteronomistic History, and they are treated as such in the Greek translations with the titles 1–4 Kingdoms

(1–2 Samuel = 1–2 Kingdoms; 1–2 Kings = 3–4 Kingdoms). Accounting for the development of Samuel–Kings has long been one of the most difficult issues in biblical scholarship. And in addition to the questions of the books' prehistory, scribes transmitting the final Hebrew version have introduced, particularly in Samuel, a significant amount of corruptions and errors. Even the most conservative exegetes admit that Samuel is highly corrupted. A prime example in 1 Samuel 14:41 can be seen in the English Bibles, which have followed the Septuagint instead of the Hebrew Bible. The italicized portion that follows is missing in Hebrew. This error was caused when the scribe copying the older Hebrew text skipped from the first "Israel" to the next and omitted everything in between.

> Then Saul said, "O Lord God of Israel, *why have you not answered your servant today? If this guilt is in me or in my son Jonathan, O Lord God of Israel, give Urim; but if this guilt is in your people Israel,* give Thummim." And Jonathan and Saul were indicated by the lot, but the people were cleared.

These scribal corruptions aside, the more interesting variations are the ones in which the Septuagint follows an alternative Hebrew version, especially in some well-known stories like David and Goliath. This story of the underdog beginning in 1 Samuel 17 has come down to us in English versions from the Hebrew Bible, which is, however, an expanded version of the story. The earlier version is preserved in the Septuagint and is significantly shorter. For example, the Greek version lacks the details about David delivering food to his brothers, his first hearing of Goliath's challenge, and his contemplation of the risk and reward of getting involved, all of which were added to the later edition (17:12–31). Other well-known episodes are also later additions to the story. The covenant Jonathan makes with David (18:1–5) and the story of Saul's evil spirit (18:10–11) were later insertions. These are only a few of the many changes made in this updated edition of the Hebrew text, and in 2 Samuel there are more. The most striking may be that in the later Hebrew edition of 2 Samuel, Jerusalem is more clearly marked out as the place of divine choice for the Temple. In 2 Samuel 15:8, the NRSV follows the oldest Greek (preserved only in a few manuscripts) in having the final two words "in Hebron": "For your servant made a vow while I lived at Geshur in Aram: If the Lord will indeed bring me back to Jerusalem, then I will worship the Lord in Hebron." The editors of the

Hebrew Bible deleted these words to ensure that their readers looked to Jerusalem alone as the proper place of worship.[11]

Solomon ascends to the throne after the death of his father and most of 1 Kings is concerned with his reign. The other major figure in this book is the prophet Elijah, and in 2 Kings the narrative is concerned to a large extent with his successor Elisha. The characterizations of each of these figures vary between the Septuagint and that of the Hebrew Bible. Many are not linguistic or translational issues but include large-scale differences: different narrative details and theological emphases in the entire Solomon narrative (1 Kings 1–11); the rearrangement of narrative sections, such as the switching of the order of 1 Kings 20 and 21; the duplication of material found elsewhere; and different versions of the same section. The account of Jeroboam's rise to power is told in 1 Kings 11–12, and in the Greek version it is retold a second time immediately after that (12:24a–z). The second story is certainly based on a Hebrew text. To explain these vastly different versions, scholars do not agree on whether the Hebrew text underlying the Septuagint was an earlier edition or even one that was a later interpretation of the one that is found in the Hebrew Bible.[12]

For many reasons, untangling the problems related to the various editions of the Deuteronomistic History (Joshua to 2 Kings) is one of the most challenging tasks for modern scholars, but the contribution of the Septuagint to resolving some of the difficulties has not always been appreciated. For example, only recently have scholars begun to recognize that the Hebrew edition used by the Septuagint translators of Samuel and Kings is most likely the same source of the writer of Chronicles. Previously, it was assumed that the Chronicler had simply retold the stories from Samuel and Kings in his own way. But the Septuagint is now clarifying the relationship by showing that the Chronicler had before him a different Hebrew source.[13] We can see in this simple overview that the Septuagint in the so-called Historical Books is strikingly different from the Hebrew Bible and consequently from our modern English versions.

Prophets and Poets

Along with the Torah and Psalms, in the history of Jewish and Christian exegesis Isaiah is paramount. The Greek translation of Isaiah is a work of art. There are, to be sure, numerous cases where the translator has misunderstood his Hebrew text, but these are often overstated. The translator follows very faithfully his Hebrew source, rendering the sense as he understands it and often producing a highly styled Greek.[14] At times he may interpret his Hebrew text according to the theological outlook of Egyptian Jews of the second century BCE but it is not always easy to determine the extent of his theological aims. The Greek Isaiah can be read as a fresh work distinct from the Hebrew Bible's version of Isaiah and thus from modern English versions of Isaiah, even if it is impossible to know whether the translator intended it to be read as such.[15] The so-called Servant Songs are influential in the theology of Paul and the early church, and one of them, Isaiah 52:13–53:12, is transformed in the Greek translation from its original meaning in the Hebrew. We have no witnesses from Qumran or elsewhere that should suggest the translator had a different Hebrew text in this passage; instead, we see his creativity at work. The translator seems not to have understood everything about the Hebrew text before him in this fourth Servant Song, just as it continues to test modern interpreters, and it is not insignificant that the apostle Paul and his later interpreters in the early church will employ these mistranslations in the formation of Christian theology.[16]

The Septuagint of Jeremiah was translated from an earlier, shorter Hebrew version such as the ones discovered at Qumran. Some 2,700 verses that are found in the later Hebrew edition, and now in our English Bible, were not part of this earlier edition. Several clear examples were discussed in the previous chapter in connection with the Qumran scrolls but we may also note a few more. In Jeremiah 31:27–34 (Septuagint 38:27–34), the Hebrew Bible features the unshakable faithfulness of God in spite of the disobedience of Israel. The key is in verse 32. In the Hebrew Bible we read "...a covenant that they broke, though I was their husband," but in the Septuagint we read "...because they did not abide in my covenant, and I was unconcerned for them." The later editors of the Hebrew Bible considered the suggestion that God was "unconcerned" for disobedient Israel out of sync with the faithfulness that writers of other scriptural texts claimed was characteristic of God. They changed this startling phrase in the text to reinforce God's faithfulness, having him say "though I was their husband," which means "though I remained faithful to them in spite of their disobedience." The Septuagint version, however, was followed in the New Testament and early Christianity: the author of Hebrews (8:9) quotes that phrase found in the Septuagint of Jeremiah, reinforcing the idea that God was "unconcerned" for disobedient Israel. Another important passage is Jeremiah 33:14–26, where the Lord promises that "David shall never lack a man to sit on the throne of the house of Israel," and it is difficult for modern readers to imagine reading Jeremiah without it. This very important passage promoting Davidic ideology is lacking in the earliest Septuagint translation but was added later into the Hebrew Bible as the significance of David's role in God's covenant with Israel was taking on new dimensions. The passage is a rich example of a Jewish theology in development and indicates that, in the second century BCE when the Septuagint of Jeremiah was translated, some Hebrew scriptural texts in circulation had not yet incorporated the emerging Davidic theology.[17]

The book of Ezekiel contains some of the most exciting language in the Bible, which inspired the visions in Revelation in the New Testament—indeed Revelation 21–22 must have been written with Ezekiel in mind—but might also have left its mark on two other writings in the Hebrew Bible: Daniel and Zechariah 1–8. Here again, because the Hebrew book itself shows many signs of heavy editorial activity, one should not be surprised to learn that the Septuagint provides evidence of a Hebrew text different from the edition of the Hebrew Bible. A very important second century CE fragment of papyrus (Papyrus 967) was discovered in 1931 in Aphroditopolis, Egypt, which may shed light on the earlier form of Ezekiel. In this fragment of the Greek Ezekiel, there are two important differences with the Hebrew Bible of Ezekiel. First, chapters 36–39 appear in the order 36–38–39–37, which means that the resurrection takes place after Gog and Magog, at the end of time. The second difference is that 36:23c–38 are missing. This is a very rich passage in which God promises to give a new heart to the people, replacing theirs of stone, and to put his spirit within them; but it is difficult for modern readers to appreciate that this was not originally in the older Hebrew text or in the earliest Septuagint text.[18]

The final collection of prophetic works in the Hebrew Bible consists of twelve shorter books by twelve different named prophets, sometimes called the Twelve Prophets and sometimes Minor Prophets. While each of these prophecies was individually composed between the eight and sixth centuries BCE and some of the early Jewish exegetical works discovered in the Judean Desert separate them and do not mention them as a whole, they have been read as a unified work as early as the first decade of the second century BCE. Ben Sira, writing the Hebrew version of the book with his name, already refers to them as a unity in 190 BCE: "May the bones of the Twelve Prophets send forth new life from where they lie, for they comforted the people of Jacob and delivered them with confident hope" (49:10). There was probably only one translator for the entire book of the Twelve, and his source was very close to the Hebrew Bible; however, there are numerous variations related to theology and style, not to mention that the order of the twelve differs. One such example of theological importance is found in the Greek translation of Zechariah where we notice the *lack of* any expectation of a return of a Davidic king, reflecting perhaps that the text's creators were content without a king.[19] For Hosea, the Hebrew text used by the translator of the Septuagint is likely to have preceded the final updating of the Hebrew Bible. One example is in Hosea 13:4, where the italicized words indicate the ones found in the Septuagint and its Hebrew version but then omitted in the later edition: "I am the Lord your God *who makes heaven firm and creates earth, whose hands created all the host of the sky. And I did not display them for you to follow after them. And I brought you up* from the land of Egypt."[20] Probably the most entertaining example reveals how the Septuagint provides a window into the development of Jewish thought in the Hellenistic period, as it leans ever more toward the eschatological. In Amos 7:1, the Hebrew Bible reports Amos's vision in which the Lord was preparing swarms of locusts to attack the land at a time that would have devastated the land. In the Septuagint, however, the meaning is transformed, and now Amos communicates that the locust attack is a symbolic army led by Gog, who makes his appearance from the Ezekiel traditions of Gog and Magog. In Hellenistic Jewish literature, an increasing fascination with Ezekiel's Gog and Magog; the well-known biblical imagery of attacking locusts from Joel and Nahum; and a new sense of expectation and impending doom allowed the translator of Amos to recreate the text. What later readers may have made of the symbolism is another discussion, but the translator certainly gave this passage a new apocalyptic dimension.[21]

Daniel was transmitted in two distinct Greek versions, the Septuagint and the version attributed to one of the three famous Greek Jewish revisers, Theodotion (the others are Aquila and Symmachus; see Chapter 7). Theodotion became the primary version of Daniel transmitted in almost all other Christian manuscripts. Here again as in Ezekiel, the study of Papyrus 967 is crucial since in Daniel it also preserves an alternative order (chapters 1–4; 7; 8; 5; 6; 9–12). The Theodotion version follows the Hebrew Bible but the Septuagint version is longer and its language more exciting. Like Esther, Daniel also accumulated additions (Chapter 6) to supplement the main text.

Job was translated into Greek prose even though large parts of the Hebrew book of Job are poetic. It is a good translation that avoids mimicking the Hebraic style often found in other books and some consider it the most unique of all the Greek translations. The Greek version raises complex questions: it is almost four hundred verses shorter than the Hebrew Bible, and as we have seen elsewhere the Greek version could reflect an alternative Hebrew edition. But here in Job it is also possible that the translator abridged the book by avoiding the Hebrew author's repetitious method and by reformulating some of the expressions he found difficult in the original Hebrew. Because of the close study of this translator's technique, we can see he works differently than the translator of, say, Samuel or Jeremiah, so the differences could be his doing rather than related to the development of the Hebrew tradition. We also see the translator at work when he seems to have softened the blow of some of Job's more vitriolic outbursts against God or rewrites sections that reveal his own distinctive theological outlook.

The Psalter was one of the most important collections of Scripture in the ancient world for Jews, and later for Christians. Along with the Torah and Isaiah it is quoted very often in the New Testament and in early Christian writings. Almost anyone who has ever encountered a Bible will know of Psalms and will have noticed that printed New Testaments often contain Psalms at the end. The Psalter's importance also means that scholars face the daunting task of trying to figure out the earliest Greek form of the collection, an overwhelming undertaking since the number of manuscripts dwarfs other books. Another complicating factor is that the brevity of these compositions meant that they were often copied and used apart from the whole collection, so that each psalm could have had its own transmission history. There are 151 psalms in the Septuagint and the divisions of the Greek Psalms do not always match the same divisions in the Hebrew; Psalms 10–148 in our English versions, following the Hebrew Bible, are numbered differently than the Greek, some of which are due to the combination of independent psalms. In the Septuagint, for example, Psalm 113 is comprised of the Hebrew Psalms 114 and 115. The translators who were responsible for the Greek Psalter follow their Hebrew source closely for the most part, but this has often been overstated. Their stylistic and theological renditions are equally impressive. In Psalm 8, for example, we find one of the most important theological innovations in the entire Bible. After Genesis 1:26–27 and 2:7, some scholars have seen Psalm 8 as the third-ranking exposition of anthropology in the Hebrew Bible.[22] The Greek translator makes a theological decision that will later impact Christian interpretation, using "angels" instead of "God" in verse 5 (verse 6 in the Septuagint). The Hebrew Bible, speaking of human beings, reads: "Yet you have made them a little lower than God..." The Septuagint translator was perhaps bothered by the suggestion that human beings were only "a little lower" than God, so he changed the passage to read: "You diminished him a little in comparison with angels." The *Common Worship Psalter* in the Anglican Church still uses the reading of the Septuagint today.[23]

The Greek translation of Proverbs reveals a number of expansionistic lines when compared with the Hebrew Bible. A number of these come from elsewhere in the Septuagint but there are good reasons to see them as part of the Hebrew version used by the translator rather than due to a creative departure from his Hebrew source. Two noticeable differences are the order of chapters in the Greek version, which may have been shuffled by the translator himself but more probably were arranged thus already in his Hebrew text, and the elimination of other personal names to ensure Solomon receives the credit for the collection, again possibly due to the translator but more probably the suppression of the names that had already been effected in his Hebrew text.[24] The translator is nonetheless responsible for some of the differences. He may reveal his knowledge of Hellenistic philosophy when in 6:8a he follows mention of the ant with a new line about the bee, not found here in the Hebrew: the progression of ant to bee and the description of the bee as "industrious" picks up the language of Aristotle's *Historia Animalium* (622B).[25]

The Final Translations

These final books were probably translated at the end of a centuries-long process that began with the Pentateuch. Scholars believe these were produced no earlier than the end of the second century BCE, but some may have been completed as late as the second century CE. Recent research on the translations indicate that at least four of the books known in Jewish tradition as the "Five Festal Scrolls"—Song of Songs, Ruth, Lamentations, Ecclesiastes, and Esther—were translated at the end of the period and are characterized by a very literal method of translation that was becoming more common at the time the Hebrew text was approaching the end of its process of formation. The finalization of the Hebrew Bible and the literal translations accentuate the development of a theological view that the precise form of the text was important to mediate the words of God. Even though the medium was Greek, representing the Hebrew form would ensure the most accurate communication of the divine word, even if the style of the Greek language had to be violated. Nonetheless, recent investigations have shown that such a view of the Hebrew did not mean the translators produced a text altogether void of elegance. Ecclesiastes, for example, stands at the far end of the spectrum in its literalism, but it has been demonstrated that even there we can find outstanding examples of Greek rhetorical and poetic devices.[26]

Esther is somewhat different. An idiosyncrasy of the book is the absence of any mention of God or of any number of major theological emphases of ancient Jewish tradition. It is thus largely a secular book that focuses on ethnic, not religious, identity. The Greek translation has been preserved in two special forms, the Septuagint and the so-called Alpha Text, but scholars are not decided on which represents the most original form or whether one is a revision of the other.[27] Both the Septuagint and the Alpha Text contain the additions to be discussed in the next chapter, but they were not present in the original translation. On the whole, the Septuagint and Alpha Text follow the Hebrew Bible very closely, a common feature of all of these Greek translations produced at the end of the translational process.

Even More Scriptures

In this chapter, we have had to talk about the Septuagint imperfectly. Because the Hebrew Bible canon was not finalized until the second century CE, it is not entirely satisfactory to focus only on these books in this chapter or to separate the ones in the next as "Apocrypha." Nonetheless, since many modern Jews and Christians conceive of the Hebrew Bible/ Old Testament in this way, we have taken a tour through the books in the Septuagint that are translations of the Hebrew and Aramaic books that were, in the centuries to come, formalized and canonized into what we now call the Hebrew Bible. In the next chapter we will learn of new writings produced between the third century BCE and the finalization of the Hebrew Bible around the second century CE, which were included in the Septuagint and treated as scriptural texts by ancient Jews and by many Christians throughout history.

6

Bird Droppings, Stoned Elephants, and Exploding Dragons

So during the forty days, ninety-four books were written.
And when the forty days were ended, the Most High spoke
to me, saying, "Make public the twenty-four books that
you wrote first, and let the worthy and the unworthy read
them; but keep the seventy that were written last, in order to
give them to the wise among your people. For in them is
the spring of understanding, the fountain of wisdom, and
the river of knowledge."

2 ESDRAS 14:44–47

"APOCRYPHA," A WORD that conveys mystery to many who have become familiar with the Bible in the Protestant tradition, is a plural Greek noun (singular: *apocryphon*) meaning "hidden," "obscure," "unknown," or "secret." From at least the late fourth century CE the term was used to refer to a collection of biblical books. There is nothing intrinsic to the books that would hint that they should have been separated from the others, and this pejorative term was applied long after they were written. The reasons for their exclusion in the Jewish and some Christian biblical canons are complex, but many early Jews and Christians treated them as scriptural texts. For this reason it would have been better to introduce them in the preceding chapters along with the other books since during the centuries of the Septuagint's formation there was nothing like the Apocrypha as we know it today. Nonetheless, because many readers have never encountered these books and many others have been taught to view them with a suspicion that mischaracterizes them, they are the subject of this chapter.

An Era of Literary Excitement

The period between c. 200 BCE and c. 200 CE was one of vibrant literary activity for both Jews and Christians. Dozens of works of various genres related to the Jewish scriptures and to scriptural figures were produced, most of them later subsumed under the name "pseudepigrapha" (from Greek: *pseudo* "false" + *epigraphein* "to inscribe") as many of them claim to have been written by a famous figure from the Jewish scriptures. Their pseudonymity, however, does not fully explain their exclusion from canonical literature: some books even within the received canons of scripture are pseudonymous—Daniel, Ecclesiastes, Ephesians, and 2 Peter, to name but a few—and some of the pseudepigrapha like *Lives of the Prophets* and *Joseph and Aseneth* are anonymous. The passage near the end of the book of 2 Esdras—written c. 100 CE and cited at the head of this chapter—seems to indicate that, at least for some, many of the books produced in this period were no less inspired than the others, even though today the word pseudepigrapha has pejorative connotations.[1]

The Christian Old Testament has thirty-nine books, but in the Hebrew Bible there are twenty-four because some are counted as one (e.g., Samuel, Kings, the Twelve Prophets). Some have assumed that when the writer of 2 Esdras mentions that twenty-four books were to be read by all, he is referring to the exact composition of the Hebrew Bible. There is no way to prove this and no way of knowing whether some of the books that made up the twenty-four were books like the Letter of Jeremiah or Sirach in place of books like Esther and Ecclesiastes, which continued to be debated for centuries. The writer also asserts that the Most High said seventy additional books should be set apart for the wise, and although the number is symbolic he was indicating a large number. In other words, they were still divine but intended only for a select readership. While many discount the value of the pseudepigrapha due to their spurious claims to authorship, it would seem that ancient readers weren't bothered with the authenticity of the authorial claims like modern readers may be. Two pseudepigrapha in particular, 1 Enoch and Jubilees, were read as authoritative scripture at Qumran, and they have always been scripture in the Ethiopian Orthodox Church.

The collection of books in the so-called Old Testament Apocrypha has a different story from that of the pseudepigrapha. They were produced by the end of the second century CE both in Palestine and elsewhere in the Diaspora, were included in the Septuagint along with those books translated from what became the canonical Hebrew Bible, but have been excluded from the canons of Scripture by all Jews and Protestant Christians. It would be a mistake to assume that the Apocrypha is a coherent, clearly defined body of writings: the books do not have the same generic or thematic relationship to one another such as might be found in the books of the Torah or the Prophets or the New Testament Gospels but were merely grouped together by later compilers of scriptural texts to set them apart from the canonical books. But if it were a mistake to fail to appreciate the diversity of the collection, it would also be mistaken to imagine that they have never been read as divine scripture.

By the second century CE, at the end of this period of creative writing, the Hebrew Bible we know today reached the end of a long process of growth. Some of the Apocrypha were composed in Greek and thus left aside, but they might also have been considered too new for inclusion. There was a premium on antiquity in the Greco-Roman world in which the Bible was finalized and recently written books were no match for the prestige and presumed sanctity of books written long before.

As we shall see, early Christians held varying opinions about the apocryphal books, but the division represented in English versions like the King James Version (KJV) or New Revised Standard Version (NRSV), which have a separate section for the Apocrypha between the Old and New Testaments, was a later innovation. The Roman Catholic Church considers several of these books "deuterocanonical," meaning "second canon," but their secondary status refers to the late date at which they were approved at the Council of Trent in 1546, not to a lesser spiritual value. Catholics distinguish between "deuterocanonical" and "apocryphal," the latter of which were not declared canonical at Trent but are still printed in the Bibles. The Orthodox Churches, however, consider all of the Apocrypha together and continue to read them in the liturgy. Hence, in the Greek Orthodox Church they are called *anagignoskomena*, "things that are read" for spiritual enrichment and instruction. There are further distinctions among the Orthodox Churches: the Armenian, Syriac, Coptic, Georgian, Slavonic, and Ethiopian churches all have different canons, and only the Ethiopian Orthodox have canonized other books like 1 Enoch and Jubilees. This lack of agreement among the churches should be borne in mind when one speaks of the Bible as "the" Christian Bible.

Some of these writings were original Greek compositions with no Semitic original and are by this feature distinguished from all the other books in the Septuagint that were translated from Hebrew and Aramaic.

A future discovery of a Semitic (Hebrew or Aramaic) original is unlikely since the style of the Greek is obviously that of an original composition and not a translation. Two of the Additions to Esther, B and E; 2, 3, and 4 Maccabees; the Prayer of Manasseh; the Wisdom of Solomon; and Baruch all fit in this latter category. Others were composed in Hebrew and Aramaic, confirmed now by the discoveries of Hebrew and Aramaic manuscripts from the Judean Desert and others from the medieval manuscripts found in Cairo: Tobit, Sirach, and Psalm 151.[2] Although there is no tangible proof at present, the style of Judith and the Letter of Jeremiah suggests that they might have been original Semitic compositions, though they could have been originally written in a Greek style marked by Semitic idiomatic features. Apparent Semitic features in a Greek text are never alone proof of an underlying Semitic source; the author could have been imitating the style of the Septuagint.[3] There are nonetheless books more likely to have been based on Semitic originals, even though we have no manuscript evidence at the moment: 1–2 Esdras; four of the Additions to Esther; 1 Maccabees; and the Additions to Daniel.[4]

Some of these books typify a common trait of authors of Hellenistic Jewish literature (including those of the pseudepigrapha): the intention to resolve perceived difficulties in the Hebrew version of the book. We shall see that the Additions to Esther are a prime example. The apocryphal writings are also of several genres—including wisdom, apocalyptic, historiographic, penitential, psalmodic, and historical fiction—and sometimes a single book contains more than one. Many of the apocryphal books do not name their author and the precise dates of the compositions are equally obscure. This is not unique to these books since the authorship and dates of most of the canonical books of the Hebrew Bible are also difficult to determine. The book of Isaiah, for example, contains material that could be dated to the eighth century BCE prophet, but the finished book contains many other elements that came from different contributors at later times. The traditions surrounding the apocryphal books and their affiliations with historic personages of Israel's past like Solomon and Jeremiah were not strong enough to ensure their inclusion in the canon, and clues within the books reveal that they were of much later date than the times of their alleged authors. The English translation of the Septuagint otherwise used in this book (New English Translation of the Septuagint: NETS) includes also the Psalms of Solomon since they appear in some early Greek manuscripts, but this collection of 18 psalms have never enjoyed canonical status in any church.[5]

Esdras A' and B'	Prayer of Manasseh
Additions to Esther	Wisdom of Solomon
Judith	Sirach
Tobit	Baruch
1–4 Maccabees	Letter of Jeremiah
Psalm 151	Additions to Daniel

Esdras A' and B'

The books bearing the title Esdras vary in several different traditions in an admittedly discombobulating way, but in the English versions 1 and 2 Esdras refer to the apocryphal books that share little in common and were composed in different periods. In the Greek manuscripts, Esdras A' and Esdras B' are parallel traditions, with some different material. Esdras A', or 1 Esdras (= 2 Esdras in Slavonic and 3 Esdras in the Appendix to the Vulgate), is the reworked account of material found in Chronicles and Ezra-Nehemiah and was translated in the second century BCE likely from a Semitic original but with attention to Greek style. Most of the book is a plain translation of Chronicles 35–36, Ezra 1–10, and Nehemiah 7:73–8:12, with the exception of a story in 3:1–5:6 not found in the Hebrew Bible. The Story of the Three Guards was written in Hebrew or Aramaic and perhaps circulated independently before it was added to the narrative to give Zerubbabel more prominence over Nehemiah. Debate continues, but it is also possible this story reflects an earlier account of the history told in Ezra-Nehemiah, which was suppressed later to elevate Nehemiah over Zerubbabel.[6] The setting for the story is the court of the Persian King Darius and concerns a wisdom contest between three young bodyguards at a banquet. The motif of a Jew displaying his wisdom in the court of a king is similar to the wisdom contest found in the *Letter of Aristeas* but is also not without canonical antecedents (e.g., Joseph, Esther, Daniel). The writer narrates that three youths display their wisdom when the king gives them a riddle and asks them to decide whether wine, the king, or women are the most powerful. We are told that the winning contestant is Zerubbabel, who answers that, while women rule both wine and the king, truth conquers all. Zerubbabel's sly retort set up his reminder that the king had vowed to rebuild the Temple and the city of Jerusalem. As champion of the contest, Zerubbabel is given the privilege to lead the people out of exile and to rebuild Jerusalem and the Temple.

The Additions to Esther

Esther acquired six supplementary passages in its Greek version, adding 107 verses to the 194 that had already existed in the Hebrew book. The Additions are spread throughout, added where it was felt the Hebrew version was deficient, and they are marked in the manuscripts by the capital letters A–F. Those who produced the Additions intended them to be read as part of the narrative.

A	Preface to Esther 1	Mordecaï's dream
B	between 3:13 and 3:14	text of Artaxerxes's edict
C	before chapter 5	prayers of Mordecai and Esther
D	replaces 5:1–2	Esther in the court
E	between 8:12 and 8:13	text of Artaxerxes's second edict
F	end of book	Mordecaï's dream understood

At least four (A, C, D, F) were based on Semitic originals and thus could have been composed in Palestine, but the style of Artaxerxes's edicts (B and E) prove these were undoubtedly written in Greek and could have been composed outside of Palestine. Because several are quoted by Josephus in his *Jewish Antiquities* (c. 93 CE), they must have been written before the end of the first century, and a note following the final Addition F indicates that at least the A and F Semitic portions had already been written by the late second or early first century BCE. The Greek translation of Esther is more intentionally pious. The Hebrew Bible version of Esther fails to mention God at all, a feature that has long troubled interpreters and led to the writing of this additional material, in which the authors add "Lord" or "God" more than fifty times. Even the Additions based on Hebrew or Aramaic originals added more religious character to the book. In the Hebrew Bible and in our English versions it is curious that Esther hides her Jewish identity and is brought without complaint into the king's harem and made queen. This proves too much for later readers, prompting the writing of Addition C in which Esther prays for God's help and confesses, "You know that I hate the glory of the lawless and abhor the bed of the uncircumcised and of any foreigner. You know my predicament—that I abhor the sign of my proud position that is upon my head on days when I appear in public. I abhor it like a menstrual cloth, and I do not wear it on the days when I am in private." She continues by professing that she had not eaten at Haman's table, had the wine of libations, and has "not rejoiced since the day of my change until now" in her new position (C:22–30).

Judith

Judith was for a long time thought to have been written in Hebrew, but there is now good reason to suppose that it was an original Greek composition.[7] It could not have been composed later than the end of the first century CE when it is mentioned in Clement of Rome's *Epistle to Corinthians* (1.55), and a Maccabean setting in the second century BCE is plausible as an early date. The author of this book provides a sympathetic depiction of feminine intelligence, strength, and beauty in his heroine Judith. Ultimately by her faith in God, but not unassisted by her charms, this pious widow kills Nebuchadnezzar's feared general Holofernes, saving her town of Bethulia and also Jerusalem. The historical claims of the story are implausible—for example, Nebuchadnezzar is king of the Assyrians—but this is conscious historical fiction. The "facts" are presented only to give it a semblance of real-world authenticity—imagine Henry VIII as the king of France in a modern work of historical fiction—and the explicit violation of historical knowledge lifts the story's message outside time and place: Vivaldi drew inspiration from Judith in *Juditha triumphans*, a celebration of the Venetian victory over the Turks during the siege of Corfu of 1716.[8] The first half of the story paints a picture of insurmountable opposition faced by Judeans as the Assyrians were setting up for war and allows the author to stun the reader when a single woman, Judith—like the biblical heroines Jael and Deborah—is used by God to defeat the enemy, but not without the assistance of her beauty. Judith goes right into the enemy camp and the Assyrians become like nervous teenage boys at a high school prom. Judith's appearance causes them to lose control of their judgment and they take her right into the tent of Holofernes. After her speech promising to turn over Bethulia to the Assyrians, Holofernes and his servants exclaim, "No other woman from one end of the earth to the other looks so beautiful or speaks so wisely!" Holofernes goes on: "You are not only beautiful in appearance, but wise in speech" (11:21–23).[9] Not only are you beautiful, Holofernes says, we're stunned that a beautiful woman could also be wise! Holofernes invites Judith to a private party, but when he becomes drunk she takes up his sword and decapitates him. Because the meaning of the name of the widowed heroine Judith (Yehudit) is "Jewess," the author may have used her as a prototypical character representing all Jews. At least one of the messages must be that God saves his people from his enemies, no matter how ferocious. There is also a Deuteronomistic theme: the Israelites were punished because of disobedience but may be saved through obedience.

Tobit

The discoveries of Hebrew and Aramaic fragments among the Dead Sea Scrolls now prove Tobit was originally composed in one of these two Semitic languages sometime in the late third or early second century BCE, followed by a Greek translation sometime thereafter.[10] It was probably written not in Palestine but in Egypt or Mesopotamia, as the book's sensitivity to Jewish Diaspora life makes certain. The imagined author is an Israelite named Tobit who lived in Nineveh, and he intends to demonstrate how God rewards faithfulness even in exile. After losing his sight when sparrow droppings fall into his eyes during the night, Tobit sends his son Tobias with a hired guide to recover some money he had deposited in Media. Later, the guide Azariah will turn out to be the angel Raphael, whose name means "God heals." On the way Tobias stops in Ecbatana at the home of Sarah, a distant relative, who had been praying that God would kill her after she had suffered the horror of marrying seven times only to see each husband die on the matrimonial night just as they were about to consummate the marriage. The servants in her home blamed her for killing the men, but the demon Asmodeus was the real murderer. Undeterred, Tobias marries her but takes no chances and performs an act to save his life. He brings out a fish he caught on the way, and when he burns the fish's heart and liver the smoke drives away Asmodeus. Tobias brings Sarah back to Nineveh and applies the gall of the fish to his father's eyes, and Tobit's sight is restored. The main themes of the efficacy of prayer and the importance of giving to the poor are paramount to Tobit's message. Anticipating the theology that develops throughout this period in books like 1 Enoch and Jubilees, several of the Dead Sea Scrolls, and then in the New Testament, Tobit is a very early text that reveals a belief in an ongoing cosmic battle between angels and demons.

1–4 Maccabees

The Babylonian and Persian empires are the oppressors in the biblical book of Daniel, but Daniel's literary contemporaries are actually 1 and 2 Maccabees. All three were written sometime between the end of the second century and start of the first BCE, but the first book of Maccabees had a Hebrew original, while the second was composed in Greek. As we saw in Chapter 2, according to Jewish sources in 167 BCE the Seleucid ruler Antiochus IV Epiphanes instigated a revolt when he profaned the Temple and unleashed a persecution of the Jews. The entire Hasmonean family is featured in 1 Maccabees, but 2 Maccabees, apparently a condensed version of a much longer history of Jason of Cyrene, focuses on Judas Maccabaeus and his family. One does not find a progression from 1 Maccabees to 2 Maccabees like one finds from 1 Samuel to 2 Samuel. Instead, 2 Maccabees begins at an earlier point in time during the reign of Seleucus IV (reigned 187–175 BCE) and the high priesthood of Onias III and ends when Judas Maccabeus kills the Seleucid general Nicanor in 161 BCE. First Maccabees aims to be taken seriously as a historiographical work (though it is not entirely that) and glorifies the Hasmonean family without expressing God's direct involvement. Second Maccabees is guided by Deuteronomistic theology, interpreting the history theologically and miraculously by attributing victory to God and glorifying the faith of the martyrs. The stories of martyrdom in 2 Maccabees have exercised an indelible influence in the history of Christian reflection. Beginning with the author of Hebrews, who apparently refers to the martyrs of 2 Maccabees in Hebrews 11:35–36, and going right through the last two millennia Christians have esteemed the Maccabean martyrs as forerunners of their own struggles. It is indeed one of the most moving portraits of religious devotion in the face of martyrdom ever to have been written. Catholic and Orthodox Bibles include 1–2 Maccabees, as they were used widely in the early church both in Greek and in early Latin translations in North Africa. In fact, 2 Maccabees 7:28 is the strongest statement in the Bible for the doctrine of creation from nothing, or creation *ex nihilo*: "I implore you, my child, to look at the heaven and the earth and see everything that is in them and recognize that God did not make them out of things that existed." This text was doubtless an influence on the champion of the doctrine, the North African theologian St. Augustine.[11]

Third Maccabees has little in common with 1–2 Maccabees. It was probably included with the other books of the Maccabees in Christian manuscripts since it tells of another time when Jews lived under foreign kings and were threatened with the pressures of Hellenization. This time the setting wasn't Judea and the power wasn't the Seleucids but was Egypt and a Ptolemaic king, Ptolemy IV Philopator (reigned 221–203 BCE). It was written in Alexandria sometime in the late second or early first century BCE in a Greek style similar to that found in the *Letter of Aristeas* and even 2 Maccabees, which likely supports the rationale for its inclusion in Christian collections alongside 1–2 Maccabees.[12] The genre is historical fiction, like Tobit or Judith, having a façade of historical reality but patently inventive. In the story, Ptolemy visits Jerusalem and is so impressed with the Jewish religion that he desires to enter the Temple. The Jews panic. In response to the high priest Simon's prayer, God strikes Philopator with paralysis before he can defile the Temple. He retreats and heads back to Egypt, begins to harass the Jews of Alexandria, and demands that they accept Greek religion if they want citizenship. Those who refuse are brought to the city and registered as slaves, but his effort is met once again with divine opposition when God causes the scribes to run out of writing materials. The king then commands the intoxication of five hundred elephants and lets them loose to trample the Jews.[13] As the elephants are released, God again intervenes:

> Then the most glorious, Almighty and true God showed forth his holy face and opened the heavenly gates from which descended two glorious angels, terrible to behold, who were apparent to all except the Judeans, and they withstood the force of the opponents and filled them with confusion and dread and bound them fast with shackles. And even the body of the king was ashudder, and forgetfulness overcame his indignant impudence. Then the beasts turned upon the armed forces accompanying them and began trampling and destroying them. (6:18–21)

In humiliation the king repents and holds a seven-day feast for the Jews. To lend legitimacy to their own festival, it is possible that this story was invented by Egyptian Jews to match the account of Purim found in the book of Esther, which was itself possibly a Diaspora equivalent to the Hanukkah of 1 Maccabees in Palestine. Like 2 Maccabees, 3 Maccabees embraces a Deuteronomistic perspective and urges faithfulness to God by reminding the reader of his divine intervention on behalf of the faithful when they are threatened.

The fourth and final of the books tied to the Maccabean name is dependent on 2 Maccabees 6–7 but is written in the Greek philosophical style known as the *diatribe*, reflecting on Greek concepts like restraint of the physical appetite in the refusal to eat pork and self-control in the face of temptation to apostatize. The chief concern of the author is to show that pious reason is superior to the passions, a focus that Eusebius recognized by referring to the book with the title *On the Sovereignty of Reason*. The martyrdoms described in 4 Maccabees are graphic—Eleazar remains faithful even when he "was being torn in his flesh by whips" and he "was dripping with blood and lacerated in his sides" (6:6); to stretch his body, the eldest brother was placed on a wheel, which "was stained on all sides with blood, the heap of coals was being quenched by the drippings of body fluids, and pieces of flesh whirled around the axles of the machine" (9:20). The deaths of the faithful become, at a very early stage in Jewish literature, atonement for the nation. The book was written possibly in Antioch, Alexandria, or one of the Greek cities of Asia Minor, but unlike 1–3 Maccabees 4 Maccabees cannot be dated before the first century CE—and it may not have been produced until after the Bar Kokhba Revolt came to its bloody end in 135 CE.[14]

Psalm 151

This psalm is actually placed in the Psalter in Septuagint manuscripts but has been separated in Bibles that print the Apocrypha as an independent section. It shows the importance of Davidic authorship of the psalms even in the Hellenistic period, as David is the presumed author and uses material from 1 Samuel 16–17 for his autobiography. The psalm was discovered in Qumran (11QPs^a) but was actually divided into two with material not found in the Greek version. We still do not know enough about how the Greek and Hebrew versions relate to one another.

The Prayer of Manasseh

2 Chronicles 33:19 recounts that God received the prayer of repentance of the wicked king Manasseh, which was then "written in the records of the seers." But there is no text of the prayer anywhere in the Hebrew Bible. King Manasseh of Judah receives a most critical review in 2 Kings 21:1–18, and we have no indication there that he ever repented of his ways. However, the Chronicler writes a more hopeful ending to his reign in

2 Chronicles 33:1–19: the king did indeed repent during his Babylonian captivity. The prayer mentioned but not written out by the Chronicler is imagined in this short apocryphon. Manasseh declares the magnificence of the glory of the God "of Abraham, Isaac, and Jacob and of their righteous offspring," confesses he has "sinned beyond the number of the sand of the sea," begs for God's mercy and offers himself up to be an example to others of how God forgives, and promises in return to praise God the rest of his life. The prayer is written in a common style, found in biblical examples in Psalm 51, Nehemiah 9, and Baruch 1:15–3:8 (for the latter see the following section). This particular prayer is, however, only one version of what may have been a Prayer of Manasseh tradition of some sort: a Dead Sea Scrolls fragment (4Q381) contains a different Hebrew prayer of Manasseh. The dating is almost impossible because the prayer is short and we have few hints in the text itself that would place it chronologically. With these problems in mind, the Prayer of Manasseh is usually dated broadly to sometime between the fourth century BCE (the possible date of Chronicles) and the third century CE where it appears in the *Didascalia*, a Christian treatise probably written originally in Greek but translated into Syriac. The Prayer of Manasseh has often been included in prayer manuals or catechetical literature, and in some biblical manuscripts it appears either at the end of Psalms or following Chronicles (as in the Vulgate).

The Wisdom of Solomon

One of the writings attributed to Solomon that was not included in the Hebrew Bible is Wisdom, also called the Book of Wisdom or the Wisdom of Solomon. There is no doubt, however, that this was an original Greek composition written in Alexandria between the second century BCE and the first CE by an author thoroughly acquainted with Hellenistic vocabulary and rhetoric and saturated in a knowledge of the Septuagint. His philosophy comes from the Greek world and like the *Letter of Aristeas* he seeks to show how, by its deep-rooted tradition and philosophical excellence, Judaism is superior to Greek thought. The author stresses that to abandon the pursuit of wisdom leads ultimately to destruction but that to embrace it leads to righteousness and eternal life. Wisdom, however, is the spirit of God, and those who cannot get beyond the physicality of the world around them are bound to miss it. While it may appear that the righteous and the evil have the same end, as the author of Ecclesiastes supposed, this author teaches that the righteous man's death is only illusory: his bodily death releases his soul into a state of immortality. By contrast, the offspring of the wicked will be cursed (3:12), and the wicked themselves "will become dishonored corpses, and an object of outrage amongst the dead for ever" (4:19). Wisdom is also one of the first Jewish texts to speak about the immortality of the soul and was extraordinarily influential in the New Testament and other early Christian theology. We will see in Chapter 8 how a text from Wisdom forms the framework for a well-known passage from the apostle Paul.

Sirach

Another apocryphon is a book known to most Christians via its name Ecclesiasticus from the Old Latin title meaning "belonging to the church," which reflects the importance of the book in early Christian worship. The Greek name Sirach is related to its Hebrew name "the book of Ben Sira," after the author Joshua ben Eleazar ben Sira. This is a much-studied book not least because Hebrew manuscripts covering two-thirds of the whole work have been discovered in fragmentary form at Qumran, Masada, and Cairo. In the prologue to the Greek translation, we learn that the translator is the grandson of the author of the Hebrew original written in Jerusalem c. 180 BCE. The unnamed grandson claims to have arrived in Egypt in the thirty-eighth year of the Ptolemy VIII Euergetes II Physcon (reigned 170–116 BCE), which would have been 132 BCE, and he translated the work some-time after that but not later than 116 BCE. This dating is generally accepted without question. The style is almost identical to the biblical book of Proverbs but goes further than its predecessor to connect success in life to Torah observance. If the book of Proverbs is devoid of any reference to the Torah as a central feature of devout Jewish life, Sirach makes amends. Typical are 15:1, "He who fears the Lord will do it, and he who has a hold on the law will lay hold of her [wisdom]"; and 24:23, "All these things are the book of the covenant of the Most High God, a law that Moses com-manded us, an inheritance for the gatherings of Jacob." Like Wisdom, Sirach engages in philosophical contemplation on psychology and meta-physics in a way that earlier Israelite wisdom never had. A hymn in praise of Israel's greatest heroes (chapters 44–50) highlights the priests Moses, Aaron, and Phineas and casts the prophets as miracle workers, but there are several notable omissions (e.g., Ezra). The last man on the list is the high priest Simon II (priest 219–196 BCE), and his appearance allows us to be certain the Hebrew original was completed no earlier than this date.

Sirach elevates the scribe as one who has unparalleled access to wisdom, and therefore to God, and appears to instruct young men for scribal careers. The author thus privileges their calling by arguing throughout that living faithfully to God requires knowledge of the commandments, and therefore the scribe, who continually studies the Torah, is the one who has the best opportunity to know God. One of the most important features of the Greek translation is its contribution to discussions over the canonical process of the Hebrew Bible. In the Prologue in which the grandson claims to have translated in Egypt, we also find a reference to "the Law and the Prophets and the other ancestral books," which some have seen as evidence that by 132 BCE the Hebrew Bible as we know it was complete. The "other ancestral books," according to this assumption, would be the Writings (*Ketuvim*). Most scholars, however, do not accept this hypothesis since the "other ancestral books" could refer to anything, including the books that never became canonical. At best it seems that the Torah and Prophets might have been a known collection by this time, but we should not read this statement in the Prologue as a confirmation of the later canon of the Hebrew Bible.

The rabbinic literature shows a mix of attitudes toward Sirach, some citing it after the Hebrew canon was fixed but others apparently prohibiting it. In the first few centuries of Christianity it was accepted as Scripture, and it is found in all the major early manuscripts of the Christian Bible.[15]

Baruch

This apocryphon claims to have been written by Jeremiah's scribe, since the prophetic book influences parts of Baruch, and early Jewish readers esteemed Baruch almost as highly as the biblical prophets. This short book shares similarities with Daniel, Sirach, and the Psalms of Solomon, convergences that could but do not necessarily mean that the author of Baruch was using these others directly; it only points to a cultural milieu in which these ideas were shared.[16] The book was almost certainly written in Greek, perhaps with the exception of the first part showing some possible links to a Semitic original, but dating is more difficult since the book is an assemblage of quite different parts. The second part has affinities with Sirach and its theological themes—its pro-Jerusalem and Torah-centered ideology—suggest a Maccabean dating in the second century BCE. There are several distinctive parts of the book that may have been independent until an editor combined them into this single work. The first part (1:1–3:8) has the language of the Deuteronomistic History: "...we have sinned before the Lord...And there have clung to us the bad things and the curse that the Lord instructed to his servant Moses..." (1:17, 20). With an outlook similar to Sirach in connecting Torah to Wisdom, the poem in the second part affirms that accepting the Torah brings life but that failing to become wise (via the Torah) brings death (3:9–4:4). Finally, the third part (4:5–5:9) has the tenor of Isaiah 40–66. Baruch was not written in the Babylonian exile as it pretends, but the writer is appealing to the timelessness of the theology of exile and return to warn his readers of disobedience and to encourage fidelity to the Torah.

Letter of Jeremiah

In the style of Jeremiah 29 this short invective against idolatry purports to be a letter sent by Jeremiah to the Jews in the Babylonian Exile and for that reason it is made an additional chapter at the end of Baruch in some Bibles. In the major Septuagint manuscripts it appears after Lamentations, also ascribed to Jeremiah. The Greek is very clumsy and was probably a bad translation of a Hebrew or Aramaic original. However, the only fragment found at Qumran is in Greek (7Q2, containing verses 43–44). The original could have been written in Palestine or elsewhere in the Diaspora, but the writer of 2 Maccabees already knew the Greek version in the second century BCE (2 Maccabees 2:1–3), and the Qumran fragment was copied c. 100 BCE. Most scholars, therefore, date the Letter of Jeremiah to the third or second century BCE.

The Additions to Daniel

There are three supplementary stories to the biblical book of Daniel attested both in the version of Theodotion and the Old Greek: the Prayer of Azariah and the Song of the Three Jews, Susanna, and Bel and the Dragon. These were added into the Greek book of Daniel by 100 BCE, but the time of their original composition is more uncertain. The Prayer of Azariah and the Song of the Three Jews was slotted in between Daniel 3:23 and 3:24 (so its sixty-eight verses are numbered 3:24–90 in Greek editions and in the New English Translation of the Septuagint: NETS), and since this addition alludes to Septuagint texts rather than to the Hebrew Bible, it may have been an original Greek composition.[17] The story is about three men more commonly known from the Hebrew Bible as

Shadrach, Meshach, and Abednego. Abednego is Azariah, who offers up a confession of sin on behalf of the community and a cry for mercy that has a strong Deuteronomistic flavor. This prayer is followed by hymn of praise for the deliverance of the three men (Shadrach is Hananiah; Meschach is Mishael) when "an angel for the Lord came down into the furnace to be with Azarias and his companions and shook the flame of the fire out of the furnace as if a moist breeze were whistling through. And the fire did not touch them at all and caused them no pain or distress" (verses 26–27 [3:49–50 NETS]). The Deuteronomistic language and the reference to the "unjust king" (verse 9 [3:32 NETS]) could point to a date of composition around or during the time of the Maccabean Revolt (160s BCE).

Susanna is placed before Daniel 1:1 in Septuagint manuscripts and in chapter 13 in the Latin Vulgate. It was probably translated from a Semitic original; the Old Greek is about a third shorter than the version of Theodotion. Susanna is odd in that it has no relation to Daniel like the other additions. The story has a timeless sensationalism about it: two voyeurs approach a young girl after watching her bathe and threaten her with blackmail if she refuses to have sex with them. When she refuses, she faces the prospect of being put to death after a sham charge of promiscuity is brought against her, but Daniel speaks up in her defense and proves the two men liars. Susanna is released, and the two men are put to death instead. This story has increasingly gained feminist appeal, as it demonstrates the ultimate acquittal of an innocent woman who would not cower to the threats of the licentious men but instead stood her ground on her own principles.

The story of Bel and the Dragon is located after Daniel 12:13 in the Septuagint but makes up chapter 14 in the Vulgate. Like Susanna, the two versions are different, but in this case they are almost the same length. Bel and the Dragon is similar to the Letter of Jeremiah and of course to the biblical book of Daniel in its opposition to idols. Like Daniel, it is set in the time of Cyrus's rule in the sixth century BCE and follows the two themes of resistance to the Babylonians and bravery in the face of persecution. Bel (the Babylonian pronunciation of Baal) is an idol worshiped by the Babylonians, who provided their idol with food and wine every night. Daniel laughs at their claim that because the food and wine was gone each morning it proved the idol was a living god. Daniel investigates, and finding footprints he shows the king that, rather than the idol, the priests and their families were coming covertly through secret doors to eat the food. The king, to his credit, was unaware the priests were deceiving him, and when Daniel revealed their sham the king allowed Daniel to destroy the idol. There was also a dragon that the king commanded Daniel to worship, but again Daniel showed that the dragon was no god at all by feeding him a cake of pitch, fat, and hair and watching the dragon explode. The people were angered at the king for destroying the idol and killing the dragon, so he handed Daniel over to them and they threw him in a lions' den normally reserved for enemies of the king. Readers looking for a supernatural deliverance are not to be disappointed: just when he was getting ready to eat his stew and bread, an angel of the Lord grabbed the prophet Habakkuk by the hair and transferred him from Judea to the den where he was commanded to feed Daniel. Nebuchadnezzar (like Darius in the biblical book of Daniel) came to the den to find Daniel sitting without a scratch, so he acknowledged the God of the Jews, removed Daniel from the pit and delivered his enemies to the den instead, "and they were immediately devoured" (verse 42).

Narrowing the Scriptures

None of these apocryphal works achieved canonical status in the Hebrew Bible, and this decision internal to early Judaism exercised a profound impact on Christian thinking for centuries to come. This same period of increased literary activity in Palestine and the Diaspora, in Hebrew and in Greek, witnessed the beginning of a new period of singularity, both in the form of the Hebrew text and in the books that were to achieve authoritative status. By the second century CE the Jewish scriptures were defined in Palestine, with debate continuing only for a few books. The debate continued because of, not as a question of, their canonical status. This was the end of the period of textual plurality. At the beginning of the period we can see multiple forms of the same biblical book, preserved now in the Septuagint (and in its Old Latin translation), the Dead Sea Scrolls, and the Samaritan Pentateuch. By the end of the period, one of the available Hebrew textual traditions will have been chosen, perhaps even unintentionally, so that almost all of the witnesses after the second century have the appearance of uniformity. Next, we will see that, since the text form of the Hebrew scriptures was becoming more or less fixed in this period, their Greek translations were also undergoing changes to reflect these new developments in the Bible's history.

7

E Pluribus Unum

*The Masoretic text was not selected in antiquity because of
its textual superiority. In fact, it was probably not selected
at all. From a certain point onward it was simply used.*

The Illusion of Merging Streams

HEBREW AND ARAMAIC manuscripts from the Judean Desert have won
most of the popular interest, but Greek manuscripts have also proven
indispensible to our understanding of the history of the Bible.[1] Prior to
these discoveries, the earliest witnesses to the Septuagint were those
of the fourth and fifth century CE codices (Sinaiticus, Vaticanus, and
Alexandrinus). The time between the Greek codices and the newly discovered Judean Desert finds was still more than half a millennium, but
they were much earlier witnesses to the Septuagint than the Aleppo and
Leningrad codices were to the Hebrew Bible. Nine fragmentary manuscripts of the Greek Pentateuch were found in the Judean Desert (five)
and in Egypt (four), and they reveal some interesting variations from the
Hebrew Bible's Torah. The oldest ones dated to the second century BCE
cover Leviticus 26:2–16 and Deuteronomy 11:4 and 11:23–28. The ones dated
to the first century BCE contain portions of Genesis 3:38, Deuteronomy
10–33 and 17–33, Exodus 28:4–7, and Leviticus 1:11–6:5, and one nearer to
or possibly from the first century CE contains Numbers 3:40–4:16.[2] While
some of the readings from these Greek fragments show only certain types
of stylistic alterations, others evince a desire to revise the text so that it conforms more to the type of text that later formed the Hebrew Bible, and others may be the oldest form of the Greek text and not revisions at all. That
this kind of revisional activity can be seen as early as the second century
BCE clearly implies that indeed some recognized divergences between the

different text traditions, and they sought to rectify what they perceived to be undesirable. One cannot fully appreciate the revisions of the biblical text without first understanding that this period was one of great textual fluidity; without the multiplicity of divergent text forms we have discussed thus far, there would have been no need to revise.

Yet we must be careful not to conclude that the revisional activity during this period between c. 200 BCE and c. 200 CE demonstrates a growing tendency to minimize the diversity of biblical texts and focus on one particular form. We need a new picture, a new vantage point from which to view the revisions. We have been looking at it backward. Although it appears there was a widespread movement to bring all texts into alignment with the sources that would make up the Hebrew Bible, we are led to this conclusion only because we look at the earlier history through the lens of a later reality. We then see a picture of all of these revisions as a shared tendency to move in the direction of the later Hebrew Bible. But since the text form of the Hebrew Bible was eventually adopted by the early rabbinic movement and soon displaced all other variations, we should expect nothing less than a distortion of the picture of the earlier variety. There may not have been a widespread desire to align with the sources of the Hebrew Bible any more than to any other text, but since these revisions agree with the Hebrew Bible that later became standard we should expect they would have been preserved and thus be more surprised to have any traces of variety left at all.

Several fragmentary Greek biblical manuscripts dated reliably to the second century BCE up to the first century CE were among the discoveries of the Dead Sea Scrolls. Some preserve small parts of the Pentateuch, and one contains a portion of the Letter of Jeremiah. The importance of these manuscript fragments is not only their early date. They also help clarify some of the attitudes to the text in this later Hellenistic period. Pentateuch fragments from the second century BCE are the earliest examples of revision toward a Hebrew text form like the Hebrew Bible. In Egypt, where the initial translation of much of the Septuagint took place, Greek papyri containing large portions of Deuteronomy and small portions of Job and Genesis were discovered, all of which can be dated to different points during this same period. A fragment of Deuteronomy, perhaps the oldest known manuscript of the Septuagint, was used along with parts of Homer's *Iliad* in a mummy cartonnage. This may tell us something about the integration of Jews in second-century Greek culture or, less likely, that non-Jewish Greeks were using the Septuagint.[3] Several of these early manuscripts contain characteristics of revision toward the Hebrew Bible, but none would do so as well as a scroll from a cave on the west side of the Dead Sea.

The most important of all the Greek manuscript discoveries in Palestine and in the Diaspora, which caused the most influential reassessment of assumptions in the history of the study of the Septuagint, was the Greek Minor Prophets Scroll from Nahal Hever. In a cave along the course of this brook leading into the western shore of the Dead Sea and near other caves in which heaps of skeletons from the Roman massacre of Jews during the Bar Kokhba Revolt (132–135 CE) were also discovered, a Greek scroll containing the Twelve Minor Prophets turned our conceptions of the development of the Septuagint on their head almost as much as some of the Hebrew manuscripts found elsewhere around the Dead Sea had done for the Hebrew Bible. The Greek Minor Prophets Scroll, dated to the first century BCE, provided us with the first glance of revisional activity happening across a larger portion of text in a systematic fashion, and even though the scroll is fragmentary like the other Pentateuchal revisions there is enough to provide us a clear picture of the methods used by these revisers. Not only was this Minor Prophets Scroll subject to revisional activity, but also the exact same traits were found in other books of the Septuagint. As noted earlier, some of the books translated in the first century in Palestine (Song of Songs, Ruth, Lamentations, and Ecclesiastes) were extremely literal translations of a source in the tradition of the Hebrew Bible. The Minor Prophets Scroll was a *revision* of an earlier Greek text, but these books had the scroll's characteristics built into their original translations. In other words, before the final books of the Septuagint had been produced, a thorough, organized effort of revision was being carried out on the other books that had been translated earlier. The evidence indicates that those who were involved in the revision of the Greek Minor Prophets Scroll and the editing of some of the previously translated books, like the Septuagint of Samuel and Kings, shared the same methodological outlook as those who made the final translations of the Septuagint of Song of Songs, Ruth, Lamentations, and Ecclesiastes. The characteristics that tie all of these books together are mostly translation equivalences: certain Hebrew words and phrases were translated in the same peculiar way, even to the extent that the new expressions violated the norms of Greek style for the sake of mirroring the Hebrew. The name given to this revision is *kaige* (pronounced KAI-geh) after one of the Greek expressions the revisers used.[4] The same methods used in the *kaige* revision found in the Minor Prophets Scroll and in the translations of these smaller books were also located in Greek manuscripts of Samuel-Kings, Joshua, and Judges and sporadically elsewhere. There is no ancient source that fully explains this particular revision activity by any single school or group; the evidence comes from the texts alone. To put it simply, these revisers were part of a process lasting several centuries through which some Jewish scribes were working to modify the oldest Greek translations so that they would conform to the tradition behind the Hebrew Bible.

Prior to the discovery of this scroll and the few papyri of the Pentateuchal books, we only knew of the revisions of Aquila, Symmachus, and Theodotion. These Greek versions were preserved mainly through the industry of the third century CE church scholar Origen, whose work we will survey later (see Chapter 12) and who probably deserves more credit than any other for keeping the work of these revisers alive. Since the discovery of earlier revisions like that in the Minor Prophets Scroll, we are able now to see that the Greek Jewish versions of Aquila, Symmachus, and Theodotion are only three among many more during this period. Origen may have chosen them because they corresponded to the Hebrew Bible as he knew it. We are probably closer to the truth if we imagine numerous revisions happening all over Palestine and maybe all around the Mediterranean world, wherever Jews were reading the Greek Scriptures, and only the ones that conformed to the Hebrew Bible continued to be passed on. Some revised for stylistic reasons, such as Symmachus, who raises the bar of Septuagint Greek by producing a more elegant text that some would call a translation rather than a revision.[5] The fragment of the Septuagint of Numbers 3:30–4:14 is also a literary revision, but even these literary revisions are motivated by the greater aim of conforming to the shape of the tradition behind the Hebrew Bible. Others revised for the same reasons as found in the Minor Prophets Scroll: not to offer a literary revision with a higher standard of Greek but to adapt more rigidly to the Hebrew Bible. Theodotion shares so many characteristics with the *kaige* revision that some have suggested the revision is one and the same with *kaige*.[6] The most peculiar of all revisions was produced by Aquila, whose literal style often abuses the Greek language: he invents new words and introduces word order unnatural to Greek to lead his readers through the Greek to the underlying Hebrew text. But even this literalism has been exaggerated in scholarly research, and when reading longer portions of Aquila's work the reader is able to see that in many cases he intensified the methodology found already in the *kaige* revision.[7] His Greek text is for the most part still understandable. The styles of Theodotion and Aquila have led to suggestions that they were the translators of Lamentations and Ecclesiastes, respectively, but the context of translation and revision in this period means that many could have been working with the same methodologies. It is merely an historical accident that we have knowledge of these persons. They were likely part of a larger network of translators and revisers.

The many textual streams that were flowing dynamically during the third and second centuries BCE, delivering a variety of biblical forms, were soon dammed up in favor of a unified current that would propose to carry forward a single, authoritative text into the Common Era. That we have the work of these revisions is probably due not to contemporary but to later attitudes toward the biblical text. As almost all of Jewish tradition coalesced around one text form after the second century CE, our view of the period is warped, and we are left with the impression that in the centuries leading up to the finalization of the Hebrew Bible the texts were being carried in this direction by an unrelenting tide.

The Masoretic Text of the Hebrew Bible

It may come as a surprise to learn that many other scriptural texts were used in antiquity besides those found in today's English versions and that the forms of the biblical texts were in a state of flux. However, the canonical process proves that numerous texts were held to various degrees of esteem by different Jewish communities throughout the ancient world: establishing a canon presupposes the existence of variability and testifies to the desire to end all variety.

From the perspective of an ancient Jewish or Christian reader there was no certainty about which of the traditions would eventually become the dominant scriptural tradition. It was simply not a question that would have entered their minds. We have seen repeatedly that the Septuagint and especially the Dead Sea Scrolls offer proof that the Hebrew Bible was not fixed before the second century CE and, perhaps more surprisingly, that many readers and users of scriptural texts before then were not bothered about it. The story of the New Testament's use of the Jewish scriptures to be discussed in the next two chapters will further substantiate this picture.

From various strands of evidence we can piece together a plausible explanation for what may have happened to bring an end to textual plurality, but we must be modest enough to admit that this is a suggestion, not an unimpeachable interpretation. Probably beginning as early as the Hasmonean period in the second century BCE, priestly-scribal leaders in Jerusalem Temple circles began to privilege one form of the Hebrew text above all others, and a certain corpus of books to the exclusion of others. We know from 2 Maccabees 2:13–15 that the Hasmoneans saw themselves as collectors and restorers of ancient documents, many of which must have been biblical writings.[8] In this same period we witness the solidification of a Torah-Prophets core of books, which may be related in part to Hasmonean ambitions to join the Hellenistic debates over the antiquity of one's own culture, for which such a "historical record" as found in the Deuteronomistic History would have been needed. The determination of what belonged to the Torah-Prophets corpus would have been made possible by the authority of the Hasmonean monarchy and high priesthood. At least part of the decision to adopt one form of the text may have had to do with priestly-scribal leadership of the Jerusalem Temple gaining a supremacy over other sectarian groups, like those at Qumran who possessed other forms of the Hebrew and Aramaic biblical texts and other books like 1 Enoch and Jubilees. The religious leaders in the Jerusalem Temple attached themselves to one text tradition, perhaps only because this tradition just happened to be the one available, but these books and their text forms were by no means used universally. This period of extensive textual plurality means that these leaders, while choosing widely accepted texts, were nonetheless making decisions to exclude others that might have been used by other Jewish groups farther away from Jerusalem. Now was the first time that authority was tied to a specific form of the text, and one readily notes how in the twenty-first century many views on the Bible find their genesis in these ancient attitudes. Instead of a focus on the theological message, every stroke of the pen became authoritative, a newly developed belief reflected in the comment of Jesus of Nazareth that not a jot or tittle of the word of God would pass away (Matthew 5:18). The form of the text was solidified, but choices were also made of which books to include, and all of these factors assured the eventual primacy of the text tradition behind the Hebrew Bible.

We already mentioned the way the books of the Hebrew Bible came together after many centuries of oral tradition, commitment to writing, supplementation with later events and emphases, modification, and growth. Yet it is one thing to ask how the biblical books came into being individually and another to ask how and why they were chosen and included in the current collection and how and why others were excluded. This final collection of books in the Hebrew Bible is what we call the biblical canon. The term "canon" is from Greek and means "straight rod" or "measuring stick," and when used in relation to a collection of books it is implied that those not on the list are somehow inferior; in relation to scriptural books it implies they are less spiritual or inspired. The first use of the term applied to biblical books came in the fourth century CE in the writing of the bishop Athanasius. There will be much more to say about the Old Testament canon in early Christianity later.[9]

Modern discussions of classical literature also utilize the word "canon" to refer to ancient literature.[10] There are radical distinctions, however, between classical and religious canons. In classical works there is a more liberal attitude and less of a desire to exclude. Quintilian (c. 35–100 CE) demonstrates this way of thinking:

> My plan is to select a few authors, those who are the most eminent. It is easy for students to decide what authors most resemble these, and so no one will have cause to complain if I happen to pass over his favourites. I admit there are more who deserve to be read than will be mentioned here.

It does not seem that Quintillian wants to exclude at all but that for him a canon is a mechanism to prioritize books rather than one to divinize them. Long before Quintillian and just before the translation of the Septuagint, in the fourth century BCE in Alexandria, out of the numbers of ancient Greek playwrights three—Aeschylus, Sophocles, and Euripides—were privileged by scholars attached to the Alexandrian Library and became the standard by which all others would be judged and to which all other works should aspire. They had already been acclaimed in Athens, but the textual scholarship of the Alexandrian Library secured their place forever, alongside Homer and Aristophanes as models of Greek literature. These three masters of dramatic poetry from the Golden Age of Athens in the fifth century BCE represented the best of Greek tragedy. Although others like Choerilus, Phrynichus, Pratinas, and Agathon had preceded and competed with the three, their works are all but lost, and we know them now only through scant mentions elsewhere. At work here, and paralleled in the formation of the biblical canon, was the selection of books by a scholarly elite but of a collection of books that were already widely regarded. On the other hand, the classical canons do not have the tinge of politics that we see in the religious canons. Thus, while the concept of canon as a collection of books against which all others are measured is surely appropriate for discussing the biblical canon, the books in the Hebrew Bible, the Christian Old Testament, and the New Testament stand apart from other canons in that they are viewed by their recipients as books of divine authorship and that those standing outside of the canon are less spiritual, or perhaps even heretical.

Nonetheless, canon is a concept applied much later than the writing of the books, and before the creation of the canon there was no way to tell which would eventually achieve authoritative status. Talking about the biblical canon is, then, inescapably retrospective. And there is an element of unfairness or prejudice in the whole discussion, because we evaluate an earlier period of religious history by later decisions. When Jesus and Peter sat down for fish and chips at a coastal café in the first century to contemplate the scriptures, they wouldn't have brought a bound copy of the Hebrew Bible with them. The reason is not only because the book form we know today had not yet been invented, but also because during this period some books may have been considered scriptural that were soon to be excluded, and some that were included may have been considered unscriptural by others. Apart from the centrality of Torah, some of the Prophets, and at least some psalms, many other Jewish works—like those we saw in the previous chapter—might have achieved authoritative status. Our modern position is not much better. When we discuss the canon, we could be talking about the canon of Judaism, of Protestantism, of Roman Catholicism, or of Eastern Orthodoxy. As we have seen, there are even different canons within the latter group, like the inclusion of 1 Enoch and Jubilees in the Ethiopian Orthodox Church. The history of Judaism is not so simple either, and in the medieval period we have evidence that the rabbinic Hebrew Bible didn't have the support of universal Judaism and that the Jews of the western Diaspora were likely still regarding apocryphal and pseudepigraphical works as scripture.[11] We will see in Chapter 10 that canon is a concept we should separate from the quite different concept of scripture. Not all of what was considered "scripture" has been included in the "canon."

The list of books only slowly came together through many centuries of acceptance of these works and belief in their divine origin. While some books like the pessimistic Ecclesiastes proved to be problematic well into the early centuries of the Common Era and their status is continually debated, during the first century CE most of the books of the Hebrew Bible we know today were treated as the authoritative scriptures of Judaism, at least in Palestine. There is no reason to believe the communities outside of Palestine did not continue using the other Hellenistic Jewish writings, including those now part of the Apocrypha. In fact, it has been argued that they did use other books, and we know from medieval debates that not all Jews accepted the scriptures that came from Palestine.[12] In the end, however, the canon of the Palestinian homeland emerged as the Hebrew Bible for almost all Jews to this day. After the destruction of the Jerusalem Temple by the Romans in 70 CE and the crisis of Jewish leadership that ensued, and without the institution of the Temple and its class of priests standing at the center of Jewish communal life the biblical text was to fill the vacuum. Even though it is true that scholars could never approve of a canonical list that had not already been accepted by at least a number of adherents, it is nonetheless necessary that some Jewish leadership decided which books to use more often than others. Given their role as de facto intellectual leaders (on account of their literacy alone), they would have been in a position to make these decisions. In this way, perhaps even in direct opposition to groups like those gathered at Qumran, canonization can be a mechanism used by authorities to define the boundaries of their groups, to determine who is in and who is out, partly by declaring which writings are in and which are out. At the end of the first century and the beginning of the second, Judaism was taking a turn toward a text centeredness it had not known before, and for the rabbis to practice their interpretations for Jewish faith and practice a stable text became necessary. It is in this context that the canon of the Hebrew Bible was fixed and closed: no longer would variant literary editions of biblical texts like those found in the Septuagint and in the Dead Sea Scrolls circulate widely, and neither would any more books be added to the twenty-four.

Some scholars have suggested that the choice of the Hebrew Bible was not in fact a choice but was a decision to use what sources were to hand. Nonetheless, we know so little about this earlier period, and there could have been sectarian interests involved in solidifying one singular, authoritative text. In any case, the new interest to establish a single authoritative text eliminated all of the beautiful diversity in early Jewish and Christian scriptural production, and both Jewish and Christian exegetes would soon be forced to develop strategies to explain away any and all disharmonious elements in the texts. Many of these alternative text forms of biblical and apocryphal books were eradicated either by the accidents of history—manuscripts that have perished, or some that still lie beneath the sands or secluded in caves—or by the decisions of religious authorities at different key moments in the past two millennia. The great variety that characterized the biblical texts prior to the start of the second century, which was normal and unproblematic for the earliest Jewish and Christian users of scripture, came to an end.

We will follow the trail of the Septuagint in the early Christian church, but first we must linger in the first century a while longer to see how the first writers of the Jesus movement continued to attest the rich variety of biblical textuality and, more importantly, how the Septuagint was most often their source. The New Testament offers some of the best examples of the variety of text forms still circulating in the first century CE.

8

The Septuagint behind the New Testament

It happened also that seven brothers and their mother were arrested and were being compelled by the king, under torture with whips and thongs, to touch the forbidden flesh of swine. One of them, acting as their spokesman, said, "What do you intend to ask and learn from us? For we are ready to die rather than transgress our ancestral laws."

2 MACCABEES 7:1–2

Women received their dead by resurrection. Others were tortured, refusing to accept release, in order to obtain a better resurrection. Others suffered mocking and flogging, and even chains and imprisonment.

HEBREWS 11:35–36

READERS OF ANY modern Bible version may be confused when they compare a citation in the New Testament with its original source in the Old Testament. The new formulation is often different from its original.[1] While it is true that the apostles used various methods of interpretation when reading the Jewish scriptures, in many cases the difference between their citation and our modern translation of the Old Testament is easier to explain: the Old Testament in modern Bibles is a translation from the Hebrew Bible, but the writers of the New Testament used almost exclusively the Greek Septuagint. We have also seen that the differences between the Septuagint and the Hebrew Bible are not merely stylistic, unlike the differences one finds between modern English versions where often the divergences are matters of English expression. Rather, the theological outlook of the

Hebrew and the Greek versions of many of the books are on different trajectories and thus lead to different conclusions. The importance of the New Testament authors' use of the Greek instead of the Hebrew cannot be overstated, and this is especially true when they preserve vestiges of the textual plurality in ways that work to their advantage. Whether they do this consciously is beside the point. We also sometimes see the New Testament authors quoting what is unquestionably the Septuagint's mistranslation of the Hebrew, which is not to say they are "wrong" by doing so. In any case one could come to such a conclusion only if one demanded of the New Testament authors absolute fidelity to the medieval Masoretic Text of the Hebrew Bible. Some do, but this is neither fair to first-century writers nor necessary for Christian theology. Jerome knew it was important to Christians how the New Testament authors used scripture, so he misleadingly insisted that they used the Hebrew Bible, wherein they found the prophecies about Christ. Augustine knew this to be a sham, and, equally aware of how important this point was for Christians, he rightly insisted on the New Testament authors' use of the Septuagint.

Nonetheless, we must still tread carefully. The distribution of citations in the New Testament is yet another confirmation that in the first century there was no complete canonical Bible as we might think of it today in our editions and translations. The evidence of the New Testament shows us the same prioritization of certain texts from the Jewish Scriptures that we found in the manuscripts from the Judean Desert, but we also find in both of these collections a variety of textual types; thus, while we can say the New Testament writers overwhelmingly used the "Septuagint," we must admit that the Septuagint itself was not a singular entity. Though for convenience we will continue to refer to the use of the Septuagint, it would be more precise to note that anyone reading the Jewish scriptures in the first century would have been exposed to a dizzying variety of textual forms. This textual plurality of the Old Testament worked to the advantage of both the New Testament and the early Christian writers we will meet in the following chapters. It allowed them to choose whichever reading best suited their purposes to open up new avenues for biblical interpretation. Yet nowhere is there any indication of a debate over the textual plurality. For the New Testament authors, finding the "original text"—a modern, often apologetically motivated concern—was not a priority.

The Jewish Background

We should not fail to remember that the first Christians were Jews, so it is not surprising that the New Testament writers did not rely solely on the scriptures we find in the Old Testament to access Jewish exegetical traditions. The burst of literary production between 200 BCE and 200 CE, surveyed in Chapter 6, provided an abundance of material for the earliest Christian writers, who would have had both formal and informal exposure to the writings that were later classified as pseudepigraphal and apocryphal. Since a biblical canon did not yet exist, we find the New Testament authors shaped by, and sometimes quoting from, these works.

The most important books outside of the canonical Hebrew Bible for the New Testament writers were Sirach, the Wisdom of Solomon, Tobit, and 2 Maccabees. It has long been pointed out that the famous Prologue of the Gospel of John (John 1:1–18), in the discourse about the divine Logos, shares many similarities with if not outright dependence on the Wisdom of Solomon. There are many other such cases where the Jewish writings, including not only apocryphal but also pseudepigraphal works, influenced the thought of the New Testament writers. For example, many interpreters will explain that Jesus' title "Son of Man" used in the Gospels comes from the book of Daniel (7:13–14; 8:16–18), but in fact this is only partially true. The Son of Man in the Gospels has been developed from both Daniel and the Book of Parables from 1 Enoch 37–71. It is striking to discover the same language in both 1 Enoch and in the Gospels: "before the sun and the signs were created, before the stars of the heaven were made, His name was named before the Lord of Spirits" (1 Enoch 48:3); and, "from the beginning the Son of Man was hidden, and the Most High preserved him in the presence of His might, and revealed him to the elect ones" (1 Enoch 62:7). The Son of Man passage in the Gospel of Matthew (25:31–46) concerning the sheep and the goats speaks of the Son of Man sitting "on the throne of his glory," which is a feature found at least three times in 1 Enoch (61:8, 62:2, and 69:27), and the whole parable shows similarities to the "Book of Parables" of 1 Enoch. There may also be a relation to 2 Esdras (= 4 Ezra), where we find the Messiah "whom the Most High has kept until the end of days, who will arise from the offspring of David" (2 Esdras 12:32). Both 1 Enoch and 2 Esdras were probably composed around the time of the Gospels or shortly thereafter, but an earlier date seems possible for Enoch given the apparent relationship between the Gospel of Matthew and Enoch. The Gospel writers, particularly the writer of the Gospel of Matthew, were indeed very much indebted to the Son of Man figure of 1 Enoch, and the writer of the Son of Man ideology in Enoch was himself developing the tradition from Daniel.[2]

As we discovered in the previous chapter, 1 Enoch achieved canonical status only in Ethiopian Orthodox Christianity, but other books in the canons of other Christian churches also influenced the writing of the New Testament. One example is in Paul's discussion of a humanity without excuse in Romans 1:18–32. This passage is, as many commentators have recognized, very similar to Wisdom of Solomon 13:1–19 and 14:22–31.[3] The apostle undoubtedly knows the apocryphal work, but here we see more significantly that Paul's own thought was shaped by it. A striking example is Romans 1:20–23, where Paul says that humans did not recognize God from the works of his hands because they were foolish; this is found also in Wisdom 13:1: "For all human beings who were ignorant of God were foolish by nature, and from the good things that are seen they were unable to know the one who is, nor, though paying attention to his works, did they recognize the craftsman. . . . " We can also understand better Paul's assertion that the lusts of the ungodly are related to, or even consequent on, their idolatry, and when Paul writes up the list of offenses the people have committed he is following a similar catalog in Wisdom 14:23–26.

In Jude 9 we have the use of noncanonical literature in an allusion and a direct citation in Jude 14. Jude 9 tells of a dispute over the body of Moses: "but when the archangel Michael contended with the devil and disputed about the body of Moses, he did not dare to bring a condemnation of slander against him, but said, 'The Lord rebuke you!'" In vain one searches the Old Testament for the allusion. Instead, it is an amalgamation of three texts: the pseudepigraphical work called *the Assumption of Moses*, in which the angel Michael is a gravedigger; Enoch, in which Michael is an accuser; and Zechariah 3:2, from which the direct quotation, "The Lord rebuke you!" is derived. In Jude 14–15 we have the only explicit citation of a noncanonical work, where 1 Enoch is cited as prophetic Scripture.

Jude 14–15	1 Enoch 1:9
It was also about these that Enoch, in the seventh generation from Adam, prophesied, saying,	
"See, the Lord is coming with tens of thousands of his holy ones,	And behold! He cometh with ten thousands of His holy ones
to execute judgement on all,	To execute judgement upon all, And to destroy all the ungodly:
and to convict everyone of all the deeds of ungodliness that they have committed in such an ungodly way,	And to convict all flesh Of all the works of their ungodliness which they have ungodly committed,
and of all the harsh things that ungodly sinners have spoken against him."	And of all the hard things which ungodly sinners have spoken against Him.

Encountering the "Sacred Writings"

The Jewish writings contained in the Septuagint, and in other writings modern scholars call pseudepigrapha, formed the theological framework for the New Testament authors. The significance of their use of the Septuagint will become clearer when we look at examples of citations in the next chapter, but first we should consider briefly how the writers of the New Testament would have accessed those scriptures. Since most liturgical use and memorization probably centered on the texts deemed most significant, we should expect the citations to be heavily concentrated on a few books. The minimal citations of apocryphal works is not an argument against their scriptural status; other parts of the Old Testament are not cited either. Jesus himself never cites Joshua, Judges, Ruth, 2 Samuel, Job, or Obadiah, but no one has suggested he did not consider them authoritative.

In a memorable passage, the apostle Paul is said to remind Timothy that he had known from childhood "the sacred writings," which the writer assures him were inspired by God and useful for his Christian formation (2 Timothy 3:14–17). But what were these "sacred writings," and how would Timothy have known them? They were not the thirty-nine books of the Protestant Old Testament. Timothy was not sat on his grandmother's knees reading out of a Bible published by the Palestine Bible Society. At best, the Torah and the Prophets had been treated as authoritative scripture by the second or early first century BCE, but the status of other writings was still disputed. Since there was uncertainty about which books should be in and which should be out, it is also possible that during this time some would have considered other books, such as the ones now called apocryphal and pseudepigraphal, to have been "sacred writings." We know this is the case at Qumran, where books like Jubilees and Enoch were treated as authoritative scripture, and some works scholars have called "rewritten scripture" were likely produced to replace biblical books. As we noted already, the writer of the late first-century Jewish apocalypse found in 2 Esdras 3–14 (and also called 4 Ezra) claimed there were many more writings that at least some Jews considered to have been useful for the same purposes for which Timothy was encouraged. This period of textual plurality and openness with regard to the boundaries of scripture means that it is even likely the earliest Christians considered books like the Wisdom of Solomon and Ecclesiasticus as part of the "sacred writings" useful for Christian formation.

Another question that arises from the exhortation to Timothy must be asked: How did the New Testament writers encounter the scriptures? If Timothy learned the sacred writings in his childhood, in what form would he have found the diverse books that were considered authoritative? Only the wealthiest members of society could have afforded to have personal ownership of multiple books of any writings, sacred or secular. There is some evidence of private possession from the second century BCE to the first CE (1 Maccabees 1:56–57; 2 Maccabees 2:13–15; 2 Timothy 4:3), but this is the exception to prove the rule. The book form we know today, in which pages are bound to a spine and covered, overtook scrolls only in the fourth century. The codex, as it was called (from Latin *caudex* "tree trunk"), comes into limited use earlier, but Jewish writings were predominantly found in scrolls. Further, while the books of the Jewish Scriptures were in written form and contained in scrolls, probably no more than 10 percent of the Jewish population in first-century Palestine were able to do more than write their name.[4] It is not insignificant that when Jesus addresses the Pharisees, Sadducees, and other leaders of the scribal and priestly classes he asks, "Have you never read" (e.g., Matthew 12:3, 12:5, 19:4, 21:16, 21:42, 22:31; Mark 2:25, 12:10, 12:26; Luke 6:3, 10:26) but that when talking to crowds he says, "You have heard it was said" (Matthew 5:21, 27, 33, 38, 43) and the crowd in John 12:34 responds, "We have heard from the law."[5] The scribes' ability to read and copy the scriptures in a largely illiterate context meant that they obtained a de facto status as experts of interpretation. The Temple and the synagogues were the most likely places one would have found the actual scrolls of the scriptures, but for most first-century

Palestinian and Diaspora Jews contact with the scriptures would have been through hearing them read aloud. One cannot imagine the use of scripture in the first century apart from its liturgical use, where it was heard but also memorized, chanted, and sung.[6] For this reason, one should expect none other than books like Genesis, Deuteronomy, Isaiah, and Psalms to have been the most quoted by New Testament writers, just as these books feature most in the scriptural citations in the Qumran manuscripts. Listeners in liturgical contexts would have been able to commit to memory excerpted passages from these books as well as the books in their entirety.[7] Some of the earliest Septuagint manuscripts already show divisions in the text, formatting elements that would have been necessary to assist reading. We know that many people in Palestine in the first century CE were able to speak Greek and that Hebrew was beginning its transformation to a strictly liturgical and academic language; even Palestinian Jews were using the Scriptures in Greek, whether by aural encounters at the synagogue, at oral performances among themselves, or in few cases through the visual medium of reading them directly.

Interpreters have often explained that discrepancies between the New Testament citations and their original source in the Old Testament were caused by the New Testament writers, who may have quoted from a faulty memory or may have intentionally modified the quote to press home a point they wished to make, and so on.[8] Others suggest that the New Testament writers gathered their Old Testament material from "testimony collections."[9] The *testimonia* hypothesis suggests that the New Testament authors used collections of excerpted citations from the Jewish scriptures arranged topically. There is evidence of these proof-text collections at Qumran, the most famous of which is the manuscript known as 4QTestimonia, often called the "Messianic Anthology" since it contains citations about a Messiah. While texts like 4QTestimonia would have been available in the first century, studies on several of the New Testament authors' use of the Old Testament texts have instead demonstrated that the authors show knowledge of the context from which they excerpted the material. Paul is a great example since he quotes from the Old Testament almost one hundred times. In some of Paul's citations he has strung together several snippets from different verses, which would seem to be just what one would find in *testimonia*.[10] Paying careful attention to the context of the citations, however, it is obvious that Paul is aware of the broader context of the source. In Romans 15:7–14, for example, the apostle strings together several different Old Testament citations from the Greek versions of Psalm 18:49 (17:50 in the Septuagint),

Romans 15:7–14	Psalm 18:49 (17:50)	Deuteronomy 32:43	Psalm 117:1 (116:1)	Isaiah 11:10
[7]Welcome one another, therefore, just as Christ has welcomed you, for the glory of God.				
[8]For I tell you that Christ has become a servant of the circumcised on behalf of the truth of God in order that he might confirm the promises given to the patriarchs,				
[9]and in order that the Gentiles might glorify God for his mercy. As it is written, "Therefore I will confess you among the Gentiles, and sing praises to your name";	Therefore I will acknowledge you among the nations, O Lord, and make music to your name…			
[10]and again he says, "Rejoice, O Gentiles, with his people";		…Be glad, O nations, with his people…		
[11]and again, "Praise the Lord, all you Gentiles, and let all the peoples praise him";			…Praise the Lord, all you nations! Commend him, all you peoples…	
[12]and again Isaiah says, "The root of Jesse shall come, the one who rises to rule the Gentiles; in him the Gentiles shall hope."				And there shall be on that day the root of Jesse, even the one who stands up to rule nations; nations shall hope in him, and his rest shall be honor.
[13]May the God of hope fill you with all joy and peace in believing, so that you may abound in hope by the power of the Holy Spirit.				
[14]I myself feel confident about you, my brothers and sisters, that you yourselves are full of goodness, filled with all knowledge, and able to instruct one another.				

Deuteronomy 32:43, Psalm 117:1 (116:1 in the Septuagint), and Isaiah 11:10.[11] If one were to look only at the direct citations, which are in agreement thematically, one may conclude that here that Paul uses some sort of *testimonia*. But look closer.

Although the citations are not exactly the same as the Septuagint text, and in fact they contain some agreements with known Septuagint revisions, this string of citations is an argument against the *testimonia* hypothesis. All of the citations show awareness of the broader context of the original sources. Romans 15:8–9, for example, shares similarities with Psalm 116:2 (117:2):

> For I tell you that Christ has become a servant of the circumcised on behalf of *the truth of God* in order that he might confirm the promises given to the patriarchs, and in order that the Gentiles might glorify God for *his mercy*…
>
> …because *his mercy* became strong toward us, and the *truth of the Lord* endures forever' (my emphases).

The links between mercy and truth in both contexts, even though the latter is not included in the citation of Romans 15:8–9, suggest that Paul was aware of the psalm from which he quoted. Moreover, although he cites Isaiah 11:10 only in Romans 15:12, the broader context and the theme of peace between Ephraim and Judah in Isaiah 11 was also in Paul's mind, as the apostle writes in Romans 15:7 and 15:14: "Welcome one another, therefore, just as Christ has welcomed you, for the glory of God… I myself feel confident about you, my brothers and sisters,* that you yourselves are full of goodness, filled with all knowledge, and able to instruct one another."

Paul's use of Deuteronomy offers further evidence. Prior to his conversion, the apostle's encounter with this book in the synagogue's liturgical contexts and in his training to be a teacher of the law would have instilled in Paul a greater awareness of certain passages over others. In addition to hearing them, he would have been familiar with key texts that he would have recited morning and evening every day. One of these was the *Shema*, originally only Deuteronomy 6:4 but later extended to a set of three passages (Deuteronomy 6:4–9, 11:13–21; Numbers 15:37–41) that continue to be part of Jewish prayer today. The essence of the Jewish faith is found there in the foundational verse of the *Shema* in Deuteronomy 6:4: "Hear, O

Israel: The Lord is our God, the Lord alone." Some of these especially sig-nificant passages made their way into Paul's writings, and the *Shema* itself was astonishingly transformed into a Christological claim in 1 Corinthians 8:6: "Yet for us there is one God, the Father, from whom are all things and for whom we exist, and one Lord, Jesus Christ, through whom are all things and through whom we exist."[12] Paul's citation of only a small phrase or sentence does not imply his ignorance of the entire book of Deuteronomy. Rather, his knowledge of the whole of Deuteronomy, and the whole of other books like Isaiah, provided the background to much of what he wrote. Even when one doesn't see it explicitly in the citation, there are other hints in and around the quote.

To be sure, there are places where Paul's citations appear so differ-ent from their source that one might imagine he either forgot or simply didn't know its original context. Paul's hermeneutical approach provides the best explanation for these cases. He wasn't unaware of the context of his source, but "Paul's 'misreading' of Scripture derives from his con-victions as a missionary theologian, not from his lack of familiarity with Israel's sacred texts."[13]

Paul may provide us with most of the evidence, but the other New Testament writers show the same tendencies. In 1 Peter, for example, one can discern the influence of Psalm 33 throughout the book, and, as we will see, the Gospel of Matthew, which perhaps arose from a formerly Pharisaic community, is thoroughly acquainted with the Jewish scrip-tures.[14] More examples could be adduced—such as from the writer of Hebrews—to show that if the New Testament authors had *testimonia* to provide them with some of their citations of the Old Testament they were only a small contribution.[15] In more cases than not, the authors appear to know well the books from which they drew their material, and some like Paul committed entire books to memory. It is most reasonable to grant that the authors would have had several means by which to interact with the scriptures, but among them the liturgical context provides the most satisfactory possibilities. Significantly, because most of their citations are based on the Septuagint, later Christians would debate whether the New Testament use of the Septuagint endowed it with an authority that was at least equal to the Hebrew. Whether the New Testament authors intention-ally chose the Septuagint over the Hebrew, whether they were aware of the different textual options, is another question altogether, but often their Septuagint readings had, even if only coincidentally, a more suitable mes-sage for their purposes than the Hebrew.[16]

We have one more issue to examine before looking at the explicit citations, and that is how the Septuagint influenced some of the theological language of the New Testament in ways that would not have been possible had the New Testament authors used the Hebrew scriptures.

Language and Theology

Right from the start we witness the influence of the Septuagint on the earliest expressions of the Christian faith.[17] In the New Testament, Jesus speaks of his blood being a *kainē diathēkē*, a "new covenant." The covenant is elucidated in Hebrews 8:8–12 and other texts, but it was preserved in the words of Jesus with this language in Luke 22:20 when at the Last Supper Jesus said, "This cup that is poured out for you is the new covenant in my blood."[18] Jesus's blood was to provide the grounds for the "new covenant," in contrast to the old one his disciples knew from the Jewish scriptures (e.g., Jeremiah 31:31–34). Thus, the earliest Christians accepted the Jewish Scriptures as prophecies about Jesus and in time began to call the collection the "Old Testament" and the writings about Jesus and early Christianity the "New Testament," since "testament" was another word for "covenant."[19] The covenant promises of God (*berith* in Hebrew) were translated in the Septuagint with the word *diathēkē*. In classical Greek *diathēkē* had meant "last will, testament," but in the Septuagint it is the chosen equivalent for God's covenant with his people. The author of Hebrews plays on the double meaning, and when Luke records Jesus' announcement at the Last Supper that his blood was instituting a "new covenant," or a "new testament," he is using the language in an explicit contrast with the old covenant, found in the Jewish scriptures. Soon, the writings that would eventually be chosen to make up the texts about the life and teachings of Jesus and the earliest expression of the Christian faith would be called the New Testament. This very distinction between the Old and New Testaments is based on the Septuagint's language.

Although Matthew is placed first, the Gospel of Mark is the earliest of the Gospel writings. Mark begins by setting forth that his writing is "the beginning of *the gospel* of Jesus Christ, the Son of God" (Mark 1:1). The word chosen by Mark, translated into English as "gospel," is the Greek word *euangelion* ("good news"), from which we also derive terms like "evangelist." In the Roman Empire, a "gospel" (Latin *evangelium*) was an announcement of good news about the emperor, sometimes a declaration of military victory, and almost always used in the plural, *evangelia*. While the hearers of the preaching about Jesus would have known that Roman use, the Christian use of the word originates in the Septuagint. In the Septuagint translation of the latter parts of Isaiah (40:9, 52:7, 60:6, and 61:1), the term *euangelion* is used in a verbal form to announce the good news of God's rule. Isaiah 52:7, for example, declares, "How beautiful upon the mountains are the feet of the messenger who announces peace, who brings good news, who announces salvation, who says to Zion, 'Your God reigns.'" This is translated into the Greek Septuagint as, "...Like season upon the mountains, like the feet of *one bringing glad tidings* of a report of peace, like *one bringing glad tidings* of good things, because I will make your salvation heard, saying to Zion, 'Your God shall reign...'" (emphasis mine). The Greek word translated into English as the "one bringing glad tidings" is a verbal form of *euangelion*. The word had probably already been in use to refer to Jesus' ministry for several decades when Mark wrote (c. 70 CE), and Mark's first-century Roman audience would have known the imperial use of the term. Mark begins his next verse (1:2) with, "As it is written in the prophet Isaiah," and he then quotes both Malachi and Isaiah. At least in this context at the beginning of his gospel it would appear that Mark's concept of *euangelion* was rooted in the Greek Isaiah, even if it was also challenging the imperial term. Even if Mark already knew the term to refer to Jesus, the lineage from the Septuagint into the early church seems clear. Mark knew well the context of Isaiah's *euangelion*, and he connected Jesus' ministry to its roots in the Jewish Scriptures. From this point on, *euangelion* became one of the most important words in the language of Christianity.[20]

New Testament terms with far-reaching theological importance are also derived from the Septuagint. The concept of the "glory of God" as it is developed in the New Testament has its roots in the Septuagint, especially in the book of Isaiah. Some of the most important terms, however, are doubtless those for "virgin" and the two titles applied to Jesus, "Lord" and "Christ," all of which came from the Septuagint. The narrative of the virgin birth is told in Matthew and Luke, but the citation of Isaiah 7:14 in Matthew 1:23 contains the prophecy: "'Look, the virgin shall conceive and bear a son, and they shall name him Emmanuel,' which means, 'God is with us.'" The Greek word for virgin is *parthenos*, but the Hebrew word in Isaiah 7:14 is *'almah*, which has the meaning "young girl." Christian tradition has read the verse as a prediction of the "virgin birth" of a Messiah, even though the translator's choice of *parthenos* was just one of several acceptable translation equivalences for the Hebrew *'almah*. Whatever the Septuagint translator intended, there can be no doubt that Matthew wished to emphasize a miraculous birth of Jesus.[21] Indeed, it is worth pondering how Matthew would have introduced the prophecy of the virgin birth had it not been for the Septuagint. It is possible, indeed quite likely, that Matthew had already known a tradition of the virgin birth of Jesus, but the Gospel writer's argument that this man is the promised Messiah could not have been made without a citation from the Jewish scriptures. It would have been one thing for Matthew to say, "This Jesus was born of a virgin according to an oral tradition," but for him to have had a text from the Jewish scriptures, provided by the Septuagint, meant that he could ground the tradition of the virgin birth in a real prophetic utterance.

Another case is the use of *kurios* referring to Jesus. For Yahweh (in English Bibles: "the LORD" in all caps), the Septuagint uses *kurios*. Although the term *kurios* usually has to do with one's authority over others, when the New Testament authors use this word from the Septuagint to refer to Jesus, they are making an extraordinary claim: Jesus of Nazareth is to be identified with Yahweh. The other no less important word in the New Testament that comes from the Septuagint is *christos*, "Christ." Christ is not part of the name of the man from Nazareth, as if "the Christs" were written above the door of his family home. Rather, "Christ" is an explicitly messianic title used by the writers of the New Testament who have learned this word from the Septuagint's translation of the Hebrew *mashiach*, "anointed," which itself is often rendered in English as "Messiah." To be sure, one detects a messianic intent on the part of the Septuagint translator in some places. Amos 4:13 may have been one of these. In the Hebrew Bible, God "reveals his thoughts to mortals," but the Septuagint has "announcing his anointed to humans." A fine distinction must be made, however, between theology that was intended by the Septuagint translators and that developed by later Christian writers. In Amos 4:13 it is merely possible we have a messianic reading, but it is unquestionably the case that the New Testament writers exploit the Septuagint's use of *christos*, in Amos and elsewhere, to messianic ends.

Direct borrowing from the language is not the only way the Septuagint influences the New Testament. Although more difficult to assess than straightforward citations, allusions to Septuagint language and thought are also pervasive, though they are sometimes difficult to determine. A few well-known allusions to the Septuagint are found in the Magnificat (the "Song of Mary" in Luke 1:46–55) and the Benedictus (the "Song of Zechariah" in Luke 1:68–79), and in Luke 1:42 the description of Mary as blessed above all other women on the earth follows the language of Judith 13:18. After this

angelic proclamation of peace brought by the coming of Jesus (Luke 2:14),
Simeon declares that he can die once he laid his eyes on the baby Jesus (Luke
2:29), exactly as Anna had said when she saw Tobit (Tobit 11:9).

The impact the Septuagint had on the language and theology of the New
Testament is clear from these examples, but we now turn to the explicit
citations of the Old Testament in the New where we see the Septuagint
from Matthew to Revelation.

9

The Septuagint in the New Testament

"...Death has been swallowed up in victory"
PAUL IN 1 CORINTHIANS 15:54, in agreement with a
Septuagint revision of Isaiah 25:8

*A single hour lovingly devoted to the text of the Septuagint
will further our exegetical knowledge of the Pauline epistles
more than a whole day spent over a commentary.*
ADOLF DEISSMANN

The Scriptures of Jesus and the Gospel Writers

WHEN WE THINK about the form of the Jewish scriptures used by the
Gospel writers, we must remember they not only wrote narrative material about the life and teachings of Jesus of Nazareth but also reported
their version and interpretation of his words.[1] How they chose to represent
Jesus' use of the scriptures is fascinating, for in these accounts they present Jesus teaching mostly from the Greek Jewish scriptures, even though
his native language was Aramaic. That is not to say Jesus could not have
read from or did not often hear the Greek Jewish scriptures in the synagogues; given his linguistic environment, he would have known at least
enough Greek to engage in basic conversation.

The writer of the Gospel of Matthew might have come out of a
first-century Jewish group like the Pharisees and would thus be the most
likely Gospel writer to have used the Hebrew scriptures. Even when
he took material from Mark and any other sources, Matthew would have
had the ability to compare, whether mentally or to a physical copy of the
Hebrew. It is surprising what we find instead. Matthew's citations of
the Jewish scriptures have been studied extensively, and some New
Testament scholars have tried to determine with statistical accuracy the
number of times the evangelist uses the Septuagint and the number of

times he uses the Hebrew scriptures.[2] But this is almost certainly an impossible calculation, because many of these citations were copied from his sources, and if he modified them at all they seem to lean toward the Hebrew form. Yet the prevalence of Greek revisions to the Hebrew scriptures around this time (see Chapter 7) means that even where Matthew follows the Hebrew word for word, he could have been using a Greek revision. Therefore, it is very difficult to make distinctions between citations based on Hebrew and those based on the Greek. In fact, none of the cases where Matthew quotes from the Jewish scriptures prove beyond doubt that his reading must have come from the Hebrew instead of a Greek revision. There is no reason to assume that this evangelist switched between Hebrew and Greek, especially since he was writing in Greek. It is more likely that Matthew's Gospel contains traces of both the old form of the Septuagint and revised versions of the Septuagint.[3] Many of the clues are small, but taken together they are very clear.

There is no reason to assume from the outset that Mark and Luke would have known the Hebrew scriptures. Mark was the first Gospel to have been written, which means that Luke and Matthew derived many of their citations from Mark and left them in their Greek form even if they made some small changes to insert the citation into their context. There is no indication in the Gospels of Mark and Luke that their writers knew Hebrew. Since Mark's sources have not survived but are hypothesized, it is difficult to be sure where he got his citations.[4] He could have drawn some from the earliest traditions of the emerging church, particularly those that are more succinct and carry some theological import. There may be no explicitly textual basis to them at all.[5] In most cases, however, it is easy to show that Mark relied on a Greek form of the Old Testament, and for this reason his use of the Septuagint has been largely undisputed.

In Mark 7:6–7, for example, Mark has Jesus make application of Isaiah 29:13. What was keeping the people from true worship? Mark's understanding is derived from the Septuagint: the people were obsessed with human tradition and teaching. In the Hebrew Isaiah, they were prevented from true worship because they had sought to follow only the formal aspects of religion, but Mark is following the Septuagint, so the connection between tradition and the teachers is explicit.[6]

One of the most striking examples of a Gospel writer's preference to have Jesus quote the Septuagint is found in Luke's Gospel. In 4:18, Jesus reads from the scroll of Isaiah to declare that his ministry is, among other

Mark 7:6–7	Isaiah 29:13 (Septuagint)	Isa. 29:13 (Hebrew)
He said to them, "Isaiah prophesied rightly about you hypocrites, as it is written,	The Lord said:	The Lord said:
'This people	"These people draw near me;	"Because these people draw near with their mouths and
honors me with their lips,	they honor me with their lips,	honor me with their lips,
but their hearts are far from me; in vain do they worship me, teaching human precepts as doctrines.'"	while their heart is far from me, and in vain do they worship me, teaching human precepts and teachings."	while their hearts are far from me, and their worship of me is a human commandment learned by rote..."

Luke 4:17–18	Isaiah 61:1 (Septuagint)	Isaiah 61:1 (Hebrew)
...And the scroll of the prophet Isaiah was given to him. He unrolled the scroll and found the place where it was written: [18]		
"The Spirit of the Lord is upon me,	The spirit of the Lord is upon me,	The spirit of the Lord God is upon me,
because he has anointed me	because he has anointed me;	because the Lord has anointed me;
	he has sent me	he has sent me
to bring good news to the poor	to bring good news to the poor,	to bring good news to the oppressed,
he has sent me	to heal the broken-hearted,	to bind up the broken-hearted,
to proclaim release to the captives	to proclaim release to the captives,	to proclaim liberty to the captives,
and recovery of sight to the blind, to let the oppressed go free...."	and recovery of sight to the blind	and release to the prisoners ....

things, to proclaim "recovery of sight to the blind." This is nowhere in the Hebrew version of Isaiah 61:1 and instead comes as a direct citation from the Septuagint.

Luke also includes another phrase that is found neither in the Hebrew nor the Greek of Isaiah 61: "to let the oppressed go free." Although in English "let the oppressed go free" looks very similar to "release to the prisoners," these are very different Hebrew phrases, so Luke is certainly not reading the Hebrew. Rather, Luke lifts the phrase from the Septuagint of Isaiah 58:6. By putting it into the flow of the citation from Isaiah 61, Luke has Jesus announce his mission as liberation for the poor and oppressed, which he later relates to the repentance of the rich (Luke 16:19–31).[7] Here we see what will become even clearer in Paul's use of the Jewish scriptures: often, the New Testament writers find in the Septuagint material to allow different theological emphases.

Matthew, Mark, and Luke are called the Synoptic Gospels in scholarship since they have a large amount of shared material: synopsis is from Greek and means seeing something together simultaneously. John's Gospel, however, is much different, not only in theological emphases but also in its lack of material shared with the Synoptics. In the fourth Gospel, we notice that sometimes the writer modifies the citation from the Septuagint but that other times he quotes directly.[8] One study suggested that, in contrast to other claims that John might have used Semitic sources, he used the Septuagint exclusively, and any deviations from the Septuagint are either his own editing of the citation or his use of a Septuagint revision.[9] An example that shows John using the Septuagint is the citation of Isaiah 40:3. In John 1:23, the evangelist quotes Isaiah 40:3 from a Greek version but makes a small adaptation for his own message.

John 1:23	Isaiah 40:3	Isaiah 40:3
He said,	(Septuagint)	(Hebrew)
"I am the voice of one	A voice of one	A voice
crying out	crying out	cries out:
in the wilderness,	in the wilderness:	"In the wilderness
'Make straight	"Prepare the way of the	prepare
the way of the Lord,'	Lord;	the way of the Lord,
as the prophet Isaiah said."	make straight	make straight
	the paths of our God."	in the desert
		a highway for our
		God."

John finds in the Greek translation a suitable vehicle to introduce the ministry of the wilderness wandering hermetic, John the Baptist. The citation in the fourth Gospel is shorter since John uses only the first part of the Isaianic citation, "prepare the way of the Lord," but he also changed the verb from "prepare" to "make straight." The decision to do so could have been because he read the two lines from Isaiah 40:3 as effectively communicating the same thing. If so, he omits the part about making straight paths and instead brings that verb into the first clause to make his citation read: "Make straight the way of the Lord." There may be another reason, however. Reading "prepare the way and make straight the paths" could suggest that John's ministry was simply preparatory and would end when Jesus arrived. By avoiding the use of the verb "prepare" and opting for "make straight," the evangelist could have been seeking an interpretation that would highlight the Baptist's role as a minister alongside of Jesus so that both are preaching the coming of the kingdom of God. This is one example of how John sometimes modifies his citations, even as it seems clear he has taken them from the Greek.[10]

Even if only briefly, we should point out an example that is often mentioned to show that John uses not only the Septuagint but also other Greek versions to which he might have had access. In citing Zechariah 12:10 in John 19:37, the writer's wording in Greek is exactly that of the Greek revision attributed to the later figure of Theodotion but that is in fact an older revision produced before the New Testament. John quotes Zechariah: "they will look on the one whom they have pierced." The Septuagint had "... and they shall look to me because they have danced triumphantly." Theodotion attempts to correct what appears to have been a reading in the Septuagint caused by the Greek translator's misunderstanding of the Hebrew, and this is the reading John adopts.

The Acts of the Apostles are thought to comprise the second of a two-volume account written by Luke, of which his Gospel was the first, so we should again expect to see the same use of the Septuagint we found in the Gospel. At the Jerusalem Council, to validate the conversion of the Gentiles James mentions with approval Simeon's story of how God includes Gentiles in his plan, because, as James says, Simeon's account "agrees with the words of the prophets." The prophet he quotes in this passage is Amos, and Acts 15:16–18 records it thus:

Acts 15:16–18	Amos 9:11–12 (Septuagint)	Amos 9:11–12 (Hebrew)
This agrees with the words of the prophets, as it is written,		
"After this I will return, and I will rebuild the dwelling of David, which has fallen;	On that day I will raise up the tent of David that is fallen,	On that day I will raise up the booth of David that is fallen,
from its ruins I will rebuild it, and I will set it up,	and rebuild its ruins, and raise up its destruction, and rebuild it as in the days of old;	and repair its breaches, and raise up its ruins, and rebuild it as in the days of old;
[17]so that all other peoples may seek the Lord— even all the Gentiles over whom my name has been called.	[12]in order that those remaining of humans and all the nations upon whom my name has been called might seek out me,[11]	[12]in order that they may possess the remnant of Edom and all the nations who are called by my name,
Thus says the Lord, who has been making these things [18]known from long ago."	says the Lord who does these things.	says the Lord who does this.

In the context of the Hebrew version, the prophecy is centered on the benefit to the people of Israel: the people are to inherit the remnant of Edom and all the other nations. In the Septuagint, the focus has shifted, and the Gentiles are seeking out the Lord, which becomes very useful in Luke's hands since he wants to legitimize the Gentile mission. Luke can use the long citations in Acts 7, 13, and 15 to support the early missionary activity to reach the Gentiles, and the Amos citations, including this one here, show both God's punishment of Israel and the renewal of Israel, whom Luke sees as Christian community of Jews and Gentiles.[12]

The Gospels and Acts provide numerous examples of the use of the Septuagint, even though we have the space to examine only a few. It would seem that if any of these writers had used the Hebrew scriptures it would have been Matthew. That he too uses the Greek Jewish scriptures is telling. It is also true that Matthew and some of the others used the revised forms of the Greek Jewish scriptures so that the Gospel writers are even witnesses to the textual plurality in the first century. We shall see presently that the chief apostle of Christianity utilizes the Greek Septuagint in more meaningful ways. Paul finds the Greek forms of scripture more suitable for his intention to announce God's message to the Gentiles.

The Apostle Paul

The pedigree Paul claims for himself ensures that he could have used the Hebrew scriptures, and one scholar has argued that Paul's use of scripture was almost entirely dependent on Hebrew and Aramaic forms.[13] Nonetheless, the consensus is now that when he quotes from the Jewish scriptures he most often, perhaps always, preferred the Greek. The reasons are sometimes related to his exegesis, but most often his choice of the Greek has to do with nothing more than the way he frequently encountered the scriptures in his liturgical and study contexts, which had mostly been in Greek. To investigate Paul's use of the Jewish scriptures and to ascertain not only whether he favored their Hebrew or Greek form but also whether it made any difference in his exegesis, one must look to none other than the book of Romans. It is critical to recognize how Paul used the scriptures Christians call the Old Testament, for they are the bedrock of his and therefore most of later Christianity's theological expression. The book of Isaiah lies at the heart of Paul's theology in his epistle to the Romans.[14]

In Romans 2, Paul acerbically condemns the Jews, calling them sinners and concluding that they, like the Gentiles, need to embrace Jesus as Lord. The most strident rhetoric is found in verses 17–24, where Paul judges the Jews for having but not obeying the law. In the final verse of this passage (24), Paul quotes Isaiah 52:5 from the Greek version. There we find a significant variation from the Hebrew.

The "because of you" in the Septuagint is used by Paul to great effect. The Greek translator had intensified the original condemnation into a

Romans 2:24	Isaiah 52:5 (Septuagint)	Isaiah 52:5 (Hebrew)
For, as it is written,	And now, why are you here? This is what the Lord says, Because my people were taken for nothing, you marvel and howl. This is what the Lord says, Because of you,	Now therefore, what am I doing here, says the Lord, seeing that my people are taken away without cause? Their rulers howl, says the Lord, and continually,
"The name of God is blasphemed among the Gentiles because of you."	my name is continually blasphemed among the nations.	all day long, my name is despised.

pointed accusation against Israel: it was their fault they remained in exile. Paul's use of this verse here in 2:24, placed before his exposition of his gospel, reveals how he intended to place himself in the prophetic tradition of Isaiah. After this verse in Isaiah, the prophet declares how the return from exile may happen. Paul does as well, but for the apostle the people of Israel will remain in exile as long as they continue to reject the Christ.[15]

The celebrated section of Romans 9–11 concerns Israel's role in God's saving plan. Once again, it is significant that when Paul writes these theological expositions he refers to the Prophets in the Septuagint. Paul argues for the inclusion of the Gentiles in God's plan for Israel, and by combining elements from the Greek version of Hosea he widens the promise to the Gentiles. Hosea 1:10 and 2:23 refer specifically to the guarantee that Israel would prosper; in Romans 9:25–26 Paul ensures this is extended to the Gentiles. Paul purposely "misreads" Hosea just as he does the Jewish scriptures elsewhere in Romans, with the intention of finding room for the Gentiles in God's plan.[16] We shall see later in Paul's use of Deuteronomy 32:43 that sometimes the Septuagint's reading better suits the apostle's purposes, whether he was choosing intentionally or not; in other cases, he takes liberties afforded him by a loose interpretation of the Septuagint to press further his inclusive understanding of God's salvation.

Another citation of Hosea 1:10 in Romans 9:26 allows Paul the same opportunities to expand the call to the Gentiles. Though the Greek editions and all English versions read similarly to the New Revised Standard Version's (NRSV's) "in the very place where it was said to them," the better reading based on textual grounds is "in the very place wherever they shall be called."[17] The former may give the impression that the people are called in a specific place, in which case the reader could assume this refers to the people of Israel alone. But Paul's play on the Septuagint allows him to call out to Gentiles wherever they might be, and the call is placed in the future tense to let them know that God was still calling them. Paul demonstrates an understanding of the entire message of the Greek Hosea; he is not merely plucking certain passages out of context. He is, however, making some modifications to the text to draw out what was already there in the Septuagint.

Romans 9:30–33 contains a citation of Isaiah 28:16 in a very important conclusion to the first part of Paul's argument in this section. Verse 33 is particularly important:

Romans 9:33	Isaiah 28:16 (Septuagint)	Isaiah 28:16 (Hebrew)
…As it is written,	…Therefore thus says the Lord,	
"See, I am laying in Zion a stone	See, I will lay for the foundations of Zion	See, I am laying in Zion a foundation stone,
that will make people stumble, a rock that will make them fall,	a precious, choice stone, A highly valued cornerstone for its foundations, And the one	a tested stone, a precious cornerstone, a sure foundation:
and whoever believes in him will not be put to shame.	who believes in him will not be put to shame.	"One who trusts will not panic."

Paul combines the ideas that a stone will be laid in Zion and will provide salvation to those who trust in it and that the stone will also be a stumbling block that many will trip over (Paul uses the same ideas in Romans 11:9–12 and 1 Corinthians 1:23). Importantly, Paul chooses the Septuagint reading, which asserts that the one who trusts "in him"—that is, in the stone—will not be "put to shame." This is different from the idea in the Hebrew book of Isaiah, where the object of one's trust is left undefined and the one who trusts is the one who "will not panic." The other aspects of this citation are very complex, but one more feature in Romans 9:33 is important.

Paul's grammatical construction is very akin to the translations of Aquila, Symmachus, and Theodotion and again suggests the apostle was possibly aware of varying text forms.[18]

In Romans 10:20–21, Paul again uses the Greek Isaiah to his advantage.

Romans 10:20–21	Isaiah 65:1–2 (Septuagint)	Isaiah 65:1–2 (Hebrew)
Then Isaiah is so bold as to say,	I became visible to those who were not seeking me;	I was ready to be sought out by those who did not ask,
"I have been found by those who did not seek me;	I was found by those who were not inquiring about me.	to be found by those who did not seek me.
I have shown myself to those who did not ask for me."	I said, "Here I am," to the nation that did not call my name.	I said, "Here I am, here I am," to a nation that did not call on my name.
[21]But of Israel he says,	I stretched out my hands all day long	[2]I held out my hands all day long
"All day long I have held out my hands to a disobedient and contrary people."	to a disobedient and contrary people, who did not walk in a true way but after their own sins.	to a rebellious people, who walk in a way that is not good, following their own devices;

In the Hebrew version of Isaiah 65:1–2, the focus is on Israel. Even though they are neither asking for nor seeking after him, God is making himself available to disobedient Israel. The translator of the Greek Isaiah made it a past event since he produced his text after the Hebrew version. So here, God became visible and was found. For Paul, however, contrasting the two was useful, and he (purposefully?) misreads the text so that Isaiah now is made to prove God's desire to accept the Gentiles. The phrasing Paul chooses—"I have become visible"—is taken directly from the Greek, even though Paul inverses the order of the first two clauses. The insertion of "But of Israel he says" is important since it allows the apostle to say that while God made himself known to the Gentiles the Israelites remained "disobedient and contrary people." Paul's language comes from the Greek and his point is damning: the fault lies with Israel.[19]

Near the end of the epistle Paul warns Christians not to be judgmental and instead urges mutual support and peacemaking within the believing community. Why should one pass judgment on other believers when all will stand before God? Paul quotes Isaiah 45:23 in Romans 14:11, but, instead of every tongue swearing (as in the Hebrew), the Septuagint and Paul say that every tongue shall acknowledge, or give praise, to God.

Romans 14:11	Isaiah 45:23 (Septuagint)	Isaiah 45:23 (Hebrew)
"As I live," says the Lord, "every knee shall bow to me, and every tongue shall give praise to God."	By myself I swear .... Because to me every knee shall bow and every tongue shall acknowledge God	By myself I have sworn. .. "To me every knee shall bow, every tongue shall swear."

The Septuagint of Deuteronomy also provided for Paul the language he needed to make explicit the reach of God's salvation to the Gentiles. In Romans 15:11, Paul cites the Greek from Deuteronomy 32:43—"Praise the Lord, all you Gentiles, and let all the peoples praise him"—in a string of citations. This Septuagint text of Deuteronomy 32:43 is from an additional part not found in the Hebrew: "Be glad, O nations, with his people, and let all the angels of God prevail for him." Regardless of whether this was in a variant Hebrew text or if the Septuagint translator simply added it himself, it is useful to Paul, since "Paul has read the Song of Moses *looking for* the inclusion of the Gentiles."[20] The Septuagint text includes an invitation to Gentiles to come worship with Israel, and by using this text Paul can answer the quandary brought about by his citation of Deuteronomy 32:21 in Romans 10:19, in which the Gentiles are seen to be included in God's salvation to provoke the Jews to jealousy so that eventually they will be saved.

The use of Isaiah 11:10 in the same section in Romans 15:12 raises similar possibilities. "The one who rises to rule the Gentiles" is nowhere to be found in the Hebrew Isaiah. It was taken from the Septuagint. In the Hebrew the root of Jesse rises to be a sign to the nations so that it might be sought out. In the Greek Isaiah, the connection in the Hebrew text between "sign" and "inquire" is eliminated. The Greek translator understood the Hebrew word for "sign" to denote a rule and authority. The translation of the Hebrew word for "inquire" as "hope" in the Greek Isaiah is unique in the Septuagint. "Hope" is usually the translation of a Hebrew word with a similar meaning, but around the time of the Greek translation of Isaiah the Hebrew word for "inquire" was being used in a sense of religious devotion, of seeking after God. It is probably this sense the Greek translator understood.[21] For Paul, this modification by the Greek translator, of "rule" for "signal" and "hope" for "inquire," provided him the text he needed to highlight Christ's rule over the nations and that Christ was the object of the hope of salvation.

There are times throughout this epistle to the Romans when Paul's use of the Greek demonstrates the textual plurality in the first century, whether or not he chooses divergent readings deliberately. For example, when Paul uses Isaiah 52:7 in Romans 10:15, his reading is found in a Greek revision, though a missionary as well traveled as Paul would have come into contact with the textual plurality depending on which geographical area he was in at the time of writing. We cannot be sure he intentionally discriminated between variants: "And how are they to proclaim him unless they are sent? As it is written, 'How beautiful are the feet of the messengers who bring good news!'"[22] Paul's citation follows the Antiochian form of the Septuagint almost exactly, and to this text he has added his own further alterations. Moreover, instead of the Hebrew, which has "How beautiful upon the mountains are the feet of the messenger who announces peace," Paul omits "on the mountains" and uses a plural "messengers" instead of the singular "messenger" found in both the Hebrew and the Septuagint. Moreover, in the Hebrew the messenger is proclaiming peace, but in the Greek the messengers announce "good news," a reference to Paul's gospel. His dependence on the Septuagint allows him "to transform Isaiah's depiction of a lone herald bringing news of the Yahweh's victory to Jerusalem into a prophecy of the numerous messengers God has sent out all over the world to proclaim the good news of Christ's lordship."[23] This verse has been especially significant in the expansion of Christianity for two thousand years, and it is therefore all the more important to recognize its roots in the Septuagint.

There are a number of places where Paul's citations are found in the Greek revisions (e.g., Romans 9:27–28, 27:33, 10:20, 11:27), and these are yet again evidences of the multiplicity of Jewish scriptural texts circulating in the first century in Greek and available to the apostle but not necessarily evidence of his intentional choices.[24] We find the same textual practices outside of the epistle to the Romans. Paul sometimes resorts to the use of the Greek revisions in 1–2 Corinthians, as we have already seen him do in Romans. In 1 Corinthians 15:54, Paul quotes Isaiah 25:8 with a phrasing similar not to the Hebrew or the Septuagint but to Theodotion.

Paul shares the reading with Theodotion: "death has been swallowed up in victory." With this reading of Isaiah, Paul was able to argue that Christ had already defeated death so the Corinthians too were victors over death.

1 Corinthians 15:54	Isaiah 25:8 (Theodotion)	Isaiah 25: 8 (Septuagint)	Isaiah 25: 8 (Hebrew)
When this perishable body puts on imperishability, and this mortal body puts on immortality, then the saying that is written will be fulfilled: "Death has been swallowed up in victory."	... Death has been swallowed up in victory	Death, having prevailed, swallowed them up	... He will swallow up death for ever.

The apostle Paul shaped Christian theology more than any other New Testament writer, even though the canonical form of the New Testament contains voices from others whose theological vision sometimes appears different, or at least nuanced differently, from that of the man from Tarsus. How was the Septuagint used in the rest of the New Testament?

Other New Testament Voices

The remainder of the New Testament outside of the books traditionally attributed to Paul consists of the epistle to the Hebrews, which makes no authorial claim; small epistles attributed to Peter, John, James, and Jude; and Revelation. All of these show evidences of their authors' use of the Septuagint and its revisions instead of the Hebrew, but we shall look at only a few examples.[25]

For the epistle to the Hebrews, there can be no question: this author demonstrates an undeniable dependence on the Septuagint and its Greek revisions. There are around three dozen direct citations and around two dozen allusions. The author frequently changes the citations such that few of them appear to resemble any of our modern editions of the Septuagint. Nonetheless, our evidence suggests that the author of Hebrews did not use the Hebrew scriptures. Even though some of his material appears to be similar to some of the Hebrew texts at Qumran, the similarities can be explained by exegetical techniques shared by Jews in this period all over the Mediterranean world. One scholar has gone so far as to say that there is not "a single Hebrew or Aramaic relic in the citations or elsewhere in Hebrews."[26]

In the Septuagint translation of Genesis 47:31, we find the parting words of Jacob to his son Joseph, and the Septuagint translator misread the Hebrew "bed" as "staff," since both nouns have the same consonantal spelling (Hebrew *mth*). In Hebrews 11:21 the writer quotes from the Septuagint, "By faith Jacob, when dying, blessed each of the sons of Joseph, 'bowing in worship over the top of his staff,'" instead of what the writer of Genesis 47:31 intended to say, "And he said, 'Swear to me'; and he swore to him. Then Israel bowed himself on the head of his bed." It is also evident the author was referring to Greek texts since his development of the idea of "rest," a very important theological concept in Hebrews, depends on a formulation in Greek, not Hebrew. In Hebrews 4:3–5, the author borrows the concept of rest from Psalm 95 and Genesis 2:2.

> For we who have believed enter that rest, just as God has said, "As in my anger I swore, 'They shall not enter my rest,'" though his works were finished at the foundation of the world. For in one place it speaks about the seventh day as follows: "And God rested on the seventh day from all his works." And again in this place it says, "They shall not enter my rest."

The Hebrew terms for rest in Psalm 95:11 and in Genesis 2:2 are different from one another, so the reader would not have made the connection if he were reading the Hebrew alone. In Greek, however, the same word is used for "rest," and by using an ancient Jewish technique of interpretation (*gezerah shawah*) whereby one passage illuminates another by verbal connections the author is able at the beginning of his epistle to set up the new theme of rest. There are more connections in this passage and surrounding ones to link the ideas: "rest" in Genesis 2:2, Psalm 95:11, and Hebrews 3:11, 4:3, and 4:4; "works" in Genesis 2:2, Psalm 95:9, and Hebrews 3:9 and 4:4; and "today" or "day" in Genesis 2:2, Psalm 95:7, and Hebrews 3:7, 3:15, and 4:4.[27] Not all of these are found in Septuagint manuscripts, however. Since some readings agree with the Alexandrian Jewish writer Philo—for example, in Philo's *On the Posterity of Cain* 64, his citation of Genesis 2:2 reads exactly as Hebrews 4:4—either the two authors used the same

Hebrews 10:5–7	Psalm 39:7–9 (Septuagint)	Psalm 40:6–8 (Hebrew and English)
Consequently, when Christ came into the world, he said, "Sacrifices and offerings you have not desired, but a body you have prepared for me; ⁶ in burnt-offerings and sin-offerings you have taken no pleasure. ⁷ Then I said, "See, God, I have come to do your will, O God" (in the scroll of the book it is written of me)."	Sacrifice and offering you did not want, But ears you fashioned for me. Whole burnt offering and one for sin you did not request. Then I said, "Look, I have come; In a scroll of a book it is written of me. To do your will, O my God, I desired— And your law, within my belly."	Sacrifice and offering you do not desire, but you have given me an open ear. Burnt-offering and sin-offering you have not required. ⁷ Then I said, "Here I am; in the scroll of the book it is written of me. ⁸ I delight to do your will, O my God; your law is within my heart."

text of Genesis or the author of Hebrews might have been directly dependent on Philo himself. There are other shared readings between Philo and Hebrews, and these too must be taken seriously; however, whether or not the author of Hebrews used Philo, he unquestionably used the Greek Jewish scriptures.

Another very well-known problem is found in Hebrews 10:5. The larger citation in 10:5–7 is taken from Psalm 40:6–8 (39:7–9 in the Septuagint), but it is Hebrews 10:5 that has caused the most problems for interpreters.

Where does the author of Hebrews get his citation? The Hebrew literally reads "ears you have dug for me," which the NRSV has appropriately rendered "you have given me an open ear." The Greek translation of Psalms has been described as a literal translation, so on this basis many scholars have judged "ears" to be the original reading and thus this as a case in which the writer of Hebrews follows neither Greek nor Hebrew. However, the arguments in favor of "ears" have not convinced everyone, and some argue that "body" is the oldest Septuagint reading that was later erased from memory due to successive revisions.[28] If this is true, the writer of Hebrews has again followed the Septuagint.

Relative to its brevity, 1 Peter contains more citations and allusions to the Old Testament than any other New Testament book, and none of them can be explained by reference to a Hebrew version.[29] Peter's use of Psalm 33 throughout his first epistle, for example, is based on the Septuagint form of the psalm and also demonstrates his extensive knowledge of the fuller context that is not included in his citation.

Finally, readers of the New Testament reach the Revelation of John, which is a special case for several reasons. While the book is strange to modern readers, popular portrayals often do not appreciate the contours of the apocalyptic genre in which Revelation was written, and often the permeation of Old Testament themes throughout this book is missed. Revelation contains no marked citations of the Old Testament, but allusions abound, and there are at least a couple of "unmarked" citations. Marked citations, as we have seen with other writers in the New Testament, are usually introduced with an attribution: "...as Isaiah said," or the like. Since his Greek throughout the book remains unrefined, would he have been more comfortable using the Hebrew Bible than the Septuagint? Like other New Testament authors, the apocalyptic seer from Asia Minor was living in a multilingual environment where Jews and Christians could move between Hebrew or Aramaic and Greek with fluency; thus, he could have been attempting to write a "Semiticized" Greek. Moreover, the citations that are recognizable are very much like the Hebrew text; on the other hand, given the abundant use of the Greek revisions in the New Testament and in the absence of positive proof for the use of Hebrew, it is unnecessary to imagine the writer using a Hebrew text.[30]

The Psalter is one resource that furnishes abundant material for the apocalyptic seer.[31] One very important unmarked citation is that of Psalm 2:1–2 in Revelation 11:15, 18 (also in Acts 4:25–26). The "rage of the nations" and "the Lord and his anointed (*christos*)" are taken from the Greek Psalter. The writer is not through with Psalm 2, however. He also writes in Revelation 2:26–27, 12:5, and 19:15 that one will come who will rule with an iron rod. This idea is based on Psalm 2:8–9: "Ask of me, and I will make the nations your heritage, and the ends of the earth your possession. You shall break them with a rod of iron, and dash them in pieces like a potter's vessel." What is important is that the author of Revelation here follows the Septuagint translation of Psalm 2:9, where the Greek translator has misunderstood the Hebrew verb or read a different Hebrew text. The Hebrew psalm reads, "Ask of me, and I will make the nations your heritage, and the ends of the earth your possession. You shall break them with a rod of iron, and dash them in pieces like a potter's vessel." The Hebrew psalmist says that the one to whom God gives authority will "break" the enemies with a rod of iron. In the Greek translation of the Hebrew, the translator has either misunderstood this verb or is reading a manuscript with a slight variant, which looks very similar in Hebrew to the verb for "rule." The revisers Aquila and Symmachus were able to spot the infelicity and their texts read "shatter" in the spirit of the Hebrew psalmist. The writer of Revelation, however, has followed the Septuagint's misunderstanding. This example is particularly important since it contains an obviously erroneous reading of an Old Testament passage that was left uncorrected by the New Testament writer. Throughout Revelation, and not only in these allusions and unmarked citations to the psalms but also to other books from the Jewish scriptures, there is no reason to expect that the writer used anything other than the Greek form of the Jewish scriptures.

The Significance of the Citations

With this survey of the New Testament writers we may now be able better to understand their use of the Jewish scriptures, which Christians would soon begin to call the Old Testament. By looking at specific types of citations we can see the significance of their choice of Septuagint over the Hebrew scriptures. Some have wondered if later Christian scribes tampered with the Septuagint to make the passages there conform to the New Testament. If this is the case, we don't really have the New Testament authors quoting the Septuagint, but the Septuagint's original wording was lost due to scribes who wanted to harmonize the two texts. The few studies that have been conducted on similar questions in the Dead Sea Scrolls and in the Samaritan Pentateuch, however, have concluded that there are no evidences of explicit sectarian readings in the manuscripts after the initial creation of the documents and thus that it is unlikely that scribes went back to the source from which they quoted to modify it drastically in light of the new. In the New Testament there are at best very few citations that might have been adjusted, but none in any significant way. Therefore, what we see in the New Testament are indeed citations from the Septuagint.[32]

We have learned in this chapter that most if not all of the citations in the New Testament are not in any way strictly dependent on the Hebrew, and in those cases where they appear to be close to the Hebrew a Greek revision can just as easily provide an explanation. Indeed, we could extend to the entire New Testament what has been proven in a study on Romans, that there is "no instance in which the hypothesis that Paul used a Greek text does not account for the data more simply and more satisfactorily than the supposition that Paul employed Hebrew and/or Aramaic texts."[33] We have also noted cases in which citations were taken from the Septuagint to make a theological point that would not have been possible had the writer cited the Hebrew version of the same text.

It would be worth the modern reader's time to ponder the significance of the New Testament authors' use of the Septuagint, to consider what theological emphases would not have been possible if the authors were using the Hebrew Bible alone. Paul's theology in Romans might be considerably different, since we have seen that his reading of the Septuagint of Isaiah provided him the theological contours he drove home. Likewise, the theme of rest in the book of Hebrews, so central to its message, would have been absent had this writer been reading the Hebrew Bible. And perhaps most shocking of all, the prophecy of the virgin birth would not have been found in the Hebrew version. The Greek Septuagint and not the Hebrew Bible gives Matthew the textual "proof" to connect Jesus to the prophecy. One inevitable objection is that Matthew was divinely inspired to transmit this theological claim about Jesus. But instead of merely claiming to have a divine vision or referring to an oral tradition, Matthew cites Isaiah to argue that Jesus was the one foretold in the Jewish scriptures. If anyone wanted to check, the "proof" was there in the Septuagint of Isaiah.

The other conclusion of this chapter reinforces those reached already: the state of the Old Testament text in the first century was still very much in flux, but this textual reality did not disturb the New Testament writers. Having examined the use of the Jewish scriptures in the New Testament, we are now ready to move forward to see how the earliest Christians read the Old Testament in the second century and beyond.

10

The New Old Testament

But also those books should not be omitted which are agreed to have been written before the advent of the Savior, because even though they are not accepted by the Jews, yet the Church of that same Savior has accepted them.

AUGUSTINE, *Speculum* 22

NATURALLY, SINCE THE earliest Christian writers wrote in Greek, they readily adopted the Greek Jewish scriptures.[1] Even though the term "Septuagint" originally referred only to the first translation of the Pentateuch in the third century BCE, its meaning was extended as early as Justin Martyr (d. c. 165) to include all of the books translated from the Hebrew Bible and some that were later called "apocrypha." The inclusion of apocryphal books led some early Christian writers to assume they too had been translations from original Hebrew scriptures. This attitude tells us two things: first, that the authoritative status of some of these books had not yet been settled; and second, that Christians were already looking to the Jewish use of scripture as a decisive criterion for their own. We shall see this unfold throughout the remainder of this book.

Because numerous Greek Jewish writings fell all along the scale from secular to sacred, it was uncertain in the first few centuries what contents would be included. A fixed collection of exactly the same books bound together between two covers would not come until much later. Instead, the "Bible" in the earliest centuries of Christianity is characterized by a loose collection of texts, circulating independently or, at best, grouped together in small sets of books. When a modern reader looks at the Table of Contents in her Bible and sees a list of Old Testament books from Genesis through to Malachi, she must recognize that this is a relatively recent innovation. The earliest Christian thinkers had at least two other challenges in addition to developing a list of books to make up the Old

Testament. They had to decide how to justify the use of Jewish writings as Christian scripture, and no later than the second century they demonstrate a certain discomfort with the differences between the Septuagint and the Hebrew scriptures that were at this time being confirmed in some Jewish circles. Christians soon realized they were theologizing on the basis of scriptural texts that were not used by their Jewish counterparts, and since the early church saw itself as the "New Israel," it was necessary to address the discrepancy. Early Christian scholars took two approaches to deal with the problem. We shall see later that some began to assume the superiority of the Hebrew Bible, but none of them knew what has become clear to us only in recent times: that the Hebrew Bible of the second century stood at the end of a long process of evolution and that the Hebrew texts used by the Septuagint translators were in many cases alternative editions of the Hebrew scriptures. Like some today are still prone to do, these church-men assumed that the Hebrew Bible in their day was the only one that had ever existed.[2] Most early Christian scholars, however, argued or at least assumed that the Greek Septuagint was the new word of God for the church, a divinely inspired text that God had delivered for the sake of bringing the message of Christianity to the world, and they had no con-cern to know how the Septuagint matched up with the Hebrew. While it may be true that most if not all assumed all of the Septuagint books had been translated from Hebrew, they mostly work in practice showing no concern for this theoretical abstraction. To the common believer, the ques-tion would not have mattered or probably never even entered their mind. As God did for the Jews in Hebrew and Aramaic, so now he had spoken in Greek for the church. This belief, deriving in part from Philo's attitude to the Septuagint, developed later into the Christian belief that God delivered a new message in Greek to prepare the world for the Christian gospel. The Jews had missed their chance.

Near the end of the first century and the completion of the writings that would comprise the New Testament, we enter into a period known as the Patristic age, characterized by the writings of the church fathers. This was a formative time during which Christians sought to define them-selves against Jews and as groups within Christianity sought to define themselves against each other. Part of that process was to determine what would constitute its authoritative body of writings. With the exception of a small Christian community arising out of Edessa that spoke Syriac, a dia-lect of Aramaic, and that translated the Hebrew Bible (nevertheless with attention both to the Septuagint and the Aramaic Targums), during this time the Septuagint was the Bible of the church: in its original Greek form, in its revisions, and in early translations into Latin used mostly in the North African church. The formation of Christianity—through preaching, teaching, apologetics, theological formation, and liturgical practices— depended almost entirely on the Septuagint as the Old Testament.[3]

Creating the Old Testament

The earliest evidence we have that some Christians were interested in defining the limits to Old Testament scripture comes only at the end of the second century and the beginning of the third, and we shall see in due course that while the New Testament was more or less fixed by the fourth century, the Old Testament remained very fluid for a surprisingly long time. Rather than citing scriptural texts only directly from scrolls, early Christian writers encountered the "text" through any number of media, such as *testimonia*, or sources with topically arranged excerpted proof texts. Many of their citations were detached from their original con- texts since they mostly served the needs of the apologetic debates by which this time was characterized.[4] Comparisons can be made even within a single writing of a Christian author like Justin Martyr, whose short cita- tions are very obviously interpolated, are modified in any number of ways, or have come from sources that had interpretative material surrounding the quote, possibly similar to the Gospels citations. His longer excerpts are very obviously copied from the Septuagint, but the shorter the citation, the more likely it came from a *testimonia* source. Nonetheless, the *testimonia* were not necessarily fixed literary forms. They were probably "traditions" of excerpted Old Testament texts that were anthologized by some writers; however, they could have varied greatly from source to source, and the textual forms within a single source may have displayed the same diversi- ty.[5] By the end of the second century writers begin to base their citations more clearly on the Septuagint text than on *testimonia* or similar (though hypothetical) sources. The Septuagint citations do not agree from author to author but Christian exegetes are using a biblical text when they cite the Old Testament. This process must have been related at least in part to the increasingly established position of the Hebrew Bible in the synagogue. As Jews were beginning to rely on a singular authoritative text, Christians also began to establish their text. But the pressure could have gone both ways. In other words, a "critical synergy" may have contributed to the fix- ing of scripture within both Jewish and Christian circles; we should not imagine that the adoption of the Jewish scriptures as the Christian Old Testament and the finalization of the Hebrew Bible in the synagogue happened at the same time by accident.[6] In these first two centuries after the New Testament, Christians had accepted the Jewish scriptures as their own and were beginning to supplement them with writings containing the teachings of Jesus and the apostles.

There was also a practical reason to adopt an established text. The technological invention of the codex, or book, in the second century facilitated the emergence of the Christian Bible. The implications for world history were enormous: not merely an artifact of antiquity, the codex was the forerunner to the modern book format. The earliest codices would have been of parts, such as a codex of the Gospels and a codex of Paul's letters. Only from the fourth century do we have evidence of both the Old and New Testament in the same codex.[7] The emergence of the codex is almost entirely the responsibility of early Christians. In the second century, only about 4 percent of the total number of surviving manuscripts are in the codex form; however, that number increases to about 80 percent by the fourth century, and the bookrolls, or scrolls, are completely overtaken by the eighth.[8] Owing to imperial support gained in the fourth century (see Chapter 12), Christian books make up more than 50 percent of the surviving books of the fifth century, where in the second they comprised only 10 percent. Why did Christians embrace the codex? Scholars have explained that the codex was more portable, easier to read than unwieldy scrolls, and less costly. But none of these factors satisfactorily explain early Christians' almost complete adoption of the codex. What is more, the artifactual evidence indicates that scrolls were not so difficult to carry, were not so unwieldy to read, and were hardly more expensive than the codex, especially since early Christian book production manifests no apparent concern to save money by writing smaller in more compact volumes. The evidence rather suggests that Christians adopted the codex for socioreligious reasons: they wanted to distinguish their own books from Jewish and pagan literature. In the codex Christians could make a claim to have a different literature than that on offer elsewhere.[9]

What Books Made Up the Old Testament?

Here we must think carefully about our use of the terms "canon" and "scripture," which are two different concepts often confusingly treated as the same. Scripture signifies only an "authoritative writing in a religious community." Canon, on the other hand, is a catalog, a list of scriptural writings. To put it simply: there can be no canon without scripture, but scripture can exist without a canon.[10] A writing must be considered scripture if it is to have any religious authority in the life of a community, but it need not make it onto a canon list to have authority. This may be difficult for modern readers to appreciate. Many of us who for one reason or another are familiar with the Bible assume that what is included in the canon and therefore printed in our Bibles is scripture, but nothing outside of the two covers of our Bibles can be called scripture. Jews in this period and Christians in the early church would not have agreed.

Like New Testament writers, early Christians rarely cite noncanonical books as scripture and instead take their biblical material almost exclusively from books found in the Hebrew Bible. Some usually appeal to this lack of citation as evidence that the early church's scriptures reflected more or less the canon of the Hebrew Bible of the synagogue. Here we see the problem with the terminology, because while the lack of citations of apocryphal books may indicate they were not treated as canonical it does not demonstrate they were regarded as unscriptural. Rather, two defining features of the Christian use of the Old Testament right up to the time of the Reformation was its role in disputes with Jews and in appeals to passages specifically used as messianic prophecies. Apologetics and messianic interpretation drove the conversation more than any other factor. Sometimes even canonical books do not feature in the citations and extended exegeses of the early church: references to Nehemiah, Obadiah, Esther, and a number of other "canonical" books are rare. As we have already seen in Qumran and in the New Testament, certain books across the Jewish and Christian spectrum were more important for exegesis than others, so the commentaries may not even tell us much about what the early church viewed as scriptural. For example, there are few traces of patristic commentaries on the apocryphal books. Origen seems to have written one on the Additions to Daniel in Book 10 of his *Stromata*, which Jerome subsequently cited in his *Commentary on Daniel* (13), and Ambrose wrote a commentary on Tobit.[11] It is possible that more existed but that later church tradition did not preserve a record of such writings. Nonetheless, the near silence of any commentarial record of apocryphal books is striking. It would seem that, in both the Jewish context and in the Greco-Roman pagan context, "to close and 'canonize' a text or literary collection is to open it up to a wealth of fresh exegetical exploration—and to invite the possibility of commentary."[12] Conversely then, not to have a commentary on a text might indicate the lack of perceived authority, whether belonging to a formal list or not. This remains a compelling line of argument against the early church's reception of the apocryphal books as scripture. Nevertheless, the suggestion is not without problems, the most significant of which is that patristic commentaries cannot be compared with Greco-Roman and Qumran commentarial literature in at least one way: the fathers selectively chose the texts on which they would comment. At least two reasons for their selectivity are that they used these texts in polemical contexts with their Jewish and pagan opponents and that they chose passages that were particularly difficult for Christians to understand. When an apocryphal book does not have a patristic commentary, it is not necessarily a proof that no one considered the book scriptural, only that it was less useful in debates with opponents or in Christological exegesis. Even commentaries on "canonical" books are often incomplete (e.g., Origen's partial commentary on Samuel), since the author was concerned only to comment on what he deemed most important. Early Christian commentaries may have laid the groundwork for the modern biblical commentary; however, they are not identical, and the texts they chose for exegesis do not tell us what the church held to be scriptural, even if they tell us what was canonical. Neither are the few canon lists drawn up by early Christian writers a sure guide to establishing the list of scriptures in the early church. There are only a few canon lists in any case, and they should not be taken to be representative of any kind of authoritative tradition or of universal belief. There was no unanimously recognized Old Testament in the early church, and indeed the diversity of canons and scriptural collections persists right down to the Reformation.

Christian canon lists in the first four centuries were in any case by no means regular or universally definitive. Perhaps putting too much confidence in the Jewish evidence like the mention of twenty-two books in Josephus' *Against Apion*, some have argued that the Christian Old Testament was established as early as the second century: the list of books was complete, some were in and some were out, and there was no further modification to the church's Old Testament. The very use of canon lists by Christian writers in the first four centuries, however, demonstrates that Christians were still debating the status of a number of books; in other words, if the Old Testament were universally recognized, there would have been no need to continue issuing canon lists.[13]

While matters of grave doctrinal importance like the nature of Christ were debated at the ecumenical councils, a formal ecumenical council was never called to address specifically the issue of the biblical canon. This might mean the demarcation of the canon was not a top priority. Instead, our understanding of the development of the Old Testament canon in the early church comes from more than a dozen canon lists issued in the first four centuries. We shall now consider only a few statements to give us a sense of the debate.[14]

The earliest list given for the Christian Old Testament canon (of which we are aware) belongs to Melito of Sardis (d. c. 190 CE). Eusebius reports that Melito took pains to find out from one called Onesimus "the accurate facts about the ancient writings, how many they are in number, and what is their order."[15] Melito reports: "I came to the east and reached the place where these things were preached and done, and learnt accurately the books of the Old Testament." He lists the books of the Hebrew Bible in roughly the same order as that found in the Septuagint. Melito's list is often said to be the earliest evidence that the Christian and Jewish Bibles were essentially the same, but this is not entirely true. Melito leaves out Esther, doesn't specify exactly what was contained in Jeremiah (in some Septuagint collections, Baruch, Lamentations, or the Letter of Jeremiah were included together), and probably includes the Wisdom of Solomon.[16] This is not exactly the same Bible, though we can see that in these early years Christians were apparently aiming to mirror Jewish attitudes to the scriptural books. It is no surprise that he does not include Esther, a book also debated within Jewish circles. We are told vaguely only that he went east, which is probably Palestine, a place where Christians had close social contacts with the Jews and would therefore be expected to adhere to a scriptural canon very like that of their contemporaries. As the later history would continue to show in numerous examples of early and medieval Christian writing, Christians nearly always aimed to match Jewish attitudes to the biblical text.[17] This earliest writer to provide a canon list does not reveal for us the final shape of the Christian Old Testament in the second century, but he shows the trajectory of Christian thinking on the canon.

Origen, whom we shall soon meet as perhaps the most important character in our entire story, also lists canonical books in a passage preserved by Eusebius, but it is clear that Origen has in mind the books of the Jewish canon; he is not affirming his own.[18] He also adds to the twenty-two books of the Hebrew canon 1–2 Maccabees, and in Jeremiah he includes the Epistle of Jeremiah. Origen's list may reflect that some Jews were still treating these as canonical in the third century, a plausible suggestion given that rabbinic literature includes debates over the status of Ecclesiasticus but also cites it as scripture.[19] In any case, while Origen treats the Hebrew tradition seriously, he also represents the practice of many other early Christian writers when he cites as scripture books not found in the Hebrew canon. He insists that Tobit, Judith, the Additions to Esther, Ecclesiasticus, and Wisdom are of divine origin and, with the exception of Baruch, cites from the noncanonical books with the introduction "it is written," the signal that he treats the writing as scripture.[20] One recent proposal suggests that Origen accepts these books only because he assumed they were originally written in Hebrew, but he makes this point just for one book, Susanna, one of the Additions to Daniel.[21] Since the context of that debate was over a book that was for the most part a Hebrew (and Aramaic) book, the concern seems to have been to prove that even the additional parts were in Hebrew, not that every book had to be an original Hebrew writing to be valid. Moreover, it is difficult to imagine that Origen, trained with a classical education and able to appreciate the quality of the Greek of books like 2 Maccabees and the Wisdom of Solomon, would have imagined all of the books were translated from Hebrew sources.[22] That Origen exegetes and does not merely comment on Wisdom 7 indicates that he accepted this book as scripture.[23] Origen was an advocate for the view that providence had delivered a new word of God for the church, and he was one of the earliest examples of Christian use of the larger Bible.

We have another list from the latter half of the third century in the Festal Letter of Athanasius, Bishop of Alexandria. Written at Easter of 367, Athanasius reveals his apologetically driven motives to solidify a canonical list. He is writing against some who were using "so-called apocryphal writings," when he could claim proudly to have followed "the traditions of our forefathers," which were "sufficient to instruct us perfectly." Athanasius claims that he bothered to investigate the matter himself so that he could give an accurate list of what was "handed down and confirmed as divine." This is by no means a man charged with the authority to settle the matter for the church universal; he is rather engaging in a polemical encounter with his own local opponents. Nevertheless, either some took note of Athanasius's list or his list reflects what was becoming standard opinion in the Near East. Two early manuscripts of the fourth century, Vaticanus and Sinaiticus, probably produced within several years either side of Athanasius' Letter, contain almost the same list as that promoted by the bishop; on the other hand, there are still important differences that prove we still do not have any sort of established canon.[24] Athanasius argued that there were three sets of books: canonical books, ecclesiastical books that could still be read for edification, and apocryphal writings that were to be avoided.[25] Baruch and the Letter of Jeremiah were included along with the prophet Jeremiah in his main canonical section, and in his second category he lists the Wisdom of Solomon, Ecclesiasticus, Esther, Judith, and Tobit. He does not specify which books he considered "apocryphal."

The most significant support for a broader Christian canon comes from the North African theologian Augustine of Hippo, whom we will meet in more detail later.[26] Of 1–2 Maccabees, Augustine writes: "These are held as canonical, not by the Jews, but by the church, on account of the extreme and wonderful sufferings of certain martyrs, who, before Christ had come in the flesh, contended for the law of God even unto death, and endured most grievous and horrible evils." In his *City of God* he refers to Tobit as scripture and also frequently defends the Wisdom of Solomon. Augustine reveals no embarrassment for having a different canon than his Jewish contemporaries and when we come to Augustine in Chapter 13, we shall see that his own situation made him the Septuagint's most ardent defender in the early church.

Several regional councils and other churchmen also mentioned the canonical collections. A broader Septuagint canon was affirmed in the Mommsen List of 360; in the 60th Canon from the Council of Laodicea in Asia Minor c. 364–365; in canon 85 of the Apostolic Canons, added c. 380 and accepted by the Orthodox Church; at the Synod of Hippo in North Africa in 393; at several Councils of Carthage also in North Africa in 397 and 419; and in the c. fifth century Galasian Decree (which restates the Carthaginian list of 419).[27] Second Esdras is likely affirmed in an old poem by Amphilochius of Iconium (c. 380), and the anonymously written sixth-century *Synopsis of Sacred Scripture* unquestionably lists that same 2 Esdras in its canon list. Although much later, in 730 St. John of Damascus goes out of his way to mention that the Wisdom of Solomon and Ecclesiasticus were not included in the Jewish canon even though they are "virtuous and noble." Even in the eighth century they must have been very important to at least some Christian communities, or he would have had no reason to mention their place in the Jewish canon.

We should also examine the material evidence. Codex Vaticanus has almost the same books as those in Athanasius' noncanonical section. One may wonder if Athanasius' separation of some of these books into separate categories reflects a current of thought that would influence Jerome several decades later (see Chapter 13). In the Septuagint, the books are not separated but are placed alongside the books of the Jewish canon: if segregated, they carry the stigma of being secondary, but if interspersed throughout the Bible alongside the canonical books their readers are more likely to treat them as scripture. The Additions to Esther are included as part of Esther; the books of the Maccabees are placed in the historical section because they were of similar value to books like Samuel and Kings; and Wisdom and Sirach (Ecclesiasticus) were placed alongside books like Proverbs because they were considered to be part of the wisdom tradition of the Old Testament. The only other fourth-century manuscript still extant, Codex Sinaiticus, is also similar to Athanasius' list except that it includes 1 and 4 Maccabees, and a space left in the binding of the manuscript reveals that the producers had intended to place 2 and 3 Maccabees there as well.[28] A fifth-century manuscript also from Alexandria (Alexandrinus) contains 1–4 Maccabees and the Psalms of Solomon.

The earliest complete manuscripts from the fourth and fifth centuries contain these additional books that were excluded from the Jewish canon, and they are placed in sections according to their genre rather than separated from the books that had achieved canonical status in the Hebrew Bible.

All of the lists from the various church councils between 363 and 397 and the witness of our manuscripts reveal that the canon was made up of a "central core, a variable fringe, and differences in arrangement."[29] What was the "variable fringe"? Even this was different in these earliest examples. Athanasius excludes Esther from his canonical list, but Baruch, the Letter of Jeremiah, and 1 Esdras are in. The two fourth-century manuscripts have seven (Vaticanus) and nine (Sinaiticus) additional writings, but the latter intended eleven since there was space for 2–3 Maccabees. In contrast to the relative stability of the New Testament canon from an early date, the Old Testament never achieved the same, and the canon of the Old Testament known today by Protestants was not found in the exact same form for more than fifteen hundred years of Christian history. The boundaries of the church's Old Testament remained loose and open well into the medieval period, at which time the diversity of the grouping of these books becomes mind-boggling. It is then that we see just how far away we really are from any sort of definitive Old Testament canon in the Christian church. In due course Jerome's biblical scholarship would eventually lead to the devaluation of the Apocrypha in the West, but the Greek Bible still in use today in the Greek Orthodox Church kept the books where they had been in the earlier Septuagint manuscripts.

There is, then, a need for caution when assessing the so-called canon lists and the statements of the few fathers who commented on the canon. Terms like "scripture" and "canon" should be used carefully. The formation of the canon in the early church was a slow process. The rough edges of the canon force us to eschew a simplistic model of a virtually unchanging Old Testament from the earliest days of Christianity. But that does not mean the borders of the Old Testament were wide open. The same core books appear on every canon list and in all of the commentaries preserved from the early church and, even though the core of the canon was relatively stable from early on, a book's omission from the canon was not a denial of scriptural authority.

Many discussions over and uses of the Old Testament arose out of polemical encounters with Jews. These specific situations determined the books to which Christians appealed and had a significant impact on the formation of the Old Testament canon in the church, but they do not tell us about what was regarded as scripture more broadly. Additionally, the early church was concerned to present itself as the "New Israel," and it was important that they followed the books of the Jewish canon to diminish the value of those the "Old Israel" had excluded. The formation of the New Testament canon in these same centuries also impacted Christian thinking on the Old Testament canon. Since the apocryphal books were mostly ignored by New Testament writers and excluded from the Jewish canon, the church would have had little incentive to add these books to their canons.[30]

We should still maintain a distinction between "canon" and "scripture" and recall that the early church treated books excluded from the canonical lists as scripture. Some Christian writers like Origen found many ideas useful for Christian instruction in books that had been excluded from the Jewish canon, and he even performed exegesis on them. Moreover, many other Christians did not share the desire to have their canonical views shaped entirely by the Hebrew Bible, and even some that did accept the core Jewish canon still permitted the use of some of the apocryphal books. Luther and the Reformers would be the only Christians in history to have definitively abandoned the broader canon.[31]

II

God's Word for the Church

*Did not Providence, who has given a foundation in the
sacred Scriptures to all the Churches of Christ, also consider
those bought with a price, for whom Christ died?*

ORIGEN, *Letter to Africanus* 4–5

THE SEPTUAGINT MADE an impression on early Christian missionary expansion, theological disputes with those both outside and inside the church, and the interpretation of the scriptures for devotional and liturgical life.[1] One of the most important claims of Christianity was that Jesus fulfilled the Jewish scriptures. Since most of the Mediterranean world in the first century spoke Greek, they were told *in Greek* that Jesus fulfilled the *Greek Jewish scriptures*, the Septuagint. In the fourth century, Eusebius could write that the Septuagint was a critical part of the *praeparatio evangelica*, "the preparation for the Gospel." Christianity was, however, a missionary religion, so Christians soon multiplied outside of the Greek world. As early as the second century, a translation of the Septuagint appeared in Latin, and the fragmentary remains from this Latin translation are now referred to collectively as the Old Latin version.[2] There is still debate over the origins of this Old Latin translation: whether it was first produced by Jews or Christians, whether there was one original translation or there were many ad hoc translations, whether it was a complete or partial translation, whether it was written or oral, and whether it was produced to be disseminated or produced only by Latin Christian writers when they discussed the biblical text.[3] The version exists today only in an extremely fragmented form, and researchers cull the readings from a few manuscripts, from marginal notations in Vulgate Bible manuscripts, and from the writings of the Latin fathers who wrote before Jerome's translation. The Old Latin version is important even in the discussion of the oldest text of the Hebrew Bible, because at times the Old Latin preserves the oldest Septuagint reading where later revisions to the Septuagint have buried the earliest text.

Many of these readings can be found in Samuel and Kings. For example, Ahaziah of Judah's reign is introduced in 2 Kings 8:25–27 in the Septuagint and in the Hebrew Bible.[4] But its placement here is awkward, and it rather belongs after 10:36 since 11:1 begins with Ahaziah's mother lamenting his death. The original order is attested in the Old Latin, but the revisions around the turn of the Common Era, which brought the Septuagint into agreement with the Hebrew Bible, have affected all later Septuagint manuscripts. This is one of several cases where our only knowledge of the older edition of the Hebrew comes through the Old Latin. Here the Old Latin has preserved the oldest form of the Greek, which in turn preserves the older form of the Hebrew.[5]

By the Carolingian Age (751–987), the Septuagint had also been translated into Coptic (an early Christian language of Egypt), Armenian, Georgian, Gothic, Slavonic, Syriac, Christian Palestinian Aramaic, Ethiopic, and Arabic.[6] Many of these local Christian communities learned the scriptures from missionaries who promptly translated the Septuagint into the local language; thus, the spread of Christianity all throughout the East owes itself in large part to the Septuagint, received by these new converts as the Christian Old Testament. Had there been no Septuagint, and had early Jewish converts remained in a Semitic world, the church may never have moved outside of its Palestinian birthplace.

Christian scholars were also becoming aware of the differences between the Bible of the synagogue and their new Old Testament. In response to this potential problem some writers developed a "chain of tradition" to explain how the Septuagint was meant for the Gentiles all along, and the most notable path taken was an elaboration on the legend of the Greek translation as told in the *Letter of Aristeas*.[7] The legend became more sensational in Christian hands, but they were not alone responsible for dramatizing the account or for transmitting it.[8] Two other Jewish writers extended the legend that we learned of in the *Letter of Aristeas* in their own ways in the first century CE, though we cannot be sure whether they knew the work or drew from another source. Philo (c. 20 BCE–c. 50 CE) and Josephus were two of the most important figures in early Jewish history, and their works are preserved mainly by Christians who saw them as part of the prehistory of the Christian gospel.[9] A philosopher, theologian, and exegete, Philo is known mostly as an expert in the allegorical interpretation of scripture, a method similar to that practiced by his fellow Jews in Palestine, for which we have evidence through the scrolls of the Judean Desert, and by the early Alexandrian Christians. Philo is also important in the study of the Septuagint because his quotations from the Jewish scriptures are, unsurprisingly, from the Greek and not the Hebrew. Even though Philo uses scripture in a highly creative way, it is still possible to read in his biblical citations some form of the Septuagint text known in the first century in Alexandria. Philo had his own interests in privileging the Septuagint. If he knew any Hebrew at all, which is unlikely, it was minimal, so he would have needed to assure his contemporaries, and himself, that the Greek biblical text found in the Septuagint translation was equal in divine inspiration to that of the Hebrew scriptures. In his work *On the Life of Moses*, Philo writes an extensive report of the origins of the Septuagint translation, but whereas the *Letter of Aristeas* only hinted at divine involvement Philo makes it explicit.[10] Through omissions of and additions to the legend, Philo creates a new story that magnifies the Greek Jewish scriptures as the vehicle through which "each nation would abandon its peculiar ways, and, throwing overboard their ancestral customs, turn to honoring our laws alone."[11] The Septuagint provided the opportunity for Jewish mission to the Gentiles, who, at least as far as Philo could imagine, spoke Greek. The apostle Paul might have felt the same way, but in the other direction: the Greek Jewish scriptures had provided for him and the early church the means to evangelize the Jews and the rest of the Mediterranean. Had these scriptures remained in Hebrew and Aramaic, they would have had a much smaller audience. But Philo believed they held a message for all, and as an Alexandrian he was quick to point out that God's word spoke to him too. To prop up Philo's belief in the validity of the Septuagint, he substituted for the *Letter of Aristeas*'s subtlety (seventy-two translators just happened to have produced a consistent translation) an unequivocal claim of divine inspiration. The translators sought a place of peace and tranquility on the island of Pharos off the coast of the Alexandrian harbor. Sitting in seclusion, they "as if possessed, prophesied, in the course of translating, not each one something different, but all of them the same nouns and verbs, as if a prompter were invisibly giving them instructions."[12]

Josephus (c. 37–c. 100 CE) was a historian writing mostly for a Roman audience; he produced a historical account on the Jewish war that led to the destruction of Jerusalem and the Temple (c. 75 CE, *The Jewish War*), an account of history in which the Jewish story was central along with an autobiography (c. 94 CE, *Antiquities of the Jews* and *Life*), and an apologetic work (c. 96 CE, *Against Apion*).[13] He also uses the Septuagint throughout his writing, but since he draws from a mixture of texts scholars have frequently turned to him to study his citations.[14] Josephus mentions the translation of the Septuagint in *Against Apion* and in *Antiquities of the Jews*. In the latter, he integrates sections of the legend from the *Letter of Aristeas*—he shows dependence on the legend like we find there and not on the one like we find in Philo—into his narrative, giving the appearance that this is his story to tell. One interesting development in Josephus is that the number of translators has now changed from seventy-two to seventy. Since "septuaginta" is the Latin word for "seventy," it is probably here with Josephus that we find the genesis of the title of our Greek translation.[15] As for the translation procedure itself, Josephus avoids any hint at a miracle, narrating only that the translators worked "ambitiously and painstakingly"; these were hard-working translators, not conduits of divine activity.[16]

With different aims, Philo and Josephus provide two accounts of the legend of the translation. Josephus had no concerns to privilege the Greek translation but merely reported the bare facts that the biblical text had been translated into Greek.[17] For Philo, the stakes to confirm the legitimacy of the Greek scriptures were higher. As a Greek-speaking Alexandrian who probably knew no Hebrew, it was important to confirm for himself and his contemporaries that the Greek translation was the very word of God. Philo makes divine involvement explicit, but like the *Letter of Aristeas* Philo had been talking only about the translation of the Law. Christian writers would amplify the legend in both ways.

From the middle of the second century with the writing of Justin Martyr, Christians continued to tell the story of the *Letter of Aristeas* with varying degrees of the fantastic. The accounts of the translation up to the first quarter of the third century indicate an interest in both historical and miraculous formulations of the legend. Other writers continued to transmit the story in later centuries, but the fourth-century version of Eusebius of Caesarea might be the most important. His *Ecclesiastical History*, finished c. 326, is the earliest comprehensive account of the church's first few centuries and became the model of subsequent histories of the church. He also wrote exegetical and apologetic works, and in his *Preparation for the Gospel* Eusebius tells his readers that the translation of the Septuagint was part of God's plan to ready the world for the coming of Christianity.[18] The prophecies of our Lord, writes Eusebius, were concealed in the Hebrew language of the Jewish scriptures, but God providentially guided a translation into Greek so that when the Savior of the world did appear the nations would recognize him. This was the time when God spoke Greek. Eusebius' claim comes in the fourth century, when the miraculous elements of the Septuagint's origins had become part of the story and when, other than the Syriac version, Christians viewed the Old Testament as the Septuagint, or the Old Latin derived from it.[19] Eusebius also wrote during the Constantinian era of imperially supported Christianity, in the new age of Christian triumphalism. For him, what God had given to the Jews was simply preparatory; Christianity superseded a Judaism that failed to recognize Jesus as the Messiah, but since God foreknew all of this he set aside his original revelation in Hebrew (and Aramaic) and prepared the world for the Gospel by speaking a new word in Greek. Eusebius's account follows the *Letter of Aristeas* to a point, but he unambiguously makes the translation part of the preparation for the Gospel.

Another writer in the late fourth century, Epiphanius of Salamis, not only narrates an extended account but also demonstrates less of a concern to tell how the translation happened than to tell his readers why the Septuagint is superior to other Greek versions. In his work *On Weights and Measures* written about 392, Epiphanius discusses the Old Testament as he knew it in its Greek translation. By this time the Septuagint was so firmly rooted in the church that Epiphanius wishes to defend what he perceived to be the original Greek translation against the later revisions and new translations that had been produced by Jews, namely, those of Aquila, Symmachus, and Theodotion. Epiphanius provides his own biographical sketches of these reviser-translators, but in doing so he cannot hide his intent to malign them and to participate in the Christian practice of stereotyping Jews as duplicitous and untrustworthy. The only conclusion Epiphanius wants his readers to reach is that the church's Septuagint alone has been handed down by the inspiration of God and that any other version is invalid and even corrupt.

By the time we come to the fourth-century writings of Eusebius and Epiphanius, the idea that the Septuagint was the inspired word of God was already so deeply rooted in the church that it allowed these writers to speak of it as the preparation for the gospel and as the superior, indeed the only, word of God for the church. If the Septuagint was indeed the Bible of the church, in what ways did it contribute to the theological and exegetical formation of the early centuries of Christianity?

The Septuagint in the Formation of Christian Theology and Piety

The use of the Septuagint in the New Testament, the persistence of the Greek language in the Mediterranean world, and the development of miraculous accounts of Septuagint origins fostered the Greek Old Testament's role in the formation of early Christian thought.[20] The writings of the Apostolic fathers (mid-first to late second century) are saturated with citations from the Septuagint when they quote the Old Testament as scripture. In the second and third centuries in the Latin West, the theologian Tertullian and the bishop Cyprian, both from Carthage (in modern Tunisia), contributed to early Christian thought in no less important ways than those writing in Greek, and their biblical texts were the Old Latin derived from the Septuagint. Among the Greek writers working directly from the Septuagint were the apologists Justin Martyr and the bishop Irenaeus, and the great lights of the Alexandrian exegetical school, Clement of Alexandria and Origen. Following on into the fourth century were Eusebius of Caesarea, Athanasius of Alexandria, Ambrose of Milan, and the Cappadocian fathers: Basil the Great and his brother Gregory of Nyssa, and their friend Gregory of Nazianzus. Although they practiced a literal, historical interpretation of the text in contrast to the allegorizing of the Alexandrians, the Antiochian exegetes also depended on the Septuagint. Thus, both Latin and Greek writers drew directly upon the Septuagint (or indirectly via its translation into Latin) in the development of early Christian doctrine. We mentioned earlier that one could assume that the fathers always regarded the Septuagint as a translation and that the only reason they treated it as authoritative scripture was because it was in their minds a faithful translation of the original Hebrew. But most of the church fathers show no concern to discover how accurately the Greek represented the Hebrew original, and indeed many would not have known how to tell anyway. Whatever their theoretical statements may indicate, their practice divulges their view of the Septuagint as not a translation but a new revelation for the church.[21] Presumably most Christians would have viewed the Hebrew Bible as strictly Jewish scripture, but the Septuagint was the treasure of the church. How was their thought shaped by the Septuagint in ways it would not have been had they been reading the Hebrew Bible?

The Septuagint translators rendered the Hebrew word Yahweh with the Greek *kurios* "lord." We saw already in Chapter 8 that the New Testament authors sometimes apply the title *Kurios* to Jesus, affirming that this man from Nazareth was the very Lord himself. When the early Christian theologians read the Septuagint, they often saw Jesus prefigured throughout the Old Testament, and this has run right through the history of Christian exegesis. There were even possibilities to find the Lord even where he may not have been. In the Septuagint of Isaiah 45:1, the prophet records, "Thus says the Lord God to my anointed, Cyrus."[22] The Greek for Cyrus was *kuros*, only one letter off from *kurios*, "Lord." Either by imagining the presence of a single letter "i" or by having a faulty manuscript tradition into which the "I" had been inserted, the fathers could read, "Thus says the Lord God to Christ my Lord." The same can be said for the title *christos*, also applied to Jesus in the New Testament, even though in the Septuagint the translators had meant for it to be only the Greek equivalent of the Hebrew word for "anointed." When Tertullian reads of the "anointed priest" in the Septuagint of Leviticus 4:5, he believes it is a reference to Christ because of how it appears in Greek (*ho hiereus ho christos*).[23] In Lamentations 4:20, the Septuagint reads, "The Lord's anointed (*christos kuriou*), the breath of our face, was captured by their destructions," which would have been impossible for the fathers to interpret as anything but a reference to Christ.[24] In the same citation, the phrase "the breath of our face" in Greek includes the word *pneuma*, which in the New Testament and early Christian literature is the word used for the Holy Spirit. Using the Septuagint allowed them to fortify their Trinitarian theology by stressing the unity of the Son and the Spirit. The Trinity also found support in a verse like Isaiah 61:1 preached by Jesus in Luke 4:18, "The spirit of the Lord is upon me." Here in this one verse, early exegetes found reference to the father from whom the spirit goes forth, to the Son who was Jesus, and to the Spirit.[25] Amos 4:13 was also read as a reference to the Trinity in the declaration, "I am the one who makes the thunder strong and creates a wind (*pneuma*) and announces his anointed (*christos*) to humans." Tertullian wrote that this verse demonstrates the individualities of the Son and the Father.[26] Concerned to protect the doctrine that the Trinitarian members were uncreated but had existed eternally, Athanasius and Ambrose argued that the created spirit (*pneuma*) here is not the Holy Spirit.[27] When Cyprian read Numbers 23:19 in the Septuagint—"God is not like human beings, to be deceived, nor like a son of man, to be threatened"[28]—he used it to criticize the Jews, whom he said nailed Christ to the cross.[29] This verse has other significant implications, because, in the Hebrew Bible and thus in our modern English translations, the text reads, "God is not a human being, that he should lie, or a mortal, that he should change his mind" (cf. 1 Samuel 15:29). The Septuagint translator of Samuel was uncomfortable with the direct association of God with man, and with even a hint that he might be capable of lying or changing his mind. The Greek translation of the Hebrew modifies the meaning: God is not *like* a man who *can be deceived*.[30]

The book of Joshua also provided opportunities for typological exegesis. Because the Greek name for Joshua (*Iēsous*) is identical to that of Jesus,
early interpreters were able to exploit the parallels: Joshua was superior to
Moses because he was able to bring the people into the land; the gospel
of Jesus is superior to Moses and the Law. Justin Martyr made such connections. When God says of the angel of the Lord leading Israel into the
Promised Land, "my name is upon him" (Exodus 23:21), he is referring to
Jesus, because it is ultimately Joshua, who according to Justin is the prefigured Jesus, who leads the people into the Promised Land. Also in his
debate with Trypho, Justin writes:

> Here is an example of what I am talking about. Jesus, as I said many
> times before, whose name had been Hosea, was named Jesus by
> Moses when he was sent out as a spy with Caleb into the land of
> Canaan. Now, you are not curious to know why he did this, nor do
> you ask or investigate the reason. Hence, you have never discovered
> Christ, and when you read you fail to understand; when you hear
> us now telling you that Jesus is our Christ, you do not study the
> question to discover that he was given this name deliberately and
> not accidentally.[31]

Typological exegesis could also be done with Susanna, one of the
Additions to Daniel. In Susanna we read of an innocent who kept quiet
while she was unjustly condemned but who in the end was vindicated.
Incredibly, Daniel says, "I am innocent of the blood of this woman," and
Hippolytus in his *Commentary on Daniel* was able to seize on it at once to
point out that Pilate had said the same to Jesus. Hippolytus would thus
also include Susanna in the genealogy of Jesus found in the Gospel of
Matthew.[32]

Not everything was as clear; in many passages where the Septuagint
was positively confusing and the meaning obscured, some of the fathers
thought that God had intentionally kept certain truths hidden. They
taught that passages that speak of hidden mysteries like Proverbs 1:6
and Tobit 12:7 referred to the way God concealed some things to test
or challenge Christians to seek a deeper level of interpretation. The
Alexandrian fathers practiced this type of allegorical method of interpretation extensively.[33] The Alexandrians are contrasted to the Antiochian
exegetes. The latter explained the scriptures not by allegory but by the
plain sense, a straightforward method that has earned the Antiochians

the distinction of being named the first historical-critical scholars.[34] The Alexandrians saw opportunity in the occasional obscurities in the Septuagint. If they felt embarrassed that the style of the Septuagint was less sophisticated than classical literature, it motivated them to devise a theological justification. Origen goes on the defensive against those who mock the poverty of the language of the scriptures, and fathers other than those in Alexandria also looked for spiritual explanations of difficult passages.[35] One striking example of a preposterous translation in the Septuagint is found in Judges 15:19. After Samson struck down a thousand men with the jawbone of a donkey, he cried out to God as he lay dying of thirst. The Hebrew says, "So God split open the hollow place that is at Lehi, and water came from it. When he drank, his spirit returned, and he revived." The Greek translator of Judges is often baffled by his Hebrew text, and here too he produces nonsense: "And God opened the wound of the jawbone, and waters came from it. And he drank, and his spirit returned in him, and he revived."[36] Attempting to make sense of the Greek, Ambrose of Milan suggested that the stream flowed from the ground when Samson threw down the jawbone.[37] A later interpreter in the south of France, Caesarius of Arles (d. 542), had no problem with the water flowing from the jawbone, because for him this was fulfilled in Christians: "for the Lord himself said, 'He who believes in me, from within him there shall flow rivers of living water.'"[38] Even later, John of Damascus (d. 749) constructed a theological interpretation in which the jawbone represented the bones of the saints: "is it unbelievable that fragrant ointment should flow from the relics of the martyrs?" A reference to baptism was also available to early Christians on account of a mistranslation of Ezekiel 47:3. The Hebrew read, "Going on eastwards with a cord in his hand, the man measured one thousand cubits, and then led me through the water; and it was ankle-deep." The Septuagint translator rendered the last phrase, "it was water of release." The Greek word *aphesis* is used in the New Testament for "forgiveness" or "remission," and this meaning may have been read into Ezekiel to see waters of remission, or baptismal waters.[39]

Early exegetes also found in the Septuagint of 2 Kings 6:5 a prediction of the crucifixion. The Hebrew text reads, "But as one was felling a log, his axe head fell into the water; he cried out, 'Alas, master! It was borrowed.'" In the Septuagint, the final phrase is, "O master! And it was borrowed!" Irenaeus wrote that this verse gives a picture of the Divine Word that had been hidden for a long time, but the wood from the axe that fell into the water symbolized the wood of the cross, which made possible the revelation of the Divine word.[40] In Isaiah 3:10 they found another anticipation of the suffering of the Christ. In the Hebrew text, the prophet proclaims, "Tell the innocent how fortunate they are, for they shall eat the fruit of their labours," for which the Septuagint has, "Let us bind the just, for he is a nuisance to us. Therefore they shall eat the fruit of their works." In other words, the prophet in the Greek Isaiah says that the just will be bound, persecuted. The writer of the *Epistle of Barnabas* read this as a reference to Christ's Passion.[41] It should not be lost on the modern reader that these early exercises in Christological exegesis were helped along in no small part by their reading of the Septuagint.

The fathers were also able to make regular use of the Septuagint in the struggle to define orthodoxy and heresy, particularly in the clash over the nature of Christ that raged in the early part of the fourth century. A local church leader named Arius (c. 250–336) was excommunicated from the church in Alexandria for teaching that Christ was created by God the Father and was therefore distinct from him and not eternal.[42] The young Alexandrian deacon Athanasius became the chief opponent of Arianism, and his victory at the Council of Nicaea in 325—which produced the Nicene Creed and anathamatized Arius and his party—propelled him to become Bishop of Alexandria the following year. For the rest of his life he would devote himself to defending what had become after Nicaea the orthodox doctrine of the Trinity. When reading the Septuagint of Genesis 19:24, "And the Lord rained on Sodom and Gomorrah sulphur and fire from the Lord out of heaven," which contained two references to the "Lord" (both *kurios*), Athanasius argued that these two Lords were the Father and the Son and thus that the Son was equal to the Father long before his incarnation. The Greek Proverbs provided many similar opportunities for interlocutors on both sides of this debate. Personified Wisdom, whom the fathers took to be Jesus, was created by God the Father and was brought forth. Two of the most important verses were Proverbs 8:22 and 25: "The Lord created me as the beginning of his ways, for the sake of his works," and "...before the mountains were established and before all the hills, he begets me." Among others, Justin Martyr, Origen, and Tertullian argued that these verses proved the dependence of the Son upon the Father. For Arius, Proverbs 8:22 proved beyond a doubt that the Son was a created being, an idea not dissimilar to the teaching about the *logos* in John and in some Pauline passages (e.g., Colossians 1:15: "He is the image of the invisible God, the firstborn of all creation."). One of the major arguments offered by Athanasius in response to these claims was that the Son was created in the sense of his incarnation alone.⁴³ Although he predated the Arian controversy, Irenaeus had explained Christ's divinity and humanity by referring to Jeremiah 17:9 in the Septuagint as a reference to Christ: "...and is a man, and who shall understand him"? In this one verse we find the affirmation of Christ's humanity and the impossibility of fully understanding him in his divinity.⁴⁴ Athanasius would also turn to the Septuagint of Jeremiah 2:13 to claim that the Father is a "fountain of living water." If the Son had not always been, the Father would be a dry fountain.⁴⁵

In addition to theological controversy, the Septuagint provided ecclesiological, devotional, and liturgical support: Irenaeus read Isaiah 60:17—"I will appoint your rulers in peace and your overseers in righteousness"—as a statement on the appointment of elders for the church, since the language used in the Septuagint for "overseers" (*episkopos*) was also used in the New Testament's ecclesiological language.⁴⁶ Personal Bibles would not become commonplace until well after the invention of the printing press in the fifteenth century; as in the New Testament age, so in these early centuries the liturgy was the means by which most encountered the scriptures.⁴⁷ The liturgical rites of the Orthodox church are steeped in the language of the Septuagint. Many Psalter prayers are taken directly from the Septuagint and inserted into the Greek liturgies. Exclamations of the greatness of the Father and the Son are as well, from addresses to God found in Isaiah 57:15 and 3 Maccabees 2:2 (*St. Clement* B.12), in Jeremiah 39:19 (*St. Clement* B.24), and throughout the Psalms (e.g., *St. James* B.44, *St. Mark* B.137). The vocabulary of the liturgies is also dependent on other parts of the Septuagint, and unique words and unique meanings of common words from the Greek Old Testament permeate, like *anaphora*, which in classical Greek could refer to anything carried but in the Septuagint refers specifically to an offering. Words like *dōra* "gift" and *thusia* "sacrifice" were also used in the same sense. In the Greek of Isaiah 9:5, the one who was to come is called the "Messenger of Great Council" (in the Hebrew: "Mighty Counselor"), the title used in the Eucharistic celebration.⁴⁸

Early Christian preaching was naturally based on the Septuagint, though it is sometimes overlooked as an important feature in the formation of Christian piety.⁴⁹ The Septuagint's role in the life of the church is also shown by the discovery of Christian amulets, charms meant to bring luck or protection, which bear prayers or other snippets from the Septuagint, and inscriptions of Septuagint verses on tombs and buildings.

From formal liturgical and homiletical expression to the use of charms and inscriptions, the evidence unambiguously tells that the Septuagint infiltrated numerous aspects of early Christian theology and piety. The scholars we will meet in the next chapter who discuss the relationship of the Septuagint to the Hebrew Bible are only a minority; most Christians would have heard the Septuagint taught and would have been shaped by it without knowing anything about its relationship to the Hebrew.

An Indispensable Role

The Septuagint stands at the heart of the early church. Except for a small number of Christians in the Syriac Church, every Christian who heard or read the Bible in the first few centuries of the Christian era would have heard the text of the Septuagint or of its translation in the Old Latin version in the languages of the East. Only a few early apologists and fathers were aware that their Bible was different from the Hebrew Bible of the synagogue, and fewer cared, even though most of them could not read Hebrew for themselves. Their interactions with Jews taught them quickly that their Septuagint had diverged significantly at points, so they went to great lengths to explain the difficulties. They argued that some of the discrepancies were errors introduced by Jews, and some were stumbling blocks placed by the Holy Spirit to drive the reader to a deeper meaning. However, for most Christians and even most of the fathers the Septuagint was simply taken for granted. It was the Christian Old Testament. Nevertheless, it did not for long remain so for all of Christendom, and in what follows we shall begin to see why.

12

The Man of Steel and the Man Who Worshipped the Sun

And many other cultured persons, since Origen's fame was noised abroad everywhere, came to him to make trial of the man's sufficiency in the sacred books. And numbers of the heretics, and not a few of the most distinguished philosophers, gave earnest heed to him, and, one might almost say, were instructed by him in secular philosophy as well as in divine things. For he used to introduce also to the study of philosophy as many as he saw were naturally gifted, imparting geometry and arithmetic and the other preliminary subjects, and then leading them on to the systems which are found among philosophers ... so that the man was proclaimed as a great philosopher even among the Greeks themselves.

EUSEBIUS, *Ecclesiastical History* 6.18

BETWEEN THE THIRD and second centuries BCE, Alexandria was home to many of the translations of the Hebrew writings that became the Septuagint, and between the second and third centuries CE it was home to Origen, nicknamed by Eusebius "Adamantius," the man of steel. Origen had become a superhero to his admirer.[1] He was arguably the most important scholar of the early church, but he unarguably had the greatest impact on the future of the Septuagint. Origen was born c. 185 in the home of devout Christian parents and his father Leonides was apparently martyred in 202 in the early stages of the Severian persecutions. He was given a Christian and a classical education that became two wells from which he drew throughout his life. At only 18 years of age (c. 203) Origen was appointed director of the Catechetical School in Alexandria where Clement had taught at the end of the second century.[2]

The years between 211 and 216 proved to be crucial in Origen's life. He met a man called Ambrose, whom he helped convert to Christianity from the Valentinian variety of Gnosticism. Origen's evangelism paid off, literally. For the rest of his career, he could dip into Ambrose's pockets, which were all too eagerly opened in a show of gratitude. Ambrose is not a little responsible for Origen's abundant output: this patron provided materials, scribes, and copyists to produce and to circulate Origen's voluminous writings.[3] Origen visited dioceses in Rome and Petra (modern Jordan), but his most important stopover was Caesarea. In 216, upon the urging of the bishops of Jerusalem and Caesarea Origen preached in the churches of Palestine; back home in Alexandria his bishop Demetrius was incensed that Origen preached without having been properly ordained. The friction between these two men began in earnest. Origen returned to Alexandria and with Ambrose's help he probably spent the next decade of his life writing.[4] He became increasingly interested in exegesis and although he could fake it, his knowledge of Hebrew probably never went beyond a traveler's grasp of a foreign language.[5] We will see presently that his textual scholarship inadvertently hastened the end of the Septuagint's prominence in the church.[6]

Another inauspicious trip to Caesarea en route to Greece in 230 would turn Origen's relationship with his bishop from bad to irretrievably damaged; in Palestine, where his preaching without ordination had caused the ire of his bishop a decade and a half earlier, he was formally ordained. Demetrius burned again with white-hot fury at Origen's insubordination, but this time because Origen sought ordination outside of his diocese. Damned if he does, damned if he doesn't.

Demetrius's rage left the scholar no other choice but to leave Alexandria and make his permanent home in Caesarea c. 232. In this last phase of his life, Origen's success as a preacher grew, as did his pastoral concerns. In contrast to his previous tenure at the Catechetical School in the philosophically rich context of Alexandria, he found himself in contact less with students than with common Christians.[7] He would live out the final two decades of his life producing a substantial exegetical literature, but following another imperial persecution unleashed by Decius, Origen succumbed to injuries and died in Tyre c. 254.[8]

Origen's works of philosophy, theology, homiletics, and exegesis have left the world in his debt. He was the first Christian to write a substantial collection of biblical commentaries, and while having roots back in the Hellenistic period the commentarial tradition in modern Christian exegesis owes almost everything to his labors. It was not an overstatement

when one of Origen's modern biographers suggested he may have been
the most prolific author in antiquity.[9] Only part of his body of work has
survived, and much of what has is only fragmentary or preserved in Latin
translations and quotations, mostly by Ambrose, Jerome, and, more unre-
liably, Rufinus. We can only imagine how much might have been lost, but
a recent find has given us hope that more of Origen's work remains to be
chanced upon: in 2012 a cataloger in the Bavarian State Library in Munich,
Germany discovered a collection of Origen's homilies on the Psalms.[10]

Origen's main concern as an exegete, theologian, and preacher was with
the interpretation of scripture. He carried out his biblical scholarship in
the service of the church.[11] In Alexandria Origen was immersed in a culture
at the center of a universe of hermeneutical methodologies. In addition to
receiving a Hellenistic education as a child, Origen was exposed to Eastern
wisdom literatures, including Iranian and Indian varieties, pagan myths,
rabbinic exegeses, and Platonic philosophy. He learned allegorical exegesis from the Greek readings of Homer and Hesiod, from Jewish methods
of interpretation championed by luminaries like Philo, and from the New
Testament writers who often spiritualized the Old, the book of Hebrews a
prime example.[12] A young educated man who inhaled the Alexandrian air
was as likely to draw in this assortment of philosophical hermeneutics as
the briny air blowing in from the Mediterranean. Caesarea was different
only to a degree, and he had already been shaped by his four and a half
decades in Alexandria before he took up residence in his new city. In that
home for the last stage of his life he found in Caesarea a regional metropo-
lis of varying influences. He made friends with Jewish teachers and began
to employ their exegetical practices.[13] Even the most determined scholar
could not have avoided the powerful force of these influences, which is
not to suggest that Origen treated the scriptures irresponsibly. On the
contrary, like any person ancient or modern Origen was profoundly influenced by the prevailing methods of interpretation that surrounded him.
Because the scriptures were so difficult to understand—Origen would
have snickered at the Reformation doctrine of the perspicuity, or clarity,
of scripture—Origen was no different from other Jewish and Christian
exegetes when he examined the text from different angles. As one modern
scholar commented, "Notable biblical exegetes on both sides cast their
nets wide in the search for useful exegetical material."[14]

During his time in Caesarea Origen became a prolific preacher, and
his homilies are characterized by the spiritual exegesis and allegorical interpretation of the Old Testament for which he stands as a prime

representative of the Alexandrian method.[15] Of utmost importance for Origen was the way the words of the scriptures opened up the Divine mysteries. This approach to interpretation, humble in its expectations of what the interpreter could achieve, became a signature of Origen's career. Others noted his antipathy to dogmatism, and he often suggested several lines of interpretation that were possible for any given passage while insisting that many of his solutions remained hypothetical. He was firm only on what was taught by the church and on everything else he refused to assert a single interpretation. Origen opened himself to correction by inviting his hearers to provide better answers than his and confessed his readiness to accept their opinions if they were convincing.[16]

A watershed in the history of the Septuagint, and thus in the history of the Christian Bible, came in the mid to late 230s. Origen began to compile what became known as the Hexapla, a "six-columned" Bible in which he placed six different biblical texts in parallel columns.[17] From left to right Origen inserted the Hebrew text (which by the third century was essentially the Hebrew Bible we now have), the Hebrew transliterated in Greek characters, the versions of Aquila, Symmachus, the Septuagint, and finally Theodotion. In the fifth column Origen used signs, mostly the asterisk and the obelus, which he must have learned from the Alexandrian classical tradition. He employed these textual notations to indicate where the Septuagint diverged from the Hebrew Bible of the synagogue.[18] Since the versions of Aquila, Symmachus, and Theodotion had harmonized the Septuagint with the emerging standard Hebrew text, Origen took readings from their columns and inserted them at points where the church's Septuagint lacked the same words or sentences and marked them off by an asterisk. Where the church's Septuagint had additional material not found in the Hebrew Bible of the synagogue—and therefore not found in the versions of Aquila, Symmachus, and Theodotion—Origen mostly did not delete but added a different sign, an obelus, to indicate where the church's Bible was expansive. Origen explained the rationale for his project in several different ways, and modern scholars have often tried to distill a singular purpose for Origen's endeavor. However, considering how often Origen contradicts himself throughout his writings, isolating one of his statements on the Hexapla would surely not exhaust Origen's motives.[19]

Origen writes in his *Letter to Africanus* (5–9) that he conducted his scholarly textual work so that he could be prepared in debates with Jews. When discussing texts he could compare the different versions to be sure that he was not building his argument on a text Jews would not accept.

On the other hand, Origen claims in his *Commentary on Matthew* (15.14) that he compiled the Hexapla as a textual project, to "heal" the Septuagint, which has usually been understood to mean he wanted to "correct" the Septuagint according to the Hebrew. But he did not know what we now know and what we have learned in Chapters 3 and 7: that the Hebrew Bible itself had undergone significant change from the initial translation of the Septuagint up to Origen's time. Origen's ambition to make the Septuagint conform to the Hebrew Bible was a problematic ambition from the outset. Still, Origen apparently had another reason to produce the Hexapla: to offer exegetes a larger Bible from which to develop interpretations of the same text. We see from Origen's later work that this may have been his chief interest, no matter what he says elsewhere.[20]

After the completion of the Hexapla, Origen continued to comment on the Septuagint, and he was well aware of the discrepancies between the church's Bible and the Hebrew Bible of the synagogue. Nonetheless, he allowed both to speak in an approach one scholar has helpfully called "exegetical maximalism," a method driven by the multiple senses of interpretation that resulted in an expansion of the size of the Bible in order to increase the exegetical possibilities.[21] Origen used the other Greek versions of Aquila, Symmachus, and Theodotion in addition to the Septuagint text so that he might work forward to a sense rather than backward toward some "original text."[22] They illuminated the meaning of the Septuagint and were not meant to undercut the church's Bible. They were "complementary rather than rival alternatives."[23] Sometimes Origen was content with multiple interpretations of one passage, while in other places he used several different interpretations from the versions in the pursuit of a single meaning.[24] Even though Jerome would use Origen's work as a springboard for his own ambitious project, he recognized the exegetical use of the Hexapla in Origen's commentaries: when he translated Origen's sermons on the Song of Songs, Jerome stated in the preface that Origen used all of the different texts to offer clear and excellent arguments.[25]

Remarkably, Origen never used the *Letter of Aristeas* legend to bolster his claim of the Septuagint's authority as his contemporaries and predecessors had. He nonetheless believed that Providence guided the translators to produce exactly what God wanted the church to have. When the Hebrew Bible and the Septuagint were at odds with one another, there were two possible explanations: copyists introduced genuine errors in the transmission of the manuscripts, or Providence introduced the divergences for the church's edification. Indeed, the "errors" could have been laid as bricks, to provide stepping-stones to reach a higher level of understanding. For instance, in his *Homilies on Jeremiah* Origen comments on variant readings that he believes were caused by scribal errors, but they are nonetheless important because they lead to meaningful exegesis.[26] This approach to scripture characterized much of early Christian interpretation in Alexandria and was another way the church's Bible was superior to the Hebrew Bible: it was richer, more pregnant with interpretive possibilities, such that even scribal errors were Spirit-produced readings for the benefit of the church. He is explicit in his *Commentary on Romans* when he notes a divergence between the Septuagint and the Hebrew Bible: he sides with the Septuagint since, he argues, the apostles recorded the reading and thereby gave their own authority to the Septuagint over the Hebrew.[27] He is not claiming that the Hebrew reading is "wrong" but that one can also follow the Septuagint.

Origen's aim was never to dislodge the Septuagint from the lecterns of the churches in favor of the Hebrew Bible. He continued, even after the Hexapla, to interpret the Septuagint and looked for ways to understand positively the divergences with the Hebrew text.[28] The appeal to other versions—Aquila, Symmachus, and Theodotion—was an appeal to the manifold ways God's word might be understood. This is why, even after finding another reading that explained more clearly what the Septuagint had left obscure, Origen claims to have "kept to the Septuagint in all respects," because he believed that "the Holy Spirit wished the forms of the mysteries to be hidden in the divine scriptures, and not to be dealt with clearly and openly."[29]

Origen's Hexapla was the beginning of the end of the Septuagint in the church, but only by accident: his attention to the Hebrew text led some later scholars to ponder whether or not the church had been missing out by ignoring it. If Origen included the Hebrew Bible in the first column of his Hexapla, didn't that imply it was worth studying? The fifth column, in which he had created a hybrid text composed of the church's Septuagint with additional readings from other Greek Jewish versions, may have begun as a scholarly tool for exegesis, apologetics, and textual analysis. But the new fifth column text was soon copied with the signs removed and was dispersed widely. It moved out from a scholarly and professional realm, where caveats could have helped to prevent its misuse, and into the church. Unintentionally, Origen's work contaminated the stream of biblical trans-mission: from the fourth century almost all Septuagint manuscripts had been influenced by the so-called Origenic, or Hexaplaric, version.

Eusebius

In the preface to his Latin translation of Chronicles completed in the final years of the fourth century, Jerome describes the *trifaria varietas*, the "threefold variety" of the Septuagint. He knew that three different versions of the Septuagint were followed in three different regions. A text attributed to Hesychius was in Egypt; a so-called Lucianic form was in the region from Constantinople to Antioch; and the Septuagint text produced from Origen's Hexapla, which Eusebius and Pamphilus assiduously copied, was in Palestine. The Hexaplaric Septuagint, named after the altered text from the fifth column of Origen's Hexapla, was evidently influential in the early church. It was supported by Eusebius and his teacher Pamphilus and spawned the translations into several other languages of the Christian East.[30]

Pamphilus was the elder of the two men responsible for copying Origen's Septuagint text, but Eusebius became the more famous of the two. More of Eusebius' writings survive than from any other author of his time, "Greek or Latin, Christian or pagan."[31] He was the first Christian writer to publish a history of the church in imitation of other grand historical narratives known in secular and Jewish literature, like Josephus' *Antiquities of the Jews*, and the *Ecclesiastical History* provides most of our information on Origen's life.[32] Eusebius' *Chronicle*, a series of chronological tables charting the history of the world, may have been inspired by the Hexapla's columnar format.[33] Pamphilus had founded a library in Caesarea that stood for several centuries and possessed an enviable stock of biblical manuscripts, lexica, dictionaries, and other etymological works, which may have begun with Origen's personal collection. The library quickly became a center of biblical and theological studies.[34] Isidore of Seville (d. 636) claimed the library had thirty thousand volumes, which was surely an exaggeration but is nonetheless an indication of its substantial holdings. Eusebius worked with Pamphilus in the library and later enlarged its collections, but their most important contribution was the revision and correction of biblical manuscripts.[35] Between 307 and 310 the two scholars prepared their *Apology for Origen*, held by a modern historian to be the single most important work in history for advancing and preserving Origen's ideas.[36] The *Apology* is a defense of Origen's theology, an attempt to forestall what was on the horizon: Origen was condemned as a heretic at the Second Council of Constantinople of 553 for his views on salvation and the Trinity, among others.[37] The *Apology* took up six volumes, the first five written by the two men while Pamphilus was in prison and the last added by Eusebius after Pamphilus' martyrdom.[38] This labor of love also found an outlet in the dissemination of Origen's commentaries. Noting Pamphilus' appreciation for Origen, Photius explains that "many of Origen's commentaries on the divine scriptures he copied with his own hand." While perhaps lost on modern readers, most scholars of Pamphilus' standing would not have lowered themselves to copy with their own hand but would have hired copyists.[39] It was a sign of genuine affection and commitment.

Eusebius and Pamphilus edited the Septuagint text between 307 and 309 CE. That they copied the fifth column of the Hexapla at all is curious. Considering their admiration for Origen and the tedious nature of copying so long a work, we might wonder if their intention was to transmit that Hexaplaric text as the preferred form of the Septuagint for the church.[40] If not, why bother? Could Eusebius have been demonstrating here his belief in the authority of the Hebrew? This seems unlikely since four years after the completion of the editorial work on the Septuagint text Eusebius wrote the *Preparation of the Gospel* (c. 313) and argued that God prompted Ptolemy Philadelphus to order the translation so that the prophecies of Christ could more easily be preached to Gentiles in the Greek-speaking Mediterranean world. If the scriptures were left to the Jews, in the Hebrew language, they would withhold them out of jealousy. By divinely orchestrating the translation of the Septuagint, God had prepared the way for the Gentiles to hear the prophecies concerning Christ.[41] Rather than taking Origen's Hexapla as a prompt to elevate the importance of the Hebrew Bible, Eusebius appears to have worked on the Hexaplaric Septuagint simply because of his esteem for Origen and his belief that his favorite scholar had produced a great work. His reasons for using the Hexaplaric Septuagint had nothing to do with a concern for the Hebrew Bible at all. We do not know how many copies of this revised Septuagint the Caesarean editors originally planned, but we know that it was copied and later used throughout Palestine. How it achieved such rapid distribution brings us to one of the most important events in the history of Christianity.

Constantine

Only six years after Origen's death in c. 254 the Roman Empire split into three regions—the Gallic, the Palmyrene, and the Roman. Eusebius was born (c. 260) in the Palmyrene region in its early years and would have known the turmoil of the so-called Crisis of the Third Century into his adulthood. Military, economic, and public health challenges nearly brought the empire to its knees, but Diocletian's institution of the Tetrarchy in 293 saved it from the brink of disaster. The system of tetrarchs ("four rulers") was formed on the idea that there would be two Augusti (emperors) and two Caesars waiting in the wings to succeed them. In the first arrangement, Diocletian became emperor of the East and Maximian of the West. Diocletian's Caesar was Galerius, and Maximian's, Constantius. The tetrarchs ("four rulers") established themselves in cities further from Rome to protect the borders, but a dizzying series of events occurred between 305 and 311 to throw the whole project into further chaos: in 305 Diocletian and Maximian both abdicated; on July 25, 306, Constantius died and his son Constantine was declared Augustus in York, England; Maxentius the son of Maximian took Rome in 310, at which time his father committed suicide; and Galerius died in 311. As Constantine recognized, the tetrarchy itself was now just as close to the end as the Roman Empire had been just years before, and it was in his mind from the start to consolidate power. In 312, Constantine's victory over his Western rival Maxentius would prove to be one of the most important events in world and in Christian history.[42]

On October 28, 312, Constantine and Maxentius fought the Battle of the Milvian Bridge, overlooking the Tiber. After the battle Maxentius entered Rome, but not as the victor: he was a soulless head on the conqueror's pike. His soldiers had not fared much better, and many of them drowned in the chilly water. The earliest account of the battle in a Latin panegyric written in 313 contains no mention of divine involvement, but in the pamphlet of Lactantius written in 314 Constantine is said to have had a dream in which he was ordered to inscribe a sign on his soldiers' shields containing a *chi-ro*, the first two letters of the name of Christ.[43] In the *Ecclesiastical History*, written in a series of editions up to 325, Eusebius attributes the victory to God but without Constantine having a vision.[44] Later, in the *Life of Constantine* written about 337, Eusebius has yielded to the myth and tells an even further embellished story to that found in Lactantius. In this latest account, Constantine is promised victory when he sees a cross in the sky several weeks before the battle: "he saw with his own eyes in the heavens a trophy of the cross arising from the light of the sun, carrying the message, *In hoc signo vinces*, or: 'In this sign, you will conquer.'"[45] There were now only two *augusti* left of the tetrarchy. Constantine and Licinius met and signed the so-called Edict of Milan in 313, guaranteeing religious toleration throughout the empire, but eleven years later Constantine finally became sole emperor after defeating his equal at Chrysopolis. The folklore of Constantine's Milvian Bridge showdown notwithstanding, there can be no doubt that his attitude to Christianity changed dramatically after the victory in 312.

Although Constantine was anything but a model disciple of Jesus' teachings, his mark on Christian history was astounding. Selfish ambition cannot alone explain Constantine's privileging of the church, especially since in the early fourth century Christians were still a tiny minority. His conversion must have been somewhat genuine, even if he only meant to add the Christian God to a collection that included Apollo and Sol Invictus.[46] The most important event, however, was when he presided personally over the First Ecumenical Council of the church at Nicaea in 325. Although not the only issue discussed at the Council, the most important (at least it became so in later tradition) was for the bishops to define the nature of the Son to the Father, in light of a challenge from Arius, the Alexandrian bishop who had taught that the Son was subordinate to the Father. The emperor's presence in a room full of bishops and his deference to the clergy on theological matters would give Christians a confidence they had never known in all the preceding years of imperial persecution and social marginalization. Some have suggested the emperor was not significantly involved in the Council, leaving everything in the hands of the bishops, while others have imagined that it was the emperor himself who supplied that all-important word, *homoousios* ("of one substance"), to describe the relationship between the Son and the Father. The most likely scenario is that the emperor only enforced the creed, after the Spaniard Ossius had presented and Alexander had defended it. The emperor, nonetheless, by virtue of his presence at the Council, once again entered the stage at a pivotal moment and was part of the proceedings that have since shaped the Christian story.[47]

Eusebius became Constantine's panegyrist—biographer is not quite accurate as Eusebius's account of Constantine's life is so tainted by his bias that it makes it impossible to take everything, or anything, in his *Life of Constantine* at face value.[48] As a Christian scholar with the ear of the emperor, he was called on to produce Bibles for distribution throughout the empire. Eusebius recounts that Constantine ordered fifty copies of the "Divine scriptures," presumably to go in the churches Constantine had begun building across the empire.[49] Constantine asked for Bibles to be made with "ornamental leather bindings, legible and convenient for portable use, to be copied by skilled calligraphists well trained in the art, copies that is of the Divine Scriptures, the provision and use of which you know very well is necessary for reading the word in the Church."[50] Constantine pressured Eusebius to act "with utmost speed" and supplied him with the materials needed for the production and with the transportation to deliver the finished product for the emperor's inspection.[51] It seems likely that Eusebius and Pamphilus had already copied the text of Origen's fifth column and preserved the Hexaplaric notes in the text before the order from the emperor came, though whether for personal gratification or some other reason we cannot be sure. It was probably from the circulation of these texts, even if locally, that the fame of Eusebius' erudition spread to the imperial court.

Origen's Septuagint text produced in the fifth column of his Hexapla didn't seep into the stream of textual transmission. It exploded onto the map and changed the course of the Septuagint's history thereafter. The devotion of Eusebius and Pamphilus to their theological hero, and the subsequent burst of scribal activity to meet the emperor's order of Bibles expedited its course from an academic text to one read and used widely in the church, now transmitted without the critical signs that the original editor had placed into it.[52] A new spirit was unleashed, and if scholars had not noticed before the divergent nature of the Septuagint and the Hebrew Bible they would soon find it impossible to ignore. The final days of the Septuagint in the West had begun.

The Man with the Burning Hand versus the Man with the Honeyed Sword

> We therefore must pass over the little streams of opinion
> and rush back to the very source from which the Gospel
> writers drew...the Hebrew words themselves must be
> presented and the opinion of all the commentators must
> be weighed, so that the reader, after considering all of these,
> may more readily discover for himself the proper way of
> thinking about the issue in question.
>
> JEROME, *Letter* 50.2

> We are right in believing that the translators of the
> Septuagint had received the spirit of prophecy; and so
> if, with its authority, they altered anything and used
> expressions in their translation different from those of the
> original, we should not doubt that these expressions also
> were divinely inspired.
>
> AUGUSTINE, *City of God* 15.23

ANTIOCHIAN REJECTION OF the excesses of the Alexandrian allegorical method distinguished these two centers of early Christian exegesis.[1]
Gradually, other changes to their exegetical system emerged: later writers like Theodore of Mopsuestia (d. 428) began to view the Septuagint as
merely a translation of the Hebrew and the Antiochians rejected Jewish
aggadic interpretation used by their Jewish neighbors. Two of the latest
of the Antiochian exegetes, John Chrysostom (d. 407) and Theodoret of
Cyrrhus (d. c. 457), created a middle way between Alexandria and Antioch,
their interpretation of messianic references in the Old Testament being
but one example.[2]

We have already noticed how Origen, the chief representative of the Alexandrian allegorical method, followed in the footsteps of the Jewish exegete Philo, who himself was also very much a part of a larger, complex web of allegorical interpretation in Alexandria. Multiple traditions— some Greek, some Persian, some Indic, and more—fused together in the Alexandrian melting pot. In similar fashion, the Antiochian school was also created not out of a vacuum but from previous models in pagan gram- matical and rhetorical traditions.[3] Opposition to the allegorical approach was not unique to the Antiochian fathers; they simply applied it to bib- lical interpretation. There were acceptable allegories, but, in contrast to what they perceived to be the Alexandrians' unrestrained application of the method, the allegories the Antiochians were ready to allow were those in which the biblical authors themselves used figurative expressions.

The Antiochians did not reject entirely the legacy of Origen, however, and they even drew from him, if only as a model of rigorous scholarship. One of the earliest Christian revisions to the Septuagint was produced in Antioch, and probably owing to their memory of Lucian's martyrdom the revision usually bears his name in the literature (the Lucianic recension). If Lucian had anything to do with it at all, he made light stylistic touches to the text after it had already been in use for some time. Scholars are now sure that the genesis of the Antiochian text goes back long before Lucian lived.[4] The Lucianic recension of the Septuagint is an invaluable witness to the development of the Christian Old Testament, even though it was far less transformative than the Hexaplaric text produced by Eusebius and Pamphilus. Because it was not as thoroughgoing as the fifth column text of Origen's Hexapla but was focused to a great deal on stylistic features, numerous passages remain unaffected by revisions to the Hebrew text; it therefore often preserves the oldest witness to the original Septuagint translation. By the fourth century, the Hexaplaric Septuagint had had such a tremendous impact on the transmission of Septuagint manuscripts that the Hexapla had indirectly affected almost every other Greek manuscript. The Antiochian Septuagint's contact with the Hexapla shows up also when it preserves traces of the three Jewish revisers Aquila, Symmachus, and Theodotion.[5]

One Antiochian in particular was a bridge connecting the past to the future of the Septuagint in the West. The modern Syrian town of Homs received global attention as the capital of the Syrian uprising that began in 2011, but in the fourth century it was the Greek city of Emesa and was on equal footing with the great cities of the Levant like Tyre, Sidon, Beirut, and Damascus. In the middle of the fourth century, another scholar with an immense storehouse of talents called Eusebius (c. 300–363) was appointed bishop of Emesa. He was a native of Edessa (modern Şanlıurfa, Turkey) but spent most of his time in Antioch, and at one point, probably in his twenties, he became a student of Eusebius of Caesarea during his tenure in the coastal city. He would doubtless have been familiar with the Hexapla kept in the library. Perhaps through these experiences, Eusebius of Emesa was driven to reject the Alexandrian method but also to embrace Origen's model of textual scholarship, of utilizing multiple versions of scripture.[6] The Hexapla's survival in Antioch—in the form of words, phrases, and whole verses taken from the Hexapla and inserted into the Antiochian Septuagint text—may owe itself at least partly to Eusebius of Emesa. Greek and Syriac fluency enabled him to bring to the exegetical task something most other fathers had not been able to do: he had a heightened awareness that the Septuagint was a translation, and as such it may have obscured or entirely miscommunicated the meaning of the original Hebrew. One may read an English translation of Tolstoy's *War and Peace*, but unless the reader knows both Russian and French a judgment about the English version's accuracy would be impossible. Eusebius may not have known Hebrew, but he was a native speaker of Syriac and therefore knew of another Bible altogether: the Peshitta ("simple"), the Syriac translation of the Hebrew Bible. Jewish converts to Christianity in Mesopotamia from about the second century CE, like the Jews of Alexandria a half millennium earlier, translated the Hebrew Bible, but chose the Hebrew as their basis instead of the Greek, for practical not ideological reasons. Syriac Jewish converts would have known the Hebrew Bible and would have chosen it by default.[7] Reading both the Peshitta and the Septuagint, Eusebius was able to recognize the limits (and the riches) of translation in ways that monolingual Greek fathers were unable to do. In his commentaries Eusebius compares different versions of the biblical text, but unlike Origen he shows some concern to establish the Hebrew reading as authoritative. The problems found in the Septuagint were not opportunities for allegorical creativity; instead, Eusebius draws his readers' attention to the divergences in the texts, and while in some cases he leaves the decision to the reader in others he makes clear that his desire is to elevate the authority of the Hebrew. Nonetheless, he stopped short of a full endorsement of the Hebrew Bible over the Septuagint, used the different versions, and cited the original Hebrew mostly to explain the problems found in the Septuagint.[8]

Eusebius never wavered from his commitment to the Septuagint as the starting point for Christian exegesis, and this is how he provides a link in our story in yet another way. The rigor of the biblical scholarship of Origen and Eusebius of Caesarea influenced him, but his rejection of Origen's allegorical method in turn later influenced one of the greatest Christian scholars of the Latin West, whose impression on the history of the Bible is felt even today. Several references to Eusebius in Jerome's writings indicate that Jerome at least knew of his work and would have been well aware of Eusebius' uniqueness in an ecclesiastical world dominated by the Septuagint. When he visited Antioch twenty years after Eusebius' burial, he found the bishop was still esteemed and missed.[9] However much or little Eusebius may have propelled Jerome to reconsider altogether the value of the Hebrew Bible, the latter radicalized the Antiochian approach far beyond what the Emesene had ever suggested.

Jerome

From 337 to 350, Constantius II was engaged in a brutal war with the Persians, and Eusebius of Emesa's reputation had attracted enough respect from the emperor that he joined the military campaigns in the late 340s.[10] Just a few years before the end of this war (c. 347), to the west of the blood-soaked Levant yet another Eusebius was born to wealthy Christian parents.[11] Eusebius Sophronius Hieronymus, better known by his Anglicized name Jerome, hailed from Stridon in the province of Dalmatia, a small town possibly close to the modern site of Ljubljana, Slovenia. His parents took a special interest in the education of their children, so Jerome and his brother had the privilege of private teachers who laid the foundations of their Christian and classical education. Jerome was sent to Rome in his preteen years so that he could study with the masters of grammar, literature, and rhetoric, like the famous scholar Aelius Donatus, one of the first advocates of punctuation in written texts. Jerome later reflected on his priveleged upbringing: "Almost from the cradle, my life has been spent in the company of grammarians, rhetoricians and philosophers"; "From my cradle, I have been nourished on Catholic milk."[12] Ready now for a career in civil service Jerome left Rome at about 20 years of age and headed for Trier, now near the German border of Luxembourg, where the Emperor Valentinian the Great had been waging wars against the Alemanni. In 367 Valentinian won the Battle of Solicinium, which would prove only to be a respite on the way to the eventual fall of the Roman Empire, and it was probably at this time that Jerome arrived in Trier. This stay would prove to be a turning point in Jerome's life. There he copied several of the writings of Hilary of Poitiers for his childhood friend Rufinus and read the most important work of monasticism in antiquity. Via Latin translations of Athanasius' *Life of Antony*, Western Christians learned of the Eastern monastic tradition. Jerome was so moved by the renunciation of the world and the commitment to the divine life exhibited by the first monk from the deserts of Egypt that he decided to give up his ambitions for civil service and devote himself entirely to God.

He spent the next decade traveling from place to place, entering into different Christian fellowships, and even gave the solitary life a try only to realize he was not cut out for monasticism. During the 370s Jerome added to his already impressive set of skills, and these new competencies would soon trigger in his mind a thought whose echo would reverberate throughout all of Christian history. During his short stint as a monk somewhere in the desert of Chalcis, Syria, Jerome tried his hand at Syriac, and more importantly he began studies of the Hebrew language with a Jewish convert to Christianity. In the last half of the decade he left behind the monastic life and in Antioch developed an impressive command of Greek. Most of the pieces were now in place for Jerome to become the most formidable biblical scholar the church had ever known: his sense of self-importance was now supplemented with linguistic competencies of which almost none of his contemporaries could boast.

Already before beginning his most pivotal contribution to Western history, Jerome's fusion of asceticism and rigorous scholarship was an innovation that has shaped monastic life down to the present day.[13] Since Jerome thousands of anonymous scholars have populated medieval monasteries throughout Western Europe, have preserved for the modern world numerous classical and biblical manuscripts, and have written other theological works of enduring value. Jerome studied Greek in Antioch, where the allegorical approach to the Old Testament was spurned, but there was an uncontrollable fire burning, a belief quickly spreading that the Hebrew Bible was superior to the Greek Septuagint. Jerome's later work shows he developed an appreciation for, and a dependence on, the work of Eusebius of Emesa, whom we have already learned was the first father to begin driving the wedge between the Septuagint and the church.

In 382 Jerome headed back to Rome. He had left more than a decade before as a graduate of Roman classical education; he returned with all that and more: he was now a master of biblical studies, possessed a profound knowledge of Greek and a decent grasp of Hebrew, and had the experience of Eastern monasticism. This rare combination of skills earned him the attention of the bishop of Rome, Pope Damasus, who made Jerome his secretary and advisor and then asked Jerome to translate Origen's homilies on the Song of Songs and to revise the existing Latin versions of Psalms and the Gospels.

Although as early as the second century the Old Testament was translated from the Septuagint into Latin in what we now call the Old Latin version, the style had not satisfied everyone. It was not that Bishop Damasus was aware of how the Old Latin Psalter diverged significantly from the Hebrew Psalter or that he would have cared. At this point, Jerome does not even show similar concerns. Rather, for a bishop in Rome, at the heart of the Roman classical education, the Old Latin translations of both the Psalter and the Gospels were inferior literary texts when compared with the Latin literature of the pagans. They were an embarrassment to Romans in a way that could not have bothered Latin Christians in North Africa. Nonetheless, Jerome's letters from this time demonstrate he was becoming more convinced of the need to study the Hebrew Bible. In Rome he began meeting with Jews and comparing the Hebrew Bible with the Septuagint and also with those Greek Jewish revisions produced by Aquila, Symmachus, and Theodotion. Seeds of doubt over the church's Bible were planted.

Jerome's experiences reading the Hebrew Bible with Jews and learning rabbinic exegetical traditions had a profound impact on his perspectives on the nature of scripture, and he knew he was one of only a handful of Latin Christians who could read the Hebrew. He now stood in a position to question the church's Bible without any more than a few objectors. The monk-turned-scholar became like a first-year student with a semester of Hebrew under his belt. He knew just enough to be dangerous. Not all were as impressed with Jerome's Hebrew scholarship as he was. In his own time, even his translation of the Gospels based on the Greek manuscripts suffered harsh judgment. The church was perfectly content with the Old Latin Gospels, and this new man on the scene seemed to have the motives of an elitist proposing to undermine the word of God. This argument will surface again in Jerome's debate with Augustine over the priority of the Septuagint.

Jerome was forced out of Rome in the late summer 385 after being found guilty on suspicions of sexual misconduct, which could have been trumped up by his opponents annoyed with his obsession to perpetuate his name.[14]

Yet while Jerome's sexual conduct remains a mystery, the idea that he was seeking to build his own legacy is no surprise to anyone who has so much as glanced at his writings. Even when writing on the topography of the Holy Land, Jerome boasts about his unrivaled knowledge of Palestine, and that put him in a unique position over those who could only read of the place.[15] The experience of banishment from Rome embittered him. Only two years after he fled Rome, he claimed that this city that celebrated its pagan culture had been pernicious to his mind.[16] In 386 Jerome moved to Bethlehem, formed a new monastic community, and began the most industrious period of his life. Not surprisingly, here in Bethlehem Jerome became more confident in his abilities with the Hebrew language and in his belief that the church had gone wrong by not following the Bible of the synagogue. It is not so difficult to imagine how Jerome's feelings on this matter will have developed. Christians had always been conscious of their apologetic interactions with the Jews and had sought to develop method-ologies that would place them on equal footing. Jerome's frustrations with the church's Bible had partly to do with apologetics, as he mentions in his preface to his translation of the Hebrew Psalms. He must have felt a little embarrassed that he was using a Bible with which his Jewish teachers and friends were unfamiliar. If the Septuagint were merely the same as the Hebrew, no one would ever have complained. These sentiments led Jerome in the 390s to attempt to overturn the four centuries tradition of the use of the Septuagint (and its Old Latin translation) in the church.

Being a confidant of the Pope had not spared Jerome the people's anger in Rome when they chased him out. Later in his life he would engage in a public humiliation of his childhood friend Rufinus over a doctrinal disagreement. One cannot help but wonder if he was always looking to score a point, and it would not be entirely unfounded to speculate whether Jerome had been driven to his revolutionary new translation of the Bible at least in part because he enjoyed having a corner on the world of knowledge that most of his Christian contemporaries could not claim. He was unpar-alleled as a biblical scholar in the Latin West, and his skill was dangerously combined with an outsized ego and an indefatigable ambition to be the architect of his own legacy. Just before he began his new translation from the Hebrew, Jerome had composed a number of works that showed off his Hebrew learning, in the form not only of exegetical treatises on Psalms and Ecclesiastes but also of books of more limited public appeal like his *Book of Hebrew Names* and his *Book of Hebrew Place Names*. Perhaps more widely read would have been his *Hebrew Questions on Genesis*, but all of these works were developing within Jerome a feeling that something was wrong in the church and in need of correction. In 391 Jerome began a new project to produce a Latin Bible based not on the Septuagint but on the Hebrew Bible. His project was motivated by a return to the *Hebraica veritas*, the "Hebrew truth," which for Jerome should be authoritative for the church. He began brazenly, acknowledging the likely fallout: "Therefore, with full knowledge and recognition (of the potential difficulties and potential criticisms), I send forth my hand into the flame."[17]

He had to expend energy later to justify his attempt to replace the church's Bible but also to explain how his own views had changed. In 383 he had censured Lucian and Hesychius, two of the producers of the *trifaria varietas*, for altering the Septuagint text, and as late as 387, a year into his new tenure in Bethlehem, he wrote affirming the authority of the Septuagint.[18] So his first step to rewriting the church's Bible was a revision of the Old Latin version of the Old Testament on the basis of the fifth column of Origen's Hexapla. Whether he was working directly from the Hexapla or from a copy of the fifth column ostensibly produced by Eusebius we cannot tell. In this revision, which has not come down to us in full and probably never covered the entire Old Testament, his intention was to bring the Old Latin into line with what he believed was a better Septuagint text. He knew that this Hexaplaric Septuagint was closer to the Hebrew Bible, and he also knew independently the versions of Aquila, Symmachus, and Theodotion.[19] Jerome's first project was only a partial measure: after his Hexaplaric revision he was more ready than ever to take that final step, and he claimed in the preface to his translation of Joshua that he was doing no different than what Origen had done before, so if everyone allowed Origen the freedom to monkey around with the Bible, why could he not pull off something as drastic?

Jerome appealed to Josephus to show that the *Letter of Aristeas* had mentioned the translation only of the Pentateuch, so applying the legend to the whole Bible was inappropriate. But he goes further: the legend is an outright lie. Jerome also undermined the authority of the Septuagint by denying its use in the New Testament.[20] We have seen just how wrong he was (Chapter 9). His attempt to connect the New Testament to the Hebrew Bible may also lie behind his claim to have seen a Semitic copy of the Gospel of Matthew, which scholars doubt ever existed, in the Library of Caesarea.

Jerome was now prepared to say that the Old Latin translations, based on the Septuagint, were full of contradictions and errors and that they could be remedied only by returning to the *Hebraica veritas*. He makes a distinction between the Septuagint translators and the original authors of scripture and charges the former as amateurs who could not get their act together to produce a consistent translation. Only the original authors of the Hebrew scriptures could be trusted because contradictions in the Septuagint and Old Latin Bibles rendered these translations untrue.[21] This is a surprising comment to anyone who has read the Hebrew Bible, even in an English translation; however, to Christians who could not read Hebrew, it was an argument that would have won Jerome favor as one who possessed the key to a mysterious treasure. The common believer could not see without his help. Included in this trust in the Hebrew Bible was a diminution of the books with which Christians had always had an ambiguous relationship, and Jerome called them "apocrypha." In a letter to parents of a young girl, Jerome urges that she avoid the apocrypha; if she must read them she should admire their stories but not treat them as truth.[22] Indeed, it may be said that Jerome invented the Apocrypha, in the sense of a catalog of books to be removed from their integration in the church's Old Testament and placed in their own section.[23] We have seen already that Athanasius made such distinctions in 367, but he was not producing a Bible that could show what this would look like. Christian ambivalence toward the apocryphal books heightens with Jerome, but even he continues to cite them. That he translates Tobit and Judith and the Additions to Esther and Daniel and includes them in his new Bible must reveal at least that, while he was prepared to take on the church's Bible in translation, he did not have the nerve to remove its books. Whenever some passages from apocryphal books could help him prove his point, he all too easily appealed to them.[24]

Jerome embarked on his final new translation in the early 390s calling it *iuxta Hebraeos* ("according to the Hebrew") to distinguish it from the Old Latin that had been rendered according to the Septuagint. He completed the translation by 405, but he did not make it easy for later interpreters to discern his motives. Jerome's ambiguousness on his motives for the move to the *Hebraica veritas* should also be seen in the political context of his day. The late fourth and early fifth centuries were tumultuous in the Roman Empire but also in relations between Jews and Christians. These years saw persecution in which Jews were often imagined to have participated with the Romans. The first Christian emperor ushered in an era of Christian triumphalism, and they now found themselves positioned above Jews. A brief interlude in which Julian sought to turn back the tide on Christian privilege was followed by a return to Christian imperialism, but in an empire that appeared ready to break apart at the seams rather than one that had the unified strength of the Constantinian age. Jerome may not have felt he could fully explain why a Christian was leaning so heavily on Jews and the Bible of the synagogue.[25]

Jerome knew enough Hebrew to translate the Old Testament, but he could not do without Aquila, Symmachus, and Theodotion. Even though these translations were in Greek, for Jerome they nevertheless represented the *Hebraica veritas* since they were faithful representations of the Hebrew Bible he knew. He also appealed to rabbinic exegetical traditions that he had learned in Bethlehem, and in some cases these dependencies led him astray and revealed just how weak his command of Hebrew really was. One of the most delightful examples of Jerome's use of the Jewish exegetical traditions is in Exodus 34:29, and even though it has provided many opportunities for readers to mock Jerome, it was not really his error. Michelangelo's sculpture in San Pietro in Vincoli is famous for its bizarre portrayal of Moses with horns; the explanation usually given is that the artist had read the Vulgate, and in this place Jerome had misunderstood his Hebrew text.[26] In the Hebrew Bible, Moses comes down from the mountain, and he "did not know that the skin of his face shone because he had been talking with God." In fact, Jerome didn't mistake the Hebrew at all but had picked up the exegetical tradition from his rabbinic sources or may have even translated none other than the Greek Jewish version of Aquila. The word is difficult, and modern interpreters continue to debate the meaning just as early readers did. The Hebrew root *qrn* can be read as a verb *qaran*, as the ancient versions and the Hebrew do here: his face was shining.[27] The Septuagint translator also does his best, and the New English Translation of the Septuagint (NETS) has translated: "the appearance of the skin of his face was charged with glory." Ancient Hebrew was written without vowels, however, so a reader could supply different ones from those that were intended. A number of Jewish exegetes either making the best sense of it they could or deliberately playing with the consonantal Hebrew text opted for the adjectival form *qeren* "horned" instead of the verb *qaran* "to shine." Moses was thus given horns in some Jewish exegetical traditions, which had also given him a halo to boot.[28] Aquila is in this same camp and renders the adjective into the Greek *keratōdēs* "horned," and Jerome translates that Greek word into Latin *cornutus*, so his Vulgate text reads of Moses: "he knew not that his face was horned from the conversation of the Lord" (Douay-Rheims).

In his translation, Jerome did not slavishly render the Hebrew as Aquila had done in Greek. His work is in many places an elegant Latin translation, and since Jerome sent most of his work to his friends in Rome, one gets the impression that he wanted to show off his acumen in the classics, with which he was far more comfortable than with Semitics. A recent study suggested some possible allusions to the Latin classics in his translation of the Hebrew Psalms, and even if these were accidental—that is, they were not intentional but were phrases recalled in Jerome's mind from his classical training—they still admit of a learned translator.[29] Because he had so radically confronted the church's Bible, many readers were disturbed by Jerome's new expressions, as many in the English-speaking world reacted to the rise in the twentieth century of new English translations to replace the King James Bible. The novelty of Jerome's language was unsettling to those who would have become comfortable with the language of the Old Latin. But it was not only a matter of style. His translation created a new Bible for the church. Outside of a small population of Christians who had been using the Syriac Peshitta based on the Hebrew Bible, it was the first time in Christian history that a Bible other than or not based on the Septuagint was promoted for use in the church. For four hundred years most Christians had heard and read from the Septuagint and its daughter translations.

At the end of the fourth century and the beginning of the fifth, after two ecumenical councils—Nicaea in 325 and Constantinople in 381—had been called to deal with challenges to the church's unity, the harmony of the universal church could not be taken for granted. The death of Theodosius I in 395 brought an end to the unified Roman Empire, and in the middle of Jerome's translation Valens became emperor of the East and Gratian of the West. Other than a brief interval under Emperor Julian (reigned 361–363) the church had been tied to imperial power since Constantine. Only the naïve or unaware would have been blind to an impending split in the church matching that of the imperial administration. In this nervous political climate, a contemporary of Jerome serving as a bishop in North Africa considered the new Latin translation a threat to the unity of an already fragile church.

The Great Debate: Jerome versus Augustine

Augustine is unique in his appeal not only in Roman Catholic tradition but also to the more recent development of Protestant Christianity. His shadow lurks behind both the Renaissance and the Reformation. From his autobiographical *Confessions* to his development of the notion of "original sin," which in turn encouraged the pessimistic Calvinist model of predestinarian theology, Augustine's theological impact on the West is incalculable. He was born in Thagaste (modern Souk Ahras, Algeria) in 354 and studied rhetoric in Carthage (modern Tunis, Tunisia). In 386, the same year Jerome had moved to Bethlehem, he underwent a dramatic conversion after reading the same book that sent Jerome into Christian ministry. The decadent sexual lifestyle he lived prior to his conversion profoundly shaped his radical theological views on sexuality, and they have ever since influenced Christian teaching on the subject.[30] In 395 he was made bishop of Hippo (modern Annaba, Algeria), and at the beginning of the fifth century Augustine established his place in the history of the Septuagint by entering into a debate with Jerome about the wisdom of introducing a new translation to the church.

Unmoved by Jerome's erudition, Augustine stood by the authority of the Septuagint as the Bible of the church. The Old Latin had transmitted the Septuagint, even though he complained about the variations in the Latin manuscripts, even worrying that one could have no confidence in texts whose variants were "intolerably numerous."[31] Nevertheless, for Augustine the Septuagint had been divinely gifted to the church and he, like earlier Christian writers, appealed twice to the legendary story of the translation for support.[32] Though Augustine knew no Hebrew and his Greek was at best mediocre, he was aware of the arguments over the differences between the Hebrew Bible and the Septuagint. These did not bother him since the Hebrew Bible belonged to the Jews and the Septuagint to the church. He appealed to the history of the Christian use of the Septuagint, beginning with the New Testament writers—in contrast to Jerome's contrived claim that the New Testament writers used the Hebrew Bible—and he noted that the churches in the East were still using the Septuagint; any change in the West might result in a schism. The disagreement between the two men was also tied to their respective philosophies of language. For Jerome the truth could be found in the Hebrew language itself; the sign was as important as the signified. This was an important feature of his philosophy of language, and in the rise of Christian Hebraism in the Renaissance and Reformation Christian scholars were attracted to theories that privileged the Hebrew language in itself, which became a crucial component in the eventual triumph of the Hebrew Bible over the Septuagint in the church.[33] On the other hand, Augustine's philosophy of language was Stoic, which meant that for him language was only a sign of what was real. God himself was the only Real; language merely pointed in God's direction, so differences between the Hebrew and Greek Bibles were no cause for concern.[34] Augustine would also argue that through obfuscations in the language, God intentionally prevents his creatures from becoming too conceited in their understanding of scripture.[35]

At the end of the fourth century, Augustine attempted to engage Jerome in a public debate through a series of letters. This type of correspondence was never meant to be private but was a way for thinkers to engage the public through the medium of apparently private communication. For a while, Jerome would hesitate to get involved in the debate, and when he finally did write he wondered if Augustine's invitation to engage was "a sword spread with honey."[36] Around 395 Augustine opened up the discussion on the Septuagint.[37] He began by praising Jerome's translations of Greek commentaries but then turned his attention to the translation of the Hebrew Bible. He writes that if Jerome should continue to translate the Hebrew he should "point out by appropriate signs the variations between your version and the Septuagint, which has such preponderant authority ...."[38] Augustine is surprised at Jerome's nerve. Could he possibly find something new in the Hebrew text that had not been found in the previous seven centuries since the original Septuagint translation? Was Jerome so confident in his Hebrew learning that he would be able to see something the original translators had missed? Who would be so arrogant not only to object to the skill of the original translators but also to suggest he could do better? If the Alexandrian translators were incapable of understanding an obscurity in the Hebrew, what gave this failed monk with a recently acquired knowledge of Hebrew the insight to break through the mystery?

As damning as Augustine's objections were, Jerome didn't see the letter for almost ten years. It would finally reach him as an attachment to another; however, in the meantime in 396 Augustine had written *On Christian Doctrine*, and in this treatise he took time to state his position more fully.[39] Augustine argued that among the available translations of the Bible, the "Itala," as he called the Old Latin, should be given preference. It was a translation from the Septuagint, which, he has already made clear, was the authoritative Bible of the church. If any corrections were to be made in the Latin tradition, they should be made according to the Septuagint, whose translators were men moved by the Holy Spirit and were guided along so that they produced what the Holy Spirit deemed "suitable for the nations." Other translations may be used but only as Origen had done: as aids to clarify the meaning of the text, not to replace it. By the time Jerome read Augustine's original letter, the latter had been mulling this for almost ten years, so he had come up with two more reasons that the Septuagint should be preferred in the churches. First, Augustine was concerned with the potential split of the church into Latin (West) and Greek (East) halves, which he saw as inevitable should the Latin church adopt a new Bible. Second, no Christian could object to Jerome's work. When using the Old Latin, it was possible to compare a reading to a Greek manuscript, because even though Augustine complained about his minimal knowledge of Greek, there were others around who could handle Greek reasonably well.[40] No Christian would be able to object to a translation from the Hebrew on linguistic grounds. Perhaps by Jerome's design, this would make him the gatekeeper of truth for the church. Augustine provided a now famous example. In Oea, a bishop read from Jerome's translation of Jonah, and because of the strange new rendering he almost lost his congregation. The Bible of the church had "gourd" in Jonah 4:6, but Jerome had changed it to "ivy." The congregation in attendance fumed upon hearing the new translation and accused it of being "Judaized." Jews were called in to explain the rendering, and they claimed that Jerome was wrong and the Septuagint was right all along. Whether this actually happened is irrelevant. Augustine has either reported a real event or has created a literary fiction, but either way he provides a window into the struggle of parting with the church's Bible in favor of Jerome's new translation.[41]

Jerome may have thought Augustine's objections unworthy of a response or may have been concerned for what the debate might do to his own reputation, so a whole year lapsed before he picked up a pen to answer his interlocutor. He blasts Augustine for not knowing that most manuscripts used in the churches already followed Origen's Hexaplaric text so already conformed to the Hebrew. But Jerome was entirely unfair on this point: he was in Palestine, where revisions to the Hebrew Bible were most likely in greater abundance than anywhere else; Augustine was in Hippo, far removed from the plethora of textual witnesses Jerome knew. Moreover, Jerome tersely responds that he shouldn't include the Hexaplaric signs to indicate where the text was different because he's translating directly from the Hebrew, not from Origen's Hexapla. Jerome also responds to Augustine's question over whether Jerome could discover something new in the Hebrew that had been missed by the original translators. He returns the favor: how could Augustine imagine that he could find something new in his commentary on the Psalms, when already at least a half dozen commentaries had been written, including one by the greatest commentator, Origen? Again, Jerome lets his impulsiveness get the best of him. Augustine wasn't denying Jerome the right to do further biblical scholarship; he was questioning whether Jerome's non-native, intermediate grasp of Hebrew was sufficient to improve what the highly regarded Alexandrian translators had produced and, even if it was, whether Jerome's new translation was the wisest course for the unity of the church. This is an altogether different criticism from the one Jerome throws back at him. Augustine was writing commentaries that built on earlier exegetes, whereas Jerome wanted to make a new Bible translation from a Semitic source. Jerome finally accuses those Jews who questioned his translation of Jonah as liars. Augustine is a nuisance to Jerome, a distraction from his essential work; it is possible some of Jerome's blatant resentment stemmed from his jealousy of Augustine's position as bishop of a historic church.[42]

Augustine may not have had the intellectual arguments for his preference for the Septuagint, but he fervently fought for the Greek Bible since, no matter his own inability to make a more compelling case, the Septuagint had for four hundred years been used in the church.[43] Unlike Jerome, Augustine was able to modify his own dogmatism and attempt to reach a more harmonious middle ground. In his final comment on the matter in *City of God*, written between 413 and 426, Augustine lauds Jerome's scholarly abilities and his gifts to the church and even announces that he has been convinced of the benefits of translating from the Hebrew Bible.[44] He nevertheless continued to insist that the Septuagint should never be corrected toward the Hebrew Bible, since the Septuagint is ultimately a new prophetic message for the church. Jerome would never be so charitable.

The conflict between Jerome and Augustine should also be read with attention to the places in which these two men worked. Augustine, the great champion of the Septuagint in the early church, was in North Africa far removed from the center of action in Jewish–Christian polemic over the nature of the Old Testament text. Jerome, on the other hand, was right in the middle of Jewish–Christian debate working in Bethlehem, intentionally engaging the rabbinic movement. There were certainly Jews in North Africa, but there is no evidence they were of the Palestinian rabbinic variety, and Jewish–Christian relations there were very different.

Tertullian wrote in the late second and early third century, and while he demonstrates knowledge of Jews and Judaism it is a superficial kind. Tertullian's "Jews" are sometimes those in the Bible and other times rhetorical figures, so it is difficult to determine when he has contemporaries in view.[45] Jews are no less opponents than pagans; neither embrace the gospel of Christ.[46] Cyprian, writing later, almost never discusses contemporary Jews, and in the one case that he does they are grouped with Gentiles and heretics as Christian opponents.[47] The archaeological record in North Africa also shows Jewish use of Latin alongside of Hebrew, but of the fourteen inscriptions dating to the second and third centuries that have been recovered only three have Hebrew.[48] It is even possible that some Jews used the Old Latin translation of the Septuagint, though this is at present a question awaiting further research. In such a context, which probably persisted into Augustine's time, there was no outside push on the Bishop of Hippo to move toward the Hebrew, while Jerome lived with the constant pressure of relating to Jews in dialogues over the biblical text. Origen too worked in Caesarea and Alexandria, both places with thriving Jewish–Christian interactions, and these pressures dictated their approach to and use of the Hebrew Bible. These are the recurring themes that will last throughout the ancient and medieval story of the church's relationship to the Old Testament.

In the following centuries in the Greek East, living in a Greek world allowed the Greek church to continue using its Greek Bible. The lack of cohesion in the West, however, along with the continued and intensifying tradition of Jewish–Christian debate, led Christians continually to assess their own Bible. Political and social upheaval also meant that the church would look to create stability within by shunning the variety of the biblical text known from the Old Latin versions and by turning to Jerome's new biblical text. Thus, they chose eventually, though not immediately, to elevate the status of Jerome's Vulgate, based on the Hebrew Bible, not because they shared his views of the "Hebrew truth" but because they wanted stability they could not find outside the church.[49]

14

A Postscript

...It is not clear which of these represents the truth... Yet both convey something important to those who read intelligently.

AUGUSTINE, On Christian Doctrine 2.17

Accordingly, when anyone claims, "Moses meant what I say," and another retorts, "No, rather what I find there," I think that I will be answering in a more religious spirit if I say, "Why not both, if both are true?" And if there is a third possibility, and a fourth, and if someone else sees an entirely different meaning in these words, why should we not think that he was aware of all of them?

AUGUSTINE, Confessions 12.31.42

AUGUSTINE WROTE THAT the lack of uniformity in the manuscripts could be helpful and that, even if multiple versions of the same biblical book exist, they could all be helpfully appropriated as Christian scripture: "This fact actually proves more of a help to interpretation than a hindrance, provided that readers are not too casual. Obscure passages are often clarified by the inspection of several manuscripts .... Each one confirms the other. One is explained by the other ...."[1] This was, however, not uniquely Augustinian, nor Western. The greatest poet of early Christianity, the Eastern Syriac theologian Ephrem, could write in the fourth century:

Who is capable of comprehending the extent of what is to be discovered in a single utterance of Yours?...Anyone who encounters Scripture should not suppose that the single one of its riches that he has found is the only one to exist; rather, he should realize that he himself is only capable of discovering that one out of the many riches which exist in it...A thirsty person rejoices because he has drunk: he is not grieved because he proved incapable of drinking the fountain dry![2]

Many modern Christians are fixated with the search for an "original text," but from the beginning it was not so. Early Christians were able to appreciate the diversity of divine communication, and even when some began to recognize the divergences between the Bible of the Jews and the Greek Christian Bible most welcomed the opportunity to learn more, showing no anxiety at the thought of not having the "original." This is a distinctively modern theological anxiety.

While the Septuagint began a long decline in the West after Jerome, it was marked by an unmatched vitality in the East, among both Jews and Christians. The reasons were often related to the political and social circumstances in both regions, but a new attitude in the Western Church would finally finish what Jerome started. Consideration of the intellectual and social context of the Reformation must take into account, among other things, the influence of medieval Christian Hebraism. Martin Luther did not just wake up one day, set out for the church with his list, his hammer, and his nail, and instigate a rush back to the Hebrew Bible as the source of truth for the Christian Old Testament. The processes had been set in place at least as early as Jerome, possibly even as early as Origen, and carried out more effectively by the Christian Hebraists of the Middle Ages.

With few exceptions, most approaches to the Septuagint between the Reformation and today have been concerned with its value as another witness to the Hebrew Bible. Even the great polyglot Bibles of the Renaissance were concerned not with the Septuagint as Christian scripture but with the humanistic enterprise of amassing knowledge of ancient sources. Rarely has the Septuagint been read on its own terms or appreciated as a witness to an *alternative* Hebrew text, to the diversity of scriptural texts before the Common Era. Even in those places where the Septuagint's translators are responsible for the divergences and there is no alternative Hebrew tradition, there might have been more interest in such a fascinatingly different Bible. As a result, the field of "Septuagint studies" is relatively small compared with the Hebrew Bible, the New Testament, and other subjects. And with fewer scholars holding posts at higher education institutions, fewer students are exposed to the Greek Bible. The situation is more perplexing in institutions of Christian learning, where the bias in favor of the Hebrew has meant that each year graduates leave school after having spent three or more years assuming that the Septuagint is an ancillary discipline, a secondary or tertiary subject that should be approached only after one has properly understood the more genuine Old Testament, the Hebrew Bible. Especially in conservative institutions students hope that by studying the Hebrew they will come closer to understanding the original words of God, which are those enshrined in the Hebrew Bible, even though, as we have seen, the Hebrew Bible very often contains late material added long after the translation of the Septuagint. At best, when biblical texts from the Dead Sea Scrolls and the Septuagint are brought into the discussion, their readings are mere "variants" of the authoritative, almost orthodox, Hebrew Bible.[3]

More recently, a few scholars have sounded as voices in the wilderness, calling for a reappropriation of the Septuagint as Christian scripture. Møgens Müller's *The First Bible of the Church: A Plea for the Septuagint* was probably overlooked since it was initially published by an academic press for a readership who may not have been interested in the modern theological implications of his argument. An article by Ross Wagner, "The Septuagint and the 'Search for the Christian Bible,'" has likewise gone unnoticed. A few attempts in French and German scholarship by both Protestant and Catholic scholars like Hartmut Gese, Hans Hübner, and Adrian Schenker have attempted to open up new vistas for Christian theological reflection, but again little traction has been made.[4]

All of this raises significant questions for Christian theologians, if not for historians. Brevard Childs wrote his *Biblical Theology of the Old and New Testaments* with the subtitle *Theological Reflection on the Christian Bible*, but based his study entirely on the Hebrew Bible, with only scant mention of the Septuagint. Anneli Aejmelaeus represents the opinions of a number of Septuagint scholars who believe that when viewed as a whole, the Hebrew Bible and the Septuagint share an almost identical theological outlook. Ross Wagner, in spite of his call for the church to read the Septuagint alongside the Hebrew Bible, agrees with Aejmelaeus' assessment on the whole. This is particularly interesting in light of Wagner's unparalleled study of Paul's use of the Septuagint of Isaiah, in which he demonstrated many unique theological opportunities provided by the Septuagint and exploited by Paul in the book of Romans. Others like Martin Rösel have charted a more optimistic course for how one might appreciate the theological contours of the Septuagint, affirming they are unquestionably different from those in the Hebrew Bible.[5] I have attempted in this book to make clear that while the Septuagint is often a straightforward translation of the Hebrew Bible we know it also contains many diverse theological trajectories. Regardless of whether the New Testament authors and the fathers thought it was a faithful translation of the Hebrew, we know now that the Septuagint translators often had different Hebrew texts, and when they did not they nevertheless introduced theological emphases that were not in the Hebrew Bible. Moreover, even though the Septuagint began as a diverse collection of translations of independent Hebrew scriptures, or at best of smaller collections of Hebrew books (like the Pentateuch), and therefore contains within itself maximal diversity, the church read it as unified holy scripture. They may not have had a full collection like we know today, but they knew that Deuteronomy was to be read as scripture in the same way Isaiah was to be read, no matter the circumstances of the original translations of these books. The canonical books of the Old Testament in the early church were Greek, not Hebrew. So if the Septuagint supported the theological expression of the New Testament writers and the theologians and exegetes who established early Christian thought, one may wonder why it has had no place in the modern church.

I would suggest that it is impossible to read the Septuagint alongside the Hebrew Bible and conclude that their theological outlooks are identical; even when the Hebrew source of the Septuagint translation is identical to the Hebrew Bible and the divergences can be attributed to the translator, his translation itself often contains theological developments in the areas of eschatology, messianism, the fulfillment of prophecy, enhancing the holiness of God (as the translator imagined was necessary), and many others.[6] One of the latter examples is in Exodus 15:3, when the militantly phrased "The Lord is a warrior, the Lord is his name" in the Hebrew text was changed to "The Lord, when he shatters wars, the Lord is his name." The translator obviously thought the Lord should not be seen as a warrior, but as one who puts an end to them.[7] In Psalm 9:21, the Lord brings fear to the nations: "Put them in fear, O Lord; let the nations know that they are only human." But in the Septuagint, he brings the law (9:21): "Set a lawgiver over them, O Lord; let nations know that they are human beings." Readings that soften the image of the punitive or warring God of the Hebrew Bible reflect either the concerns of the Greek translators or of the editors of divergent Hebrew texts underlying the Greek translation. Regardless of which explanation explains each deviation, one is hard pressed to claim the theological visions of the Septuagint and the Hebrew Bible are identical. On the other hand, neither can one claim that the theological vision of the Septuagint is entirely uniform. While passages in the Pentateuch and Psalms seem to downplay the militarism of the Lord, others speak of God in terms of omnipotence identical to the Hebrew Bible. We realize, then, that to speak of the theology of the Septuagint is fraught with the same problems one faces when speaking of the theology of the Hebrew Bible. Like we have seen in the diversity of the forms of the biblical text in antiquity, so also the theological trajectories of the biblical books are often different from one another and sometimes even within the same book. This lack of uniformity has led many Hebrew Bible scholars to abandon the search for biblical theology, an attitude that has affected a similar desertion of the search for a theology of the Septuagint. Nonetheless, for Christian theology Adrian Schenker insists that the divine word can reside in both the Hebrew Bible and the Septuagint. Schenker's view is very much like that of Augustine and most of the writers in the early Church. This perspective suggests that the scriptures used by the New Testament writers and early church fathers have been unjustifiably neglected in Christian theology.

What would modern Christian theology look like if its theologians returned the Septuagint to the place it occupied at the foundation of the church, or at least began to read it alongside the Hebrew Bible, as a witness to the story of the Bible and in acknowledgment of its role in shaping Christianity? The Septuagint has already affected some of Christian theology, but mostly only where the New Testament writers mediate its readings. We saw earlier that the Septuagint, almost exclusively, molds Paul's theology in Romans, and the same can be said for the author of Hebrews. There may be further ideas still, but because the Septuagint has not attracted significant attention from theologians its value for modern Christian thought is yet unknown.

A full-scale exploration awaits an energetic thinker, but for now it is interesting that even while interest in the theological interpretation of the Bible is increasing the Septuagint has not been given the part it deserves in the drama of the church's reception and use of scripture. For those who wish to pursue such questions as a "Search for the Christian Bible" entails, who wish to consider the theological implications of the Septuagint's role in the history of the church, I have tried to do the work of the historian, and perhaps now the door is open wide enough for the theologians to walk through it.

Notes

CHAPTER 2

1. F.C. Babbitt, trans., *Plutarch's Moralia*, vol. 4 (Loeb Classical Library, Cambridge, MA: Harvard University Press, 1936).

2. The account is translated in A.K. Grayson, *Assyrian and Babylonian Chronicles* (Locust Valley, NY: J.J. Augustin, 1975), number 5.

3. Cyrus Cylinder, lines 20–22a. The text of and introduction to the Cyrus Cylinder can be found in W.W. Hallo, *The Context of Scripture: Monumental Inscriptions from the Biblical World*, vol. 2 (Leiden: Brill, 2000), 314–316. See also A. Kuhrt, "The Cyrus Cylinder and Achaemenid Imperial Policy," *Journal for the Study of the Old Testament* 25 (1983): 83–97; Kuhrt, *The Persian Empire: A Corpus of Sources of the Achaemenid Period* (London: Routledge, 2007).

4. The best work on the Persian Empire is P. Briant, *From Cyrus to Alexander: A History of the Persian Empire* (Winona Lake, IN: Eisenbrauns, 2002); but see also J. Wiesehöfer, *Ancient Persia*, 4th ed. (London: I.B. Tauris, 1996).

5. See H.G.M. Williamson, "The Aramaic Documents in Ezra Revisited," *Journal of Theological Studies* 59.1 (2008): 41–62 for a positive assessment; for a negative view, see L.L. Grabbe, "The 'Persian Documents' in the Book of Ezra: Are They Authentic?" in O. Lipschits and M. Oeming (eds.), *Judah and the Judeans in the Persian Period* (Winona Lake, IN: Eisenbrauns, 2006), 531–570.

6. Assuming the biblical account of return, this would be the case especially since the exiles were mostly elites forcibly removed from a context in which they would have been leaders of their community. Upon return, they would have expected to regain their influence immediately without imagining they had been forgotten and life had moved on. See D. Smith-Christopher, *The Religion of the Landless: The Social Context of the Babylonian Exile* (Bloomington, IN: Meyer Stone, 1989); Smith-Christopher, *A Biblical Theology of Exile* (Minneapolis: Fortress Press, 2002).

7. D.M. Carr, *The Formation of the Hebrew Bible* (New York: Oxford University Press, 2011), 217–221. The Persian Imperial Authorization was first suggested by P. Frei, "Zentralgewalt und Lokalautonomie im Achämenidenreich," in P. Frei and K. Koch (eds.), *Reichsidee und Reichsorganisation im Perserreich* (Göttingen: Vandenhoeck & Ruprecht, 1984), 8–43. His English article summarized the state of the question in 2001; Frei, "Persian Imperial Authorization: A Summary," in J.W. Watts (ed.), *Persia and Torah: The Theory of Imperial Authorization of the Pentateuch* (Atlanta: Society of Biblical Literature, 2001), 1–40. The most recent monograph is now K.-J. Lee, *The Authority and Authorization of the Torah in the Persian Period* (Leuven: Peeters, 2011).

8. E. Bresciani, "The Persian Occupation of Egypt," *Cambridge History of Iran*, vol. 2 (Cambridge: Cambridge University Press, 1985), 507–509; J.D. Ray, "Egypt 525–405 B.C.," *Cambridge Ancient History*, vol. 4 (Cambridge: Cambridge University Press, 1988), 262–264; Lee, *Authority and Authorization of the Torah*, 31–211.

9. See, for example, C. Meier, *A Culture of Freedom: Ancient Greece and the Origins of Europe* (Oxford: Oxford University Press, 2011).

10. S. Schwartz, *Imperialism and Jewish Society: 200 BCE to 640 CE* (Princeton, NJ: Princeton University Press, 2001), 22–31.

11. A helpful way of discussing these various degrees of enculturation is found in J.M.G. Barclay, *Jews in the Mediterranean Diaspora* (Berkeley: University of California Press, 1996).

12. Schwartz, *Imperialism and Jewish Society*, 24–25.

13. R. Lane Fox, "Hellenistic Culture and Literature," in J. Boardman, J. Griffin, and O. Murray (eds.), *The Oxford History of Greece and the Hellenistic World* (Oxford: Oxford University Press, 2001), 391.

14. Deuteronomy 28:25: "And you shall be in dispersion in all the kingdoms of the earth." The term is more ancient than the Septuagint, but then it meant the infiltration of dominant Greeks into newly conquered territories.

15. J. Modrzejewski, *The Jews of Egypt: from Rameses II to Emperor Hadrian* (Philadelphia: Jewish Publication Society, 1995), 73, notes the lack of barriers preventing Jews from migrating to Egypt between 302 and 198. K. Mueller, *Settlements of the Ptolemies: City Foundations and New Settlement in the Hellenistic World* (Leuven: Peeters, 2006), 180, notes that, by the end of the third century BCE, "long-distance and large-scaled immigration had ceased," even though inner-Egyptian migratory patterns continued into the second.

16. On the Jewish presence in Egypt during Ptolemaic times, see Modrzejewski, *Jews of Egypt*; Barclay, *Jews in the Mediterranean Diaspora*, 19–47; T. Rajak, *Translation and Survival: The Greek Bible of the Ancient Jewish Diaspora* (Oxford: Oxford University Press, 2009), 64–91. On the synagogue, see L.I. Levine, *The Ancient Synagogue: The First Thousand Years*, 2d ed. (New Haven, CT: Yale University Press, 2005).

17. Though see J. Ma, "Relire les *Institutions des Séleucides* de Bikerman," in
    S. Benoist (ed.), *Rome, a City and Its Empire in Perspective: The Impact of the
    Roman World through Fergus Millar's Research* (Leiden: Brill, 2012), 59–84, who
    argues that the Jewish account is fictionalized and does not cohere with what is
    known about Seleucid policy.

CHAPTER 3

1. The quote is cited from Ulrich, *The Dead Sea Scrolls and the Origins of the Bible*
    (Grand Rapids, MI: Eerdmans, 1999), 17.
2. Of course the translation committees also refer occasionally to other versions,
    but these are mostly used to adopt readings where the Masoretic Text is deemed
    difficult or for some other reason inferior to the others.
3. The story of their discovery is told in G. Vermes, *The Story of the Scrolls: The
    Miraculous Discovery and True Significance of the Dead Sea Scrolls* (London:
    Penguin, 2010).
4. E. Tov's *Textual Criticism of the Hebrew Bible* has long been the standard text
    for this discussion, and it is now in its third edition (Minneapolis: Fortress
    Press, 2012). An overview is now in his "The Qumran Hebrew Texts and the
    Septuagint—an Overview," in S. Kreuzer et al. (eds.), *Die Septuaginta: Entstehung,
    Sprache, Geschichte* (Tübingen: Mohr Siebeck, 2012), 3–17.
5. W. Smelik, "The Languages of Roman Palestine," in C. Hezser (ed.), *The Oxford
    Handbook of Jewish Daily Life in Roman Palestine* (Oxford: Oxford University
    Press, 2010), 125.
6. It is not easy to compare Hebrew to English since the semantic value of Hebrew
    words is based in its root consonants and may thus restrain wildly divergent
    readings.
7. In addition to this layer of vowels, the Masoretes added other reading aids
    (e.g., accents) and cross-referencing notations.
8. See I. Yeiven, *Introduction to the Tiberian Masorah*, trans. E.J. Revell (Missoula,
    MT: Scholars Press, 1980); A. Sáenz Badillos, *A History of the Hebrew Language*,
    trans. J. Elwolde (Cambridge: Cambridge University Press, 1993), 76–111. The
    newest handbook by G. Khan, *A Short Introduction to the Tiberian Masoretic
    Bible and Its Reading Tradition* (Piscataway, NJ: Gorgias Press, 2012), is now the
    place to begin.
9. Tov, *Textual Criticism*, 11–12.
10. Tov repeats this often, but see ibid., ch. 2; Tov, "The Status of the Masoretic
    Text in Modern Text Editions of the Hebrew Bible: The Relevance of Canon,"
    in L.M. McDonald and J.A. Sanders (eds.), *The Canon Debate* (Peabody, MA:
    Hendrickson, 2002), 242–243; Tov, "The Dead Sea Scrolls and the Textual
    History of the Masoretic Text," in N. Dávid et al. (eds.), *The Hebrew Bible in Light
    of the Dead Sea Scrolls* (Göttingen: Vandenhoeck & Ruprecht, 2012), 41–53. Also,

see E. Ulrich, "The Fundamental Importance of the Biblical Qumran Scrolls," in Dávid et al., *Hebrew Bible in Light of the Dead Sea Scrolls*, 54–59.

11. See now M. Kartveit, *The Origin of the Samaritans* (Leiden: Brill, 2009), 290–295; Tov, *Textual Criticism*, 88, n. 139.

12. For example, see the categorization proposed by Tov, *Textual Criticism*, 107–110.

13. The statistics here are (cautiously) culled from ibid., 96–97.

14. Ibid., 108.

15. Typical is the "Introduction" in McDonald and Sanders, *Canon Debate*, 4.

16. I leave aside the complicated issue of authoritativeness, but it is discussed in E. Ulrich, "From Literature to Scripture: Reflections on the Growth of a Text's Authoritativeness," *Dead Sea Discoveries* 10.1 (2003): 3–25.

17. J.E. Sanderson, *An Exodus Scroll from Qumran: 4QpaleoExod^m and the Samaritan Tradition* (Atlanta: Society of Biblical Literature, 1986), 11–13, 310; A. Salvesen, "The Tabernacle Accounts in LXX Exodus and their Reception in Hellenistic Judaism," in T.M. Law, M. Liljeström, and K. De Troyer (eds.), *On the Trail: Studies in Honour of Anneli Aejmelaeus* (CBET; Leuven: Peeters, 2013).

18. These are the categories in M. Zahn, *Rethinking Rewritten Scripture: Composition and Exegesis in the 4QReworked Pentateuch Manuscripts* (Leiden: Brill, 2011).

19. Ibid., 58–62.

20. M. Segal, "Biblical Exegesis in 4Q158: Techniques and Genre," *Textus* 19 (1998): 45–62; Zahn, *Rethinking Rewritten Scripture*, 63–67.

21. Zahn, *Rethinking Rewritten Scripture*, 239–240.

22. Ulrich, *Dead Sea Scrolls and the Origins of the Bible*, 8.

23. On Isaiah 38:20–22, see the discussion in Tov, *Textual Criticism*, 310–311; but cf. J. Stromberg, "The Role of Redaction Criticism in the Evaluation of a Textual Variant: Another Look at 1QIsaa XXXII 14 (38:21–22)," *Dead Sea Discoveries* 16.2 (2009): 155–189.

24. See the discussion in Ulrich, *Dead Sea Scrolls and the Origins of the Bible*, 34–50.

25. See Tov, *Textual Criticism*, 286–294.

26. P.-M. Bogaert, "De Baruch à Jérémie: Les deux rédactions conservées du livre de Jérémie," in P.-M. Bogaert (ed.), *Le Livre de Jérémie: Le prophète et son milieu. Les oracles et leur transmission* (Leuven: Leuven University Press, 1981), 169, 172; W.L. Holladay, *Jeremiah 2: A Commentary on the Book of the Prophet Jeremiah, Chapters 26–52* (Minneapolis: Fortress Press, 1989), 313–314; A. Aejmelaeus, "Jeremiah at the Turning-Point of History: The Function of Jer. XXV 1–14 in the Book of Jeremiah," *Vetus Testamentum* 52 (2002): 459–482.

27. The Samuel Scrolls do not confirm the Septuagint in the way we saw in Jeremiah, by providing a Hebrew text that matches almost exactly the Greek. Rather, the verbal and redactional connections showed that we had variant texts. See now P. Hugo and A. Schenker (eds.), *The Archaeology of the Books of Samuel: The Entangling of the Textual and Literary History* (Leiden: Brill, 2010).

28. On the sectarians, and especially the debate on their connection to the Essenes, see M.D. Goodman, "The Qumran Sectarians and the Temple in Jerusalem," in C. Hempel (ed.), *The Dead Sea Scrolls: Texts and Context* (Leiden: Brill, 2010), 263–273.

29. See S. Talmon, *The World of Qumran from Within: Collected Studies* (Jerusalem: Magnes Press, 1989), 74.

30. Ulrich, "The Absence of 'Sectarian Variants' in the Jewish Scriptural Scrolls Found at Qumran" in E.D. Herbert and E. Tov (eds.), *The Bible as Book: The Hebrew Bible and the Judean Desert Discoveries* (London: British Library, 2002), esp. 191.

CHAPTER 4

1. The discussion of translation in the ancient world follows A. Wasserstein and D.J. Wasserstein, *The Legend of the Septuagint: From Classical Antiquity to Today* (Cambridge: Cambridge University Press, 2006), 1–4.

2. See J.N. Adams, M. Janse, and S. Swain (eds.), *Bilingualism in Ancient Society* (Oxford: Oxford University Press, 2002); also, now specifically on Egypt, A. Papaconstantinou (ed.), *The Multilingual Experience in Egypt, from the Ptolemies to the Abbasids* (Farnham, UK: Ashgate, 2010).

3. See W.W. Hallo, *Origins: The Ancient Near Eastern Background of Some Modern Western Institutions* (Leiden: Brill, 1996); Hallo, *The World's Oldest Literature: Studies in Sumerian Belles-Lettres* (Leiden: Brill, 2010); G. Deutscher, *Syntactic Change in Akkadian* (Oxford: Oxford University Press, 2007).

4. Herodotus, *Histories* 2.154 and 4.87; Thucydides 4.50.

5. M. von Albrecht, *A History of Roman Literature: From Livius Andronicus to Boethius: With Special Regard to Its Influence on World Literature*, 2 vols. (Leiden: Brill, 1997), 112–119; noted also in T. Rajak, *Translation and Survival: The Greek Bible of the Ancient Jewish Diaspora* (Oxford: Oxford University Press, 2009), 25. On Egypt specifically, see A. Papaconstantinou (ed.), *The Multilingual Experience in Egypt, from the Ptolemies to the Abbasids* (Farnham, UK: Ashgate, 2010).

6. See the questions raised in K. De Troyer, "When Did the Pentateuch Come into Existence? An Uncomfortable Perspective," in M. Karrer and W. Kraus (eds.), *Die Septuaginta: Texte, Kontexte, Lebenswelten* (Tübingen: Mohr Siebeck, 2008), 269–286.

7. Wasserstein and Wasserstein, *Legend of the Septuagint*, 16.

8. Thus the title of Rajak: *Translation and Survival*.

9. J. Dines, *The Septuagint* (London: Continuum), 42.

10. De Crom, "The *Letter of Aristeas* and the Authority of the Septuagint," *Journal for the Study of the Pseudepigrapha* 17.2 (2008): 144–147.

11. Honigman, "The Narrative Function of the King and the Library in the *Letter of Aristeas*," in T. Rajak et al. (eds.), *Jewish Perspectives on Hellenistic Rulers* (Berkeley: University of California Press, 2007), 131–132.

12. De Crom, "*Letter of Aristeas*," 148, likens Demetrius to Ezra, but here I follow A. Kovelman, *Between Alexandria and Jerusalem: The Dynamic of Jewish and Hellenistic Culture* (Leiden: Brill, 2005), 124.

13. B.G. Wright has written perhaps more on Aristeas than any other Septuagint scholar and represents this negative assessment well. See, for example, "The *Letter of Aristeas* and the Question of Septuagint Origins Redux," *Journal of Ancient Judaism* 2.3 (2011): 304–326.

14. Rajak, *Translation and Survival*, 24–63, makes such a case.

15. This idea guides S. Honigman, *The Septuagint and Homeric Scholarship in Alexandria: A Study in the Narrative of the Letter of Aristeas* (London: Taylor & Francis, 2003).

16. See E. Bickerman, *The Jews in the Greek Age* (Cambridge, MA: Harvard University Press, 1988), 253–254; C. Boyd-Taylor, "Robbers, Pirates and Licentious Women: Echoes of an Anti-Dionysiac Polemic in the Septuagint," in Karrer and Kraus, *Die Septuaginta*, 559–571.

17. J.A. Lee, *A Lexical Study of the Septuagint Version of the Pentateuch* (Chico, CA: Scholars Press, 1983), 115; J. Joosten, "To See God: Conflicting Exegetical Tendencies in the Septuagint," in Karrer and Kraus, *Die Septuaginta*, 297–298.

18. The new collection of essays edited by E. Bons and T.J. Kraus aims to open up the discussion of the Septuagint's Greek style, one imagines in response to the ideas behind the Interlinear Paradigm. See especially Joosten, "Rhetorical Ornamentation in the Septuagint: The Case of Grammatical Variation," in E. Bons and T.J. Kraus (eds.), *Et sapienter et eloquenter: Studies on Rhetorical and Stylistic Features of the Septuagint* (Göttingen: Vandenhoeck & Ruprecht, 2011), 11–22, who mentions the relationship of the Septuagint to an author like Polybius.

19. See the comments in Dines, *Septuagint*, 123. M. Rösel, *Übersetzung als Vollendung der Auslegung: Studien zur Genesis-Septuaginta* (Berlin: De Gruyter, 1994); Evans, *Verbal Syntax in the Greek Pentateuch*, should be consulted.

20. J.K. Aitken, "The Significance of Rhetoric in the Greek Pentateuch," in J.K. Aitken et al. (eds.), *On Stone and Scroll: Essays in Honour of Graham Ivor Davies* (Berlin: De Gruyter, 2012), 507–522.

21. Mélèze-Modrzejewski, *Jews of Egypt*, 99–106, defends the theory. See Honigman, *Septuagint and Homeric Scholarship*, 198–213; Rajak, *Translation and Survival*, 84–86.

22. The "Interlinear Paradigm" was popularized by A. Pietersma, "A New Paradigm for Addressing Old Questions," in J. Cook (ed.), *Bible and Computer: Stellenbosch AIBI 6 Conference* (Leiden: Brill, 2002), 337–364. The most recent articulation of the position is that of C. Boyd-Taylor, *Reading between the Lines: The Interlinear Paradigm for Septuagint Studies* (Leuven: Peeters, 2011). The quote here comes from the Preface, vii.

23. Boyd-Taylor, *Reading between the Lines*, 93–95.

24. See a clear distinction in Wright, "*Letter of Aristeas.*"
25. See recently Carr, *Formation of the Hebrew Bible*, 153–179.
26. J.K. Aitken, private communication.

CHAPTER 5

1. J. Dines, *The Septuagint* (London: Continuum), 14.
2. K.H. Jobes and M. Silva, *Invitation to the Septuagint* (Grand Rapids, MI: Baker, 2000), 213; M. Rösel, "Translators as Interpreters: Scriptural Interpretation in the Septuagint," in M. Henze (ed.), *A Companion to Biblical Interpretation in Early Judaism* (Grand Rapids, MI: Eerdmans, 2012), 85–86.
3. Rösel, "Translators as Interpreters," 86. NETS reads: "his recourse is to you, and you will rule over him."
4. Dines, *Septuagint*, 14.
5. See A. Salvesen, "Textual and Literary Criticism and the Book of Exodus: The Role of the Greek Versions," in T.M. Law, M. Liljeström, and K. De Troyer (eds.), *On the Trail: Studies in Honour of Anneli Aejmelaeus* (CBET; Leuven: Peeters, 2013).
6. See G.J. Brooke, "The Temple Scroll and LXX Exodus 35–40," in G.J. Brooke and B. Lindars (eds.), *Septuagint, Scrolls and Cognate Writings* (Atlanta: Scholars Press, 1992), 81–106.
7. I. Kislev, "The Vocabulary of the Septuagint and Literary Criticism: The Case of Numbers 27, 15–23," *Biblica* 90 (2009): 59–67.
8. The connection was made clear to me in conversation with David Lincicum.
9. This is disputed, but see T.M. Law, "The Fanciful Portraits of Solomon: From the Deuteronomists to Josephus," in *Annali di Storia dell'Esegesi* 30/1 (2013).
10. See, for example, the work of M. van der Meer, *Formulation and Reformulation: The Redaction of the Book of Joshua in the Light of the Oldest Textual Witnesses* (Leiden: Brill, 2004).
11. See P. Hugo, "The Jerusalem Temple Seen in 2 Samuel according to the Masoretic Text and the Septuagint," in M.K. Peters (ed.), *XIII Congress of the International Organization for Septuagint and Cognate Studies, Ljubljana 2007* (Atlanta: Society of Biblical Literature, 2008), 192–195.
12. For a summation of this research and the significant contributions of A. Schenker, J. Trebolle, Z. Talshir, and now P. Hugo, see T.M. Law, "3–4 Kingdoms," in J.K. Aitken (ed.), *The T&T Clark Companion to the Septuagint* (London: Continuum, 2013).
13. This has been suggested often by Julio Trebolle Barrera. See, for example, Barrera, "Kings (MT/LXX) and Chronicles: The Double and Triple Textual Tradition," in R. Rezetko et al. (eds.), *Reflection and Refraction: Studies in Biblical Historiography in Honour of A. Graeme Auld* (Leiden: Brill, 2007), 483–501. Now, R. Klein's commentary on 2 Chronicles demonstrates it: Klein, *2 Chronicles* (Minneapolis: Fortress Press, 2012).

14. One of John Lee's lectures in his series of Grinfield Lectures showed the high style of the Greek translator of Isaiah compared with other Hellenistic works.

15. R.E. de Sousa, *Eschatology and Messianism in LXX Isaiah 1–12* (London: Continuum, 2010), 13–18; cf. A. Van der Kooij, *The Oracle of Tyre: The Septuagint of Isaiah XXIII as Version and Vision* (Leiden: Brill, 1998).

16. See F. Watson, "Mistranslation and the Death of Christ: Isaiah 53 LXX and Its Pauline Reception," in S.E. Porter and M.J. Boda (eds.), *Translating the New Testament: Text, Translation, Theology* (Grand Rapids, MI: Eerdmans), 215–250.

17. On which, see the short study of A. Schenker, *Das Neue am neuen Bund und das Alte Testament. Jer 31 in der hebräischen und griechischen Bibel* (Göttingen: Vandenhoeck & Ruprecht, 2006).

18. On the question, see now the study of I.E. Lilly, *Two Books of Ezekiel: Papyrus 967 and the Masoretic Text as Variant Literary Editions* (Leiden: Brill, 2012).

19. See P. Ahearne-Kroll, "LXX/OG Zechariah 1–6 and the Portrayal of Joshua Centuries after the Restoration of the Temple," in W. Kraus and R.G. Wooden (eds.), *Septuagint Research: Issues and Challenges in the Study of the Greek Jewish Scriptures* (Atlanta: Society of Biblical Literature, 2006), 179–192.

20. Noted by A.A. Macintosh, *A Critical and Exegetical Commentary on Hosea* (Edinburgh: T&T Clark, 1997), lxxiv–lxxix. The NRSV has made stylistic changes that obscure the awkwardness of the Hebrew Bible in Hosea 13:4: "Yet I have been the Lord your God ever since the land of Egypt...."

21. See M. Theocharous, *Lexical Dependence and Intertextual Allusion in the Septuagint of the Twelve Prophets: Studies in Hosea, Amos and Micah* (London: Continuum, 2012), 223–239. The other Hellenistic texts are the Sibylline Oracles 3.319–22, 512–13, 635–51, 657–731; Jubilees 7:19; 8:25; 9:7–8; and 4Q161.

22. K. Seybold, *Introducing the Psalms*, trans. R.G. Dunphy (Edinburgh: T&T Clark, 1990), 153.

23. See A. Pietersma, "Not Quite Angels: A Commentary on Psalm 8 in Greek," in A. Voitila and J. Jokiranta (eds.), *Scripture in Transition: Essays on Septuagint, Hebrew Bible, and Dead Sea Scrolls in Honour of Raija Sollamo* (Leiden: Brill, 2008), 255–274.

24. See L. Cuppi, "The Treatment of Personal Names in the Book of Proverbs from the Septuagint to the Masoretic Text," in T.M. Law and A. Salvesen (eds.), *Greek Scripture and the Rabbis* (Leuven: Peeters, 2012), 19–38.

25. J. Cook, *The Septuagint of Proverbs: Jewish and/or Hellenistic Proverbs? Concerning the Hellenistic Colouring of LXX Proverbs* (Leiden: Brill, 1997), esp. 154–200.

26. J.K. Aitken, "Rhetoric and Poetry in Greek Ecclesiastes," *Bulletin of the International Organization for Septuagint and Cognate Studies* 38 (2005): 55–77.

27. The NRSV has translated the Septuagint text in its Apocrypha section.

CHAPTER 6

1. See C.A. Evans, *Ancient Texts for New Testament Studies* (Peabody, MA: Hendrickson, 2005), 27.

2. J.K. Aitken, in James R. Royse, P. Kyle McCarter, and James K. Aitken "Text Criticism", in M.D. Coogan (ed.), *The Oxford Encyclopedia of the Books of the Bible* (Oxford: Oxford University Press, 2011, e-reference edition), http://www.oxford-booksofthebible.com/entry?entry=t280.e138-s2 (accessed 2 February 2012), rightly cautions the use of the Cairo material, since some of these were late retranslations from Greek (or possibly Syriac).

3. See Aitken, "Apocrypha"; Davila, "(How) Can We Tell If a Greek Apocryphon or Pseudepigraphon Has Been Translated from Hebrew or Aramaic?" *Journal for the Study of the Pseudepigrapha* 15 (2005): 3–61.

4. Jan Joosten, however, makes a strong case for the Prayer of Azariah as an original Greek composition. See Joosten, "The Prayer of Azariah (DanLXX 3): Sources and Origin," in J. Cook (ed.), *Septuagint and Reception: Essays Prepared for the Association for the Study of the Septuagint in South Africa* (Leiden: Brill, 2009), 5–16.

5. For all of these books, a good place to start since it has the latest research presented in summary form and has provided guidance for this chapter is in the individual articles in M.D. Coogan (ed.), *Oxford Encyclopedia of the Books of the Bible* (Oxford: Oxford University Press, 2012), and in the summative article of A. Salvesen, "The Growth of the Apocrypha," in J. Rogerson and J. Lieu (eds.), *The Oxford Handbook of Biblical Studies* (Oxford: Oxford University Press, 2006), 489–517.

6. See L. Fried (ed.), *Was 1 Esdras First? An Investigation into the Priority and Nature of 1 Esdras* (Atlanta: Socity of Biblical Literature, 2011), for the most recent debate on the relationship between the Septuagint and Hebrew Bible.

7. See B. Otzen, *Tobit and Judith* (London: Sheffield Academic Press, 2002), 140–141.

8. The full title is *Juditha triumphans devicta Holofernis barbarie* (Judith triumphant over the barbarians of Holofernes). See D. Levine Gera, "Judith," in Coogan, *Oxford Encyclopedia.*

9. I prefer NRSV to NETS here.

10. The texts have been edited by S. Weeks et al. (eds.), *The Book of Tobit: Texts from the Principal Ancient and Medieval Traditions with Synopsis, Concordances, and Annotated Texts in Aramaic, Hebrew, Greek, Latin, and Syriac* (Berlin: De Gruyer, 2004).

11. See N.J. Torchia, *Creatio ex nihilo and the Theology of St. Augustine: the Anti-Manichaean Polemic and Beyond* (New York: Peter Lang, 1999).

12. This was shown long ago by C.W. Emmet, "The Third Book of Maccabees," in R.H. Charles (ed.), *The Apocrypha and Pseudepigrapha of the Old Testament*

in English (Oxford: Clarendon Press, 1913), vol. 1, 155–173; and more recently by N.C. Croy, *3 Maccabees* (Leiden: Brill, 2006).

13. This event is recalled in Josephus's *Against Apion* (2.50–55), but under Ptolemy VIII Physcon (reigned 145–116 BCE).

14. J.M. van Henten, "A Jewish Epitaph in a Literary Text: 4 Macc 17:8–10," in J.W. van Henten and P.W. van der Horst (eds.), *Studies in Early Jewish Epigraphy* (Leiden: Brill, 1994), 44–69. See also now the discussion in D.A. DeSilva, *4 Maccabees: Introduction and Commentary on the Greek text in Codex Sinaiticus* (Leiden: Brill, 2006).

15. A. Segal, *Sefer Ben-Sirah ha-Shalem* (Jerusalem: Bialik Institute, 1958), notes eighty-five citations of the book in rabbinic literature up to the tenth century CE.

16. *2 Baruch* 78–87, also called the *Letter of Baruch*, is included in the canon of the church of the East, and *4 Baruch* is found in the Ethiopian Orthodox canon.

17. Joosten, "Prayer of Azariah (DanLXX 3)."

CHAPTER 7

1. The quotation comes from E. Tov, "The Status of the Masoretic Text in Modern Text Editions of the Hebrew Bible: The Relevance of Canon," in L.M. McDonald and J.A. Sanders (eds.), *The Canon Debate* (Peabody, MA: Hendrickson, 2002), 242–243.

2. The standard index is only in German: A. Rahlfs and D. Fraenkel, *Verzeichnis der griechischen Handschriften des Alten Testaments*, I.1 (Göttingen: Vandenhoek & Ruprecht, 2004).

3. As noted by J. Dines, *The Septuagint* (London: Continuum), 5. The manuscript is PRyl 458 (Rahlfs 957), containing Deuteronomy 23:24–24:3; 25:1–3; 26:12, 17–19; 27:15; 28:2; and 28:31–33.

4. A recent assessment is given in Law, "Kaige, Aquila, and Jewish Revision," in T.M. Law and A. Salvesen (eds.), *Greek Scripture and the Rabbis* (Leuven: Peeters, 2012), 39–64.

5. The most creative work on Symmachus has been done by A. Salvesen. See Salvesen, *Symmachus in the Pentateuch* (Manchester: Manchester University Press, 1991); more recently, see Salvesen, "Midrash in Greek? An Exploration of the Versions of Aquila and Symmachus in Exodus," in J.K. Aitken et al., *On Stone and Scroll: Essays in Honour of Graham Ivor Davies* (Berlin: De Gruyter, 2012), 523–536; Salvesen, "Did Aquila and Symmachus Shelter under the Rabbinic Umbrella?" in Law and Salvesen, *Greek Scripture and the Rabbis*, 107–126.

6. Cf. P.J. Gentry, *The Asterisked Materials in the Greek Job* (Atlanta: Scholars Press, 1995).

7. Law, "Kaige, Aquila, and Jewish Revision."

8. My account follows closely that of Carr, *Formation of the Hebrew Bible*, 158–159, but where he adds to the evidence the cessation of textual plurality and the increase of revisional activity in this period, I depart. As I explained just before

this section, I believe we have the *appearance* of the cessation of textual plurality and the increase in revisions, simply because the later triumph of the Hebrew Bible distorts our view.

9. The Muratorian fragment should probably be dated later than the traditional second-century date.

10. See T. Hägg, "Canon Formation in Greek Literary Culture," in E. Thomassen (ed.), *Canon and Canonicity: The Formation and Use of Scripture* (Copenhagen: Museum Tusculanum Press, 2010), 109–128. The quote from Quintillian is also via Hägg, from D.A. Russell, trans., *Quintillian: The Orator's Education* (Loeb Classical Library, Cambridge, MA: Harvard University Press, 2002).

11. A. Edrei and D. Mendels, "A Split Jewish Diaspora: Its Dramatic Consequences," *Journal of the Study of the Pseudepigrapha* 16.2 (2007): 91–137.

12. Ibid. See also A. Wasserstein and D.J. Wasserstein, *The Legend of the Septuagint: From Classical Antiquity to Today* (Cambridge: Cambridge University Press, 2006), 217–237.

CHAPTER 8

1. The citation of 2 Maccabees 7:1–2 follows NETS, except for the phrase "to touch the forbidden flesh of swine," for which NETS has "to partake of unlawful swine's flesh." The sense is rather that these brothers would not even touch the forbidden flesh, much less go further by eating it. For this interpretation and translation, see D.R. Schwartz, *2 Maccabees* (Berlin: De Gruyter, 2008), 296, 300–301.

2. D.A. DeSilva, *The Jewish Teachers of Jesus, James, and Jude: What Earliest Christianity Learned from the Apocrypha and Pseudepigrapha* (New York: Oxford University Press, 2012), 127–140.

3. See J.A. Fitzmyer, *Romans: A New Translation with Introduction and Commentary* (New York: Doubleday, 1993), 269–295.

4. C. Hezser, *Jewish Literacy in Roman Palestine* (Tübingen: Mohr Siebeck, 2001), 503–504.

5. D. Lincicum, *Paul and the Early Jewish Encounter with Deuteronomy* (Tübingen: Mohr Siebeck, 2010), 25, n. 12.

6. See Lincicum, *Paul and the Early Jewish Encounter with Deuteronomy* (Tübingen: Mohr Siebeck, 2011), 21–28; E. Tov, "The Background of Sense Divisions in the Biblical Texts," in M.C.A. Korpel and J.M. Oesch (eds.), *Delimitation Criticism: A New Tool in Biblical Scholarship* (Assen: Van Gorcum, 2000), 312–350.

7. J.R. Wagner, *Heralds of the Good News: Isaiah and Paul in Concert in the Letter to the Romans* (Leiden: Brill, 2002), convincingly argues Paul knew the Greek Isaiah by heart.

8. The argument on text-based memorization by D.M. Carr, *The Formation of the Hebrew Bible* (New York: Oxford University Press, 2011), 3–149, could be used in a study on the citations in the New Testament.

9. The clearest statement of this position is in M.C. Albl, *"And Scripture Cannot Be Broken": The Form and Function of the Early Christian Testimonia Collections* (Leiden: Brill, 1999).

10. Lincicum, *Early Jewish Encounter*, 56–57, also rebuts the suggestion that Paul made random scribbling in notebooks from which he later culled the citations.

11. This example is based on the excellent discussion in F. Wilk, "The Letters of Paul as Witnesses to and for the Septuagint Text," in W. Kraus and R.G. Wooden (eds.), *Septuagint Research: Issues and Challenges in the Study of the Greek Jewish Scriptures* (Atlanta: Society of Biblical Literature, 2006), 262–263.

12. Lincicum, *Early Jewish Encounter*, 1–58, 138–140.

13. Wagner, *Heralds of the Good News*, 25.

14. See K. Jobes's assessment of the Septuagint in 1 Peter: "The Septuagint Textual Tradition in 1 Peter," in Kraus and Wooden, *Septuagint Research*, 311–333.

15. G.J. Steyn, *A Quest for the Assumed LXX Vorlage of the Explicit Citations in Hebrews* (Göttingen: Vandenhoeck & Ruprecht, 2011), shows the author of Hebrews almost certainly didn't use *testimonia*. See in particular his example (pp. 54–56) of the use of Psalm 2 and 2 Samuel 7 in Hebrew 1:5.

16. J. Norton, *Contours in the Text: Textual Variation in the Writings of Paul, Josephus, and the Yahad* (London: Continuum, 2011), is the first study that attempts to prove the ancient authors had knowledge of the textual plurality and exploited it to their ends.

17. See C. Boyd-Taylor's appropriate cautions on Septuagint lexicography; Boyd-Taylor, "The Semantics of Biblical Language *Redux*," in R.J.V. Hiebert (ed.), *"Translation Is Required": The Septuagint in Retrospect and Prospect* (Atlanta: Society of Biblical Literature, 2010), 41–58.

18. It may well be that the adjective "new" was a latter addition to Jesus's original words.

19. The first attested use of the terminology is in 2 Corinthians 3, even though it does not carry the same sense as a collection of books.

20. See R.E. Watts, *Isaiah's New Exodus in Mark* (Tübingen: Mohr Siebeck, 1997); M.D. Hooker, "Isaiah in Mark's Gospel," in S. Moyise and M.J.J. Menken (eds.), *Isaiah in the New Testament* (London: Continuum, 2005), 35–50.

21. R. de Sousa, "Is the Choice of ΠΑΡΘΕΝΟΣ in LXX Isa. 7:14 Theologically Motivated?" *Journal of Semitic Studies* 53.2 (2008): 211–232.

CHAPTER 9

1. The quote from Deissmann is found in K.H. Jobes and M. Silva, *Invitation to the Septuagint* (Grand Rapids, MI: Baker, 2000), 23; originally from A. Deissmann, *The Philology of the Greek Bible* (London: Hodder & Stoughton, 1908), 12.

2. R.H. Gundry, *The Use of the Old Testament in St. Matthew's Gospel* (Leiden: Brill, 1967); R.H. Longenecker, *Biblical Exegesis in the Apostolic Period* (Grand Rapids, MI: Eerdmans, 1999).

3. M.J.J. Menken, *Matthew's Bible: The Old Testament Text of the Evangelist* (Leuven: Peeters, 2004), 9.

4. This is not the place to enter into the disputed territory of the relationship between Matthew, Mark, and Luke, but a readable account is in M. Goodacre, *The Synoptic Problem: A Way through the Maze* (London: T&T Clark, 2001).

5. S. Moyise, "Deuteronomy in Mark's Gospel," in S. Moyise and M.J.J. Menken (eds.), *Deuteronomy in the New Testament* (London: Continuum, 2007), 27–41.

6. M. Hooker, "Isaiah in the Gospel of Mark," in S. Moyise and M.J.J. Menken (eds.), *Isaiah in the New Testament* (London: Continuum, 2005), 39–41; R. Watts, *Isaiah's New Exodus in Mark* (Tübingen: Mohr Siebeck, 1997), 216–218.

7. B.J. Koet, "Isaiah in Luke-Acts," in Moyise and Menken, *Isaiah in the New Testament*, 84.

8. I find little to which I would object in M.J.J. Menken, *Old Testament Quotations in the Fourth Gospel: Studies in Textual Form* (Kampen: Kok Pharos, 1996), and my analysis favors his. See his work for more extensive argumentation of these and other examples.

9. B.G. Schuchard, *Scripture within Scripture: The Interrelationship of Form and Function in the Explicit Old Testament Citations of the Gospel of John* (Atlanta: Scholars Press, 1992).

10. See Menken, *Old Testament Quotations in the Fourth Gospel*; Schuchard, *Scripture within Scripture*, 1–15.

11. The direct object "me" is lacking in the Greek but supplied by the NETS translator.

12. See also W. Kraus, "The Role of the Septuagint in the New Testament: Amos 9:11–12 as a Test Case," in R.J.V. Hiebert (ed.), *"Translation Is Required": The Septuagint in Retrospect and Prospect* (Atlanta: Society of Biblical Literature, 2010), 171–190; H. Utzschneider, "Flourishing Bones—The Minor Prophets in the New Testament," in Kraus and Wooden, *Septuagint Research*, 273–292.

13. T.H. Lim, *Holy Scripture in the Qumran Commentaries and Pauline Letters* (Oxford: Oxford University Press, 1997).

14. For elaborations on these examples of Paul's use of Isaiah in Romans, readers should consult the relevant passages and arguments in Wagner, *Heralds of the Good News*, which is the most convincing argument to date on Paul's use of the Septuagint in Romans and the source that guides much of this discussion.

15. Ibid., 176–178.

16. Ibid., 82.

17. The reading adopted in v. 26 goes against the NRSV and all English versions, which have followed the Greek text in the edition of NA[27]. More compelling on text-critical grounds is the reading proposed in ibid., 84, n. 126 and 127.

18. Ibid., 126–151.

19. Ibid., 205–216.

20. Lincicum, *Early Jewish Encounter*, 165 (italics in original).

21. See R.E. de Sousa, *Eschatology and Messianism in LXX Isaiah 1–12* (London: Continuum, 2010), 151.

22. NRSV has "of those," but following the Greek I use "the messengers" to make clear the Septuagint's role in this citation.

23. Wagner, *Heralds of the Good News*, 170–174, 346.

24. J. Norton, *Contours in the Text: Textual Variation in the Writings of Paul, Josephus, and the Yahad* (London: Continuum, 2011); see also F. Wilk, "The Letters of Paul as Witnesses to and for the Septuagint Text," in W. Kraus and R.G. Wooden (eds.), *Septuagint Research: Issues and Challenges in the Study of the Greek Jewish Scriptures* (Atlanta: Society of Biblical Literature, 2006), 266.

25. See the new work of D.A. DeSilva, *The Jewish Teachers of Jesus, James, and Jude: What Earliest Christianity Learned from the Apocrypha and Pseudepigrapha* (New York: Oxford University Press, 2012).

26. M. Karrer, "The Epistle to the Hebrews and the Septuagint," in Kraus and Wooden, *Septuagint Research*, 339.

27. On these, see G.J. Steyn, *A Quest for the Assumed LXX Vorlage of the Explicit Citations in Hebrews* (Göttingen: Vandenhoeck & Ruprecht, 2011), 196–204. See also H. Attridge, "The Epistle to the Hebrews and the Scrolls," in A.J. Avery-Peck et al. (eds.), *When Judaism and Christianity Began* (Leiden: Brill, 2004), 2:315–42, esp. 316, n.5.

28. See M. Karrer, "Epistle to the Hebrews and the Septuagint," 347–349, against Jobes and Silva, *Invitation to the Septuagint*, 195–198. The majority of the manuscripts for the Greek Psalms actually have "body" (Greek *soma*) in 39:7, including an early papyrus (Bodmer 24). Hebrews 10:5 is probably a citation from the oldest Septuagint text, which read "body." The translation, "you have prepared a body for me," while not literally following the Hebrew, would have been chosen as a sensible way to understand what the psalmist meant. The Greek Psalms do on the whole display a degree of literalism, but they also show an occasional freedom; this is just such a case when one might see a more idiomatic translation, since the digging of ears might have been hard to understand. Therefore, it has been argued more convincingly that Hebrews 10:5 is a translation of the oldest Septuagint text. The later revision of the Septuagint towards the text of the Hebrew Bible introduced "ears," and the more we understand about the revisions of the Septuagint this is exactly what we should expect.

29. K. Jobes, "The Septuagint Textual Tradition in 1 Peter," in Kraus and Wooden, *Septuagint Research*, 311.

30. Also S. Moyise, *The Old Testament in the Book of Revelation* (Sheffield: Sheffield Academic Press, 1995), 17.

31. On this section, see more extensive discussion in Moyise, "The Psalms in the Book of Revelation," in S. Moyise and M.J.J. Menken (eds.), *The Psalms in the New Testament* (London: Continuum, 2004), 231–246.

32. The studies were done on the Dead Sea Scrolls by E. Ulrich, and on the Samaritan Penateuch by S. Schorch, as noted by E. Tov, "The Septuagint

between Judaism and Christianity," in T.S. Caulley and H. Lichtenberger (eds.), *Die Septuaginta und das frühe Christentum/The Septuagint and Christian Origins* (Tübingen: Mohr Siebeck, 2011), 16, n. 73. On the New Testament, see R.A. Kraft, "Christian Transmission of Greek Jewish Scriptures: A Methodological Probe," in A. Benoit et al. (eds.), *Paganisme, Judaïsme, Christianisme: Influences et affrontements dans le Monde Antique (Mélanges M. Simon* (Paris: E. de Boccard, 1978), 207–226. Examples of Christian "tampering" with the Septuagint in the light of the New Testament citation has always been scant according to Tov, "Septuagint between Judaism and Christianity," 3–25, here 15–21.

33. Wagner, *Heralds of the Good News*, 345, n. 8, contra Lim, *Holy Scripture in the Qumran Commentaries*.

CHAPTER 10

1. Augustine's quote is from E.L. Gallagher, *Hebrew Scripture in Patristic Biblical Theory* (Leiden: Brill, 2012), 53.

2. A case in point is the treatment of the evidence in E.R. Brotzman, *Old Testament Textual Criticism* (Grand Rapids, MI: Baker, 1993).

3. M. Harl, "Le Septante chez les Pères Grecs et dans la vie des chrétiens," in M. Harl, G. Dorival, and O. Munnich (eds.), *La Bible Grecque des Septante* (Paris: Cerf, 1994), 289: "This historical fact is undeniable: The Fathers of the Church...worked with the Septuagint, and the Septuagint alone, as the Old Testament." ["Ce fait historique est indéniable: les Pères de l'Église...travaillé avec la LXX comme "AT," et seulement avec elle."]

4. For more on the *testimonia* and the citation of the Septuagint and how they are explained here, see O. Skarsaune, "Scriptural Interpretation in the Second and Third Centuries," in M. Sæbo (ed.), *Hebrew Bible/Old Testament: The History of its Interpretation*, I.1 (Göttingen: Vandenhoeck & Ruprecht, 1996), 418–421. Skarsaune's work on Justin Martyr is also still recommended; Skarsaune, *The Proof from Prophecy: A Study in Justin Martyr's Proof-Text Tradition: Text-Type, Provenance, Theological Profile* (Leiden: Brill, 1987).

5. M.C. Albl, *"And Scripture Cannot Be Broken": The Form and Function of the Early Christian Testimonia Collections* (Leiden: Brill, 1999). Studies on manuscripts could also be consulted: see, for example, A. Falcetta, "A Testimony Collection in Manchester: Papyrus Rylands Greek 460," *Bulletin of the John Rylands University Library of Manchester* 83 (2001): 3–19.

6. P.S. Alexander, "The Biblical Canon in Rabbinic Judaism," in P.S. Alexander and J.-D. Kaestli (eds.), *The Canon of Scripture in Jewish and Christian Tradition/ Le canon des Écritures dans les traditions juive et chrétienne* (Lausanne: Éditions du Zèbre, 2007), 57–58.

7. The best discussion now on Christian book production is that of L. Hurtado and C. Keith, "Book Writing and Production in the Hellenistic and Roman Era," in J.C. Paget and J. Schaper (eds.), *The New Cambridge: Cambridge University Press,*

History of the Bible: From Beginnings to 600 (Cambridge: Cambridge University Press, 2013).

8. See the *Leuven Database of Ancient Books*, http://www.trismegistos.org/ldab/; W.A. Johnson, "The Ancient Book," in R.S. Bagnall (ed.), *The Oxford Handbook of Papyrology* (Oxford: Oxford University Press, 2009), 266.

9. L. Hurtado, *The Earliest Christian Artifacts: Manuscripts and Christian Origins* (Grand Rapids, MI: Eerdmans, 2006), 43–95. The revolution that the book brought to Christianity is also narrated eloquently by A. Grafton and M.H. Williams, *Christianity and the Transformation of the Book: Origen, Eusebius, and the Library of Caesarea* (Cambridge, MA: Harvard University Press, 2006).

10. M.W. Holmes, "The Biblical Canon," in S.A. Harvey and D. Hunter (eds.), *The Oxford Handbook of Early Christian Studies* (Oxford: Oxford University Press, 2008), 405–406. Eugene Ulrich, in his numerous publications (see "Further Reading," especially under the heading for the Dead Sea Scrolls), has often made similar comments.

11. R.E. Heine, "Origen and the Eternal Boundaries," in T.S. Caulley and H. Lichtenberger (eds.), *Die Septuaginta und das frühe Christentum/The Septuagint and Christian Origins* (Tübingen: Mohr Siebeck, 2011), 402.

12. M. Bockmuehl, "The Dead Sea Scrolls and the Origins of Biblical Commentary," in R.A. Clements and D.R. Schwartz (eds.), *Text, Thought, and Practice in Qumran and Early Christianity* (Leiden: Brill, 2009), 6.

13. A very conservative but problematic assessment is in R. Beckwith, "The Formation of the Hebrew Bible," in M.J. Mulder (ed.), *Mikra: Text, Translation, Reading & Interpretation of the Hebrew Bible in Ancient Judaism & Early Christianity* (Peabody, MA: Hendrickson Publishers, 2004), 39–86.

14. Gallagher counts twelve in the Greek Church alone: see Gallagher, *Hebrew Scripture*, 25–30.

15. Eusebius, *Ecclesiastical History* 4.26.12–14.

16. Gallagher, *Hebrew Scripture*, 22, who reads Wisdom as another title for Proverbs. I am unconvinced, but even if Wisdom is another title for Proverbs it proves that Melito's canonical list was influenced by contact with Jewish sources, which we will see later continued to exercise an influence on Christian thinking.

17. See also H. von Campenhausen, *The Formation of the Christian Bible* (Philadelphia: Fortress Press, 1972), 65; M. Hengel, *The Septuagint as Christian Scripture* (Edinburg: T&T Clark, 2002), 60–61.

18. See Eusebius's comment in *Ecclesiastical History* 6.25.1–2.

19. *b.Hagigah* 13a; *y.Hagigah* 77c; *b.Yebamoth* 63b; *Genesis Rabah* 8:2b; *Erubin* 54a; *b.Baba Kamma* 92b.

20. For example, in his *Homilies on Numbers* 27.1. See J.N.B. Carleton Paget, "The Christian Exegesis of the Old Testament in the Alexandrian Tradition," in Sæbo, *Hebrew Bible/Old Testament*, 502–503; now R.E. Heine, *Origen: Scholarship in the Service of the Church* (Oxford: Oxford University Press, 2010), 68–76.

21. Gallagher, *Hebrew Scripture*, 63–104.

22. Gallagher, *Hebrew Scripture*, 95–98, discusses this for the fathers more broadly.

23. Heine, "Origen and the Eternal Boundaries," 396. See also Gallagher, *Hebrew Scripture*, 38–46, where he does not deny the possibility that Origen saw the Wisdom of Solomon both as scripture and perhaps as canonical.

24. Grafton and Williams, *Christianity and the Transformation of the Book*, 220–221; B. Metzger, *Manuscripts of the Greek Bible* (New York: Oxford University Press, 1991), for Vaticanus; D. Jongkind, *Scribal Habits of Codex Sinaiticus* (Piscataway, NJ: Gorgias Press, 2007), for Sinaiticus.

25. Gallagher, *Hebrew Scripture*, 27–29.

26. *On Christian Doctrine* 2.8.13.

27. There are questions surrounding the authenticity of the 60th Canon from the Laodicean Council, but proof is inconclusive either way.

28. I owe this point to Dirk Jongkind.

29. Holmes, "Biblical Canon," 413. For the lists, see L.M. McDonald, *The Biblical Canon: Its Origin, Transmission, and Authority* (Peabody, MA: Hendrickson, 2007).

30. E. Zenger, *Einleitung in das Alte Testament*, 8th ed. (Stuttgart: Kohlhammer, 2012), 28–31.

31. In the Middle Ages there were some Latin Bible manuscripts like Gregory the Great's that left out the apocryphal books; this never stuck, and these cases remain rare exceptions.

CHAPTER 11

1. My translation of Origen's comment is close to E.L. Gallagher, *Hebrew Scripture in Patristic Biblical Theory* (Leiden: Brill, 2012), 57, but with some modification.

2. The origins of the Old Latin are contested. For a recent overview, see P.-M. Bogaert, "The Latin Bible, c. 600 to c. 900," in R. Marsden and E.A. Matter (eds.), *The New Cambridge: Cambridge University Press, History of the Bible: From 600 to 1450* (Cambridge: Cambridge University Press, 2012), 69–92.

3. See P.M. Bogaert, "Vetus Latina," in A. Salvesen and T.M. Law (eds.), *The Oxford Handbook of the Septuagint* (Oxford: Oxford University Press, forthcoming).

4. See J. Trebolle Barrera, "Textual Pluralism and Composition of the Books of Kings," in H. Ausloos et al. (eds.), *After Qumran: Old and Modern Editions of the Biblical Texts: The Historical Books* (Leuven: Peeters, 2012), 225–226.

5. The catchy title of two of J. Trebolle Barrera's articles has often been cited: Barrera, "From the "Old Latin" through the "Old Greek" to the "Old Hebrew" (2 Kings 10:23–35)," *Textus* 11 (1984): 17–36; Barrera, "Old Latin, Old Greek and Old Hebrew in the Books of Kings (1 Ki 18:27 and 2 Ki 20:11)," *Textus* 13 (1986): 85–95. The probability is made all the stronger when readings, like this one, appear also in the Antiochian version of the Septuagint.

6. See A. Salvesen, "A Well-Watered Garden (Isaiah 58:11): Investigating the Influence of the Septuagint," in R.J.V. Hiebert (ed.), *"Translation Is Required": The Septuagint in Retrospect and Prospect* (Atlanta: Society of Biblical Literature, 2010), 191–208; A. Salvesen and T.M. Law (eds.), *The Oxford Handbook of the Septuagint* (Oxford: Oxford University Press, forthcoming).

7. The chain is discussed in A. Kamesar, *Jerome, Greek Scholarship and the Hebrew Bible: A Study of the Quaestiones Hebraicae in Genesim* (Oxford: Oxford University Press, 1993), 29–34.

8. The full history of the legend is told in A. Wasserstein and D. Wasserstein, *The Legend of the Septuagint: From Classical Antiquity to Today* (Cambridge: Cambridge University Press, 2006). The early Christian writers are treated in chapter 5, 95–131.

9. T. Rajak, *Translation and Survival: The Greek Bible of the Ancient Jewish Diaspora* (Oxford: Oxford University Press, 2009), 280–282.

10. 2.25–44.

11. 2.43–44.

12. On Philo here, see Gallagher, *Hebrew Scripture*, 148. The translation here is from A. Kamesar, "Biblical Interpretation in Philo," in Kamesar (ed.), *The Cambridge Companion to Philo* (Cambridge: Cambridge University Press, 2009), 65–91.

13. The best introduction to Josephus is still T. Rajak, *Josephus: The Historian and His Society* (London: Duckworth, 2002), now in a second edition. But for Josephus's use of the Antiochian revision of the Septuagint, see the cautious assessment now in T. Kauhanen, *The Proto-Lucianic Problem in 1 Samuel* (Göttingen: Vandenhoeck & Ruprecht, 2012).

14. The new study J. Norton, *Contours in the Text: Textual Variation in the Writings of Paul, Josephus, and the Yahad* (London: Continuum, 2011), argues that ancient writers had an awareness of textual plurality.

15. *Antiquities* 12.7. See Wasserstein and Wasserstein, *Legend of the Septuagint*, 47.

16. *Antiquities* 12.104.

17. On the use of the *Letter of Aristeas* in Philo and Josephus, see F. Borchardt, "The LXX Myth and the Rise of Textual Fixity," *Journal of the Study of Judaism* 43 (2012): 1–21.

18. *Preparation for the Gospel* 8.

19. The Armenian version was probably made not long after Eusebius but probably not before the late fourth century at the earliest and most likely not until the fifth.

20. The old introduction to the Septuagint of H.B. Swete, *An Introduction to the Old Testament in Greek* (Cambridge: Cambridge University Press, 1914); and the newer French edition of M. Harl, G. Dorival, and O. Munnich (eds.), *La Bible Grecque des Septante* (Paris: Cerf, 1994), 289–320, provide examples of how the Septuagint impacted the early church, some of which are presented here. Readers may also see these and many more examples by perusing the relevant volumes

of the Ancient Christian Commentary on Scripture. Although imperfect for many reasons, this series at least provides glimpses of early Christian exegesis. In any case, this is an area in which more research is needed.

21. Gallagher, *Hebrew Scripture*, is the strongest recent statement against my view here.

22. *Epistle of Barnabas* 12:11; Tertullian, *Against Praxeas* 28, *Against the Jews* 7; Cyprian, *Testimonies against the Jews* 1.21.

23. *On Baptism* 7.

24. Justin Martyr, *First Apology* 1.55; Irenaeus, *Against Heresies* 3.10.2; Tertullian, *Against Marcionism* 3.6.

25. Irenaeus, *Against Heresies* 3.18.3.

26. *Against Praxeas* 28

27. *On the Holy Spirit* 2.6.

28. NETS reads more awkwardly: "God is not to be put upon like a man, nor is he to be threatened like a son of man."

29. Cyprian, *Testimonies against the Jews* 2.20.

30. On this issue in the reading in 1 Samuel, see A. Aejmelaeus, "A Kingdom at Stake: Reconstructing the Old Greek—Deconstructing the Textus Receptus," in A. Voitila and J. Jokiranta (eds.), *Scripture in Transition: Essays on Septuagint, Hebrew Bible, and Dead Sea Scrolls in Honour of Raija Sollamo* (Leiden: Brill, 2008), 362–364.

31. The texts are Justin Martyr, *Dialogue with Trypho*, 75.1 and 113.1, in Saint Justin Martyr, *Dialogue with Trypho*, trans. T.B. Falls, rev. ed. T.P. Halton, ed. M. Slusser (Washington, DC: Catholic University of America Press, 2003).

32. Hippolytus, *Commentary on Daniel* 6.8–14. C.L. de Wet, "The Reception of the Susanna Narrative (Dan. XIII; LXX) in Early Christianity," in J. Cook (ed.), *Septuagint and Reception: Essays Prepared for the Association for the Study of the Septuagint in South Africa* (Leiden: Brill, 2009), 240–242.

33. Looking beyond the plain meaning of a text to discover a deeper insight was not an invention of Christian exegetes. Philo was part of a culture of allegorical interpretation in the Greco-Roman world and had already followed this method in his own exposition of scripture. See especially J. Dillon, "Philo and the Greek Tradition of Allegorical Exegesis," in *Society of Biblical Literature Seminar Papers* 33 (Atlanta: Society of Biblical Literature, 1994), 69–80; V. Nikiprowetzky, *Le commentaire de l'Écriture chez Philon d'Alexandrie: son caractère et sa portée, observations philologiques* (Leiden: Brill, 1977).

34. As in J. Barton, *The Nature of Biblical Criticism* (Louisville, KY: Westminster John Knox, 2007).

35. Origen, *Philocalia* iv, xv.

36. Codex Alexandrinus. In Codex Vaticanus: "And God broke open the pit in the jawbone...."

37. *Letter* 19.

38. *Sermon* 119.4.
39. Cf. *Epistle of Barnabas* 11.
40. Irenaeus, *Against Heresies* 5.17.4.
41. Epistle of Barnabas 6:7.
42. A more sympathetic picture of Arius emerges from R. Williams, *Arius: Heresy and Tradition*, rev. ed. (Grand Rapids, MI: Eerdmans, 2002), who demonstrates the *creation* of the Arian controversy in the polemical writings of Athanasius.
43. C. Kannengiesser, *Handbook of Patristic Exegesis: The Bible in Ancient Christianity* (Leiden: Brill, 2006), 301–302.
44. *Against Heresies* 3.18.3; 3.19.2; Cf. Kannengiesser, *Handbook of Patristic Exegesis*, 314.
45. *Defence of the Nicene Definition* 3.12; *Against the Arians* 1.19. Cf. Kannengiesser, *Handbook of Patristic Exegesis*, 315.
46. *Against Heresies* 4.26.5.
47. W. Horbury, "Old Testament Interpretation in the Writings of the Church Fathers," in M.J. Mulder (ed.), *Mikra: Text, Translation, Reading & Interpretation of the Hebrew Bible in Ancient Judaism & Early Christianity* (Peabody, MA: Hendrickson, 2004), 748–750; M.E. Johnson, "The Apostolic Tradition," in G. Wainwright and K.B. Westerfield Tucker (eds.), *The Oxford History of Christian Worship* (Oxford: Oxford University Press, 2006), 32–75. On early liturgy, see R.F. Taft, "The Interpolation of the Sanctus into the Anaphora: When and Where? A Review of the Dossier," *Orientalia Christiana Periodica* 57 (1991): 281–308; 58 (1992) 83–121; G. Rouwhorst, "Continuity and Discontinuity between Jewish and Christian Liturgy," *Bijdragen* 54 (1993): 72–83; Rouwhorst, "The Reception of the Jewish Sabbath in Early Christianity," in P. Post et al. (eds.), *Christian Feast and Festival* (Leuven: Peeters, 2001), 223–266; Rouwhorst, "The Reading of Scripture in Early Christian Liturgy," in L.V. Rutgers (ed.), *What Athens Has to Do with Jerusalem* (Leuven: Peeters, 2002), 305–331.
48. Hippolytus, *Apostolic Tradition* 2.4.
49. See M. Alexandre, "Pâques, la vie nouvelle," in A. Spira and C. Klock (eds.), *The Easter Sermons of Gregory of Nyssa* (Cambridge, MA: Harvard University Press, 1981), 153–194.

CHAPTER 12

1. The citation is from J.E.L. Oulton, trans., *Eusebius, Ecclesiastical History: Books 6–10*, vol. 2 (Cambridge, MA: Harvard University Press, Loeb Classical Library, 1932). The nickname Adamantius is from Eusebius, and A. Grafton and M.H. Williams, *Christianity and the Transformation of the Book: Origen, Eusebius, and the Library of Caesarea* (Cambridge, MA: Harvard University Press, 2006), 21, characterize it as part of Eusebius's adoration for his teacher, as he "portrayed Origen as a kind of superhero of Christian piety and scholarship."

2. For some time scholars considered Clement's "school" a private and unofficial endeavor, which was formalized only during Origen's leadership; it is now considered more likely that Origen came to the helm of an ecclesiastical institution that was already in business. See A. Van den Hoek, "The "Catechetical" School of Early Christian Alexandria and Its Philonic Heritage," *Harvard Theological Review* 90 (1997): 59–87; H.F. Hägg, *Clement of Alexandria and the Beginnings of Christian Apophaticism* (Oxford: Oxford University Press, 2006), 56–59.

3. Eusebius, *Ecclesiastical History* 6.18; 6.23; 6.36.

4. Eusebius, *Ecclesiastical History* 6.23; Jerome, *On Illustrious Men* 61.

5. See N. de Lange, *Origen and the Jews* (Cambridge: Cambridge University Press, 1976), 21–23.

6. See A. Salvesen, "A Convergence of the Ways? The Judaizing of Christian Scripture by Origen and Jerome," in A.H. Becker and A. Yoshiko Reed (eds.), *The Ways that Never Parted: Jews and Christians in Late Antiquity and the Early Middle Ages* (Tübingen: Mohr Siebeck, 2003), 233–258.

7. See also H. Crouzel, *Origène* (Paris: Lethielleux, 1985), 46.

8. Eusebius, *Ecclesiastical History* 6.39.5, 7.1. Cf. R.M. Grant, *Eusebius as Church Historian* (Oxford: Oxford University Press, 1980), 20 and 31; Crouzel, *Origène*, 59.

9. Crouzel, *Origène*, 63.

10. Lorenzo Perrone (Bologna) identified the fragments and will soon publish his findings.

11. R.E. Heine's title for his excellent work is *Origen: Scholarship in the Service of the Church* (Oxford: Oxford University Press, 2011). M.J. Edwards, *Origen against Plato* (Aldershot, UK: Ashgate, 2002), 1, notes that in the scholarship of Simonetti and Crouzel it became "clearer to the modern world that Origen was before all else a churchman, who availed himself of philosophy in the service of exegesis and the defense of the ecclesiastic tradition." In his exegesis he often shows he is concerned to deal with opponents, whether real or imagined, for the health of the church. See, for example, *On First Principles*, book 4 and *Commentary on John*, book 6.

12. Crouzel, *Origène*, 112.

13. De Lange, *Origen and the Jews*; Crouzel, *Origène*, 112.

14. De Lange, *Origen and the Jews*, 103–21.

15. Cf. also Crouzel, *Origène et la "connaissance mystique"* (Paris: Desclée de Brouwer, 1961), 281–285.

16. Crouzel, *Origène*, 109, 217.

17. See T.M. Law, "Origen's Parallel Bible: Textual Criticism, Apologetics, or Exegesis?" *Journal of Theological Studies* 59.1 (2008): 1–21.

18. J. Dines, *The Septuagint* (London: Continuum, 2004), 101; Fernández Marcos, *The Septuagint in Context* (Leiden: Brill, 2000), 213–215, are skeptical that the signs were in the fifth column in the first place, allowing the possibility that

Origen's followers later added the signs. Grafton and Williams, *Christianity and the Transformation of the Book*, 116–117, however, are unequivocal.

19. For the texts and the fuller treatment of the following, see Law, "Origen's Parallel Bible." An admirably detailed discussion of the significance of the Hexapla is in Grafton and Williams, *Christianity and the Transformation of the Book*, 86–132.

20. Kamesar, *Jerome, Greek Scholarship*; Law, "Origen's Parallel Bible."

21. Kamesar, *Jerome, Greek Scholarship*, 19.

22. Kamesar, *Jerome, Greek Scholarship*, 25; cf. G. Sgherri, "Sulla valutazione origeniana dei LXX," *Biblica* 58.1 (1977): 1–28 (here 2–6).

23. Romeny, *A Syrian in Greek Dress: The Use of Greek, Hebrew, and Syriac Biblical Texts in Eusebius of Emesa's Commentary on Genesis* (Leuven: Peeters, 1997), 116.

24. Sgherri, "Sulla valutazione," 2–4.

25. Noted in Kamesar, *Jerome, Greek Scholarship*, 28, n. 79.

26. 14.3. Kamesar, *Jerome, Greek Scholarship*, 18. Cf. R.P.C. Hanson, *Allegory and Event: A Study of the Sources and Significance of Origen's Interpretation of Scripture* (Louisville, KY: SCM, 2002), 175.

27. *Commentary on Romans* 8.6–7. See Heine, *Origen*, 73.

28. Contra Nautin, *Origène: Sa vie et son oeuvre* (Paris: Beauchesne, 1977), 351–353. See also Law, "Origen's Parallel Bible"; Romeny, *Syrian in Greek Dress*, 114.

29. Book 10 in Song of Songs 1.3.14. See also Romeny, *Syrian in Greek Dress*, 117; Kamesar, *Jerome, Greek Scholarship*, 20–21.

30. Jerome (however reservedly), *Apology against Rufinus* 2.27.; *Letters* 106.2.2. See also Kamesar, *Jerome, Greek Scholarship*, 35: " ... this text did not achieve any kind of official status, nor did its appearance deter further recensional activity."

31. T.D. Barnes, *Constantine and Eusebius* (Cambridge: Cambridge University Press, 1981), v.

32. Some now doubt whether Eusebius intended to write this history of the church or whether its parts were stitched together later. See the problem in R.W. Burgess, "The Dates and Editions of Eusebius' *Chronici canones* and *Historia ecclesiastica*," *Journal of Theological Studies* 48 (1997) 471–504.

33. Photius, *Bibliotheca* 118. Cf. Jerome, *On Distinguished Men* 75; Barnes, *Constantine and Eusebius*, 120.

34. Grafton and Williams, *Christianity and the Transformation of the Book*, 178–240; Barnes, *Constantine and Eusebius*, 93; also, in two places, Jerome notes the fervor of two bishops of Caesarea, Acacius and his successor Euzoïus, to preserve the library (*Letters* 34.1; *On Distinguished Men* 113). *Etymologies* 6.6.1. In J. Oroz Reta, Manuel-A. Marcos Casquero, and Manuel C. Diaz y Diaz (eds.), *Etimologías: Edicion Bilingüe*, vol. 1 (Madrid: Editorial Católica, 1982), 580, the editors suggest that the 30,000 volumes were the combined number from two libraries. There is now an English translation of the Etymologies: S.A. Barney, *The Etymologies of Isidore of Seville* (Cambridge: Cambridge University Press, 2006). Jerome (*On Distinguished Men* 3) claims that the library possessed a copy

of the original text of Matthew's gospel in Hebrew, a theory of Matthean origins no longer considered plausible by modern scholarship.

35. They had no small impact on the transmission of the New Testament text down to the present day. See B.M. Metzger, *Chapters in the History of New Testament Criticism* (Leiden: Brill, 1963), 42–72.

36. J.W. Trigg, *Origen* (London: Routledge, 1998), 3. See Nautin's analysis of the *Apology* in *Origène*, 99–153.

37. Heine, *Origen*, asks for a reassessment of Origen's status as a heretic. On the proceedings, see now the edited two volume set of translated texts, with commentary and annotations, on the Council, in R. Price, *The Acts of the Council of Constantinople of 553* (Liverpool: Liverpool University Press, 2009).

38. However, because the original work has been lost in its entirety, we only have recourse to a Latin translation of the first book alone, from an author, Rufinus, whose reliability is disputed.

39. Photius, *Bibliotheca* 118; See R.S. Bagnall, *Reading Papyri, Writing Ancient History* (London: Routledge, 1995), 25; L. Hurtado and C. Keith, "Book Writing and Production in the Hellenistic and Roman Era," in J.C. Page and J. Schaper (eds.), *The New Cambridge: Cambridge University Press, History of the Bible: From Beginnings to 600* (Cambridge: Cambridge University Press, 2013). Jerome also noted that Pamphilus undertook to copy with his own hand because he "was on fire with such love for the sacred library" (*On Illustrious Men* 75).

40. The colophons at the end of 2 Esdras and Esther in Codex Sinaiticus also bear witness to their position on the priority of the Hexaplaric LXX. Thanks to an international collaboration, the Codex Sinaiticus can now be viewed online at http://www.codexsinaiticus.com.

41. *Preparation of the Gospel* 8.1.6–7.

42. A. Cameron, *The Later Roman Empire, AD 284–430* (London: Routledge, 1993), 30–65.

43. *On the Death of the Persecutors* 44.4–6. On the sources here, see A. Cameron, *The Later Roman Empire, AD 284–430* (London: Fontana Press, 1993), 56.

44. *Ecclesiastical History* 9.9. See A. Louth, "The Date of Eusebius' *Historia ecclesiastica*," *Journal of Theological Studies* 41 (1990): 111–123; R.W. Burgess, "The Dates and Editions of Eusebius' *Chronici canones* and *Historia ecclesiastica*."

45. *Life of Constantine* 1.27–28.

46. Cameron, *Later Roman Empire*, 47–65.

47. M. Edwards, "Alexander of Alexandria and the *Homoousion*," *Vigiliae Christianae* 66 (2012): 1–21; Edwards, "The First Council of Nicaea," in M.M. Mitchell and F.M. Young (eds.), *The Cambridge History of Christianity*, vol. 1, (Cambridge: Cambridge University Press, 2006), 552–567 (esp. 560–561). D. MacCulloch, *A History of Christianity* (London: Penguin, 2009), 214, imagines a greater role for Constantine, but Cameron, *Later Roman Empire*, 68, suggests that Constantine's involvement remained ambiguous and that he deferred all decisions to the bishops.

48. Cameron, *Later Roman Empire*, 47. See the edition with introduction in A. Cameron and S. Hall, *Life of Constantine* (Oxford: Clarendon Press, 1999).

49. *Life of Constantine* 4.36. For Constantine's building program, see T.E. Gregory, *A History of Byzantium*, 2d ed. (Chichester, UK: Wiley-Blackwell, 2010), 148–159.

50. *Life of Constantine* 4.36.2. Some scholars have suggested that *Codex Vaticanus* and *Codex Sinaiticus* were among the fifty copies, but this is merely a guess. See T.C. Skeat, "The Codex Sinaiticus, the Codex Vaticanus, and Constantine," *Journal of Theological Studies* 50 (1999): 583–625; Grafton and Williams, *Christianity and the Transformation of the Book*, 216–221.

51. *Life of Constantine*, 4.36.3–4; 37. Cf. Barnes, *Constantine and Eusebius*, 125, unlikely suggestion that Eusebius only sent Constantine copies of the New Testament.

52. The sigla no doubt fell out of use in the transmission of the Greek manuscripts in the next several hundred years, probably because copyists did not see the need for them or did not understand them.

CHAPTER 13

1. These citations are from A. Cain, *The Letters of Jerome: Asceticism, Biblical Exegesis, and the Construction of Christian Authority in Late Antiquity* (Oxford: Oxford University Press, 2009), 55; and R.W. Dyson's translation in his *Augustine: The City of God against the Pagans* (Cambridge: Cambridge University Press, 1998).

2. B. ter Haar Romeny, *A Syrian in Greek Dress: The Use of Greek, Hebrew, and Syriac Biblical Texts in Eusebius of Emesa's Commentary on Genesis* (Leuven: Peeters, 1997), 91.

3. On this entire discussion of the Antiochians, the literature is deep. See the Further Reading, but also throughout this section see Romeny, *Syrian in Greek Dress*, and bibliography cited there.

4. Scholars refer to the earlier stages as the "proto-Lucianic." See N. Fernández Marcos, *The Septuagint in Context* (Leiden: Brill, 2000), 223–238.

5. See, for instance, Law, "Symmachus in Antioch?: The Translation of Symmachus in the Antiochian Recension of 1 Kings (3 Reigns)," *Textus* 25 (2010): 29–48, and the bibliography cited there. The improbability of the versions of the three Jewish revisers circulating independently of the Hexapla in early Christianity has been convincingly argued by R. Ceulemans, "Greek Christian Access to 'the Three,' 250–600 CE," in T.M. Law and A. Salvesen (eds.), *Greek Scripture and the Rabbis* (Leuven: Peeters, 2012), 165–191.

6. Romeny, *Syrian in Greek Dress*, 8. Also now the excellent R.E. Winn, *Eusebius of Emessa: Church and Theology in the Mid-Fourth Century* (Washington, DC: Catholic University of America Press, 2011).

7. See both of my articles "Syriac, Bible translations of" and "Aramaic and Syriac" in the *Encyclopedia of Ancient History* (Oxford: Wiley-Blackwell, 2013).

8. Romeny, *Syrian in Greek Dress*, 110–112.
9. Winn, *Eusebius of Emessa*, 37–41.
10. D. Woods, "Ammianus Marcellinus and Bishop Eusebius of Emesa," *Journal of Theological Studies* 54 (2003): 587; Winn, *Eusebius of Emessa*, 2, 45–46.
11. My own reading of Jerome is similar to A. Cain, *The Letters of Jerome* (Oxford: Oxford University Press, 2009), who emphasizes Jerome's propagandistic self-portraiture. See also the collection of essays in A. Cain and J. Lössl (eds.), *Jerome of Stridon: His Life, Writings and Legacy* (Farnham, UK: Ashgate, 2009). The best recent biographical portrait is M.H. Williams's excellent *The Monk and the Book* (Chicago: University of Chicago Press, 2006); see also A. Kamesar, *Jerome, Greek Scholarship, and the Hebrew Bible: A Study of the Quaestiones Hebraicae in Genesim* (Oxford: Clarendon Press, 1993). On Jerome's Hebrew knowledge, see M. Graves, *Jerome's Hebrew Philology: A Study Based on His Commentary on Jeremiah* (Leiden: Brill, 2007).
12. *Preface IH Job*, and *Letter* 82.2.
13. This is one aspect is highlighted by Williams, *The Monk and the Book*, esp. 1–24, 167–200.
14. Cain, *Letters of Jerome*, 114–124, 131, for the irony of Jerome targeting other clerics for legacy hunting.
15. See A.S. Jacobs, *Remains of the Jews: The Holy Land and Christian Empire in Late Antiquity* (Stanford: Stanford University Press, 2004), esp. 56–60, 67–100.
16. Cain, *Letters of Jerome*, 99–128.
17. *Preface to Isaiah*.
18. *Preface to the Gospel* and *Preface to the Books of Solomon according to the Septuagint*.
19. Though see Ceulemans, "Greek Christian Access."
20. Prologue to the *Hebrew Questions on Genesis*.
21. *Letter* 27.1.
22. *Letter* 107.12. See E. Gallagher, "The Old Testament 'Apocrypha' in Jerome's Canonical Theory," *Journal of Early Christian Studies* 20 (2012): 313–333.
23. Gallagher, *Hebrew Scripture*, 51, also considers this to be innovative, at least in Jerome's mind.
24. Salvesen, "Convergence of the Ways," 236.
25. Salvesen, "Convergence of the Ways," 251.
26. D. MacCulloch, *Reformation: Europe's House Divided 1490–1700* (London: Penguin, 2004), 82.
27. The etymology of this Hebrew word is disputed, but there is good support for the meaning "to shine." See C. Houtman, *Exodus*, vol. 3 (Leuven: Peeters, 1999), 730–733.
28. On the Jewish traditions, see H. Schreckenberg and K. Schubert, *Jewish Historiography and Iconography in Early and Medieval Christianity* (Assen: Van Gorcum, 1992), xv–xvii.

29. J. Cameron, "The Vir Triculus: An Investigation of the Classical, Jewish and Christian Influences on Jerome's Translation of the Psalter Iuxta Hebraeos" (Unpublished DPhil thesis, Oxford, 2006).

30. MacCulloch, *History of Christianity*, 302–303.

31. *Letter* 71.6; the phrase in the translation of W. Parsons, *Saint Augustine: Letters*, vol. 1 (Washington, DC: Catholic University of America Press, 1951). Cf. *On Christian Doctrine* 2.16.

32. *On Christian Doctrine* 2.15.22; *City of God* 18.43.

33. J. Friedman, *The Most Ancient Testimony: Sixteenth-Century Christian-Hebraica in the age of Renaissance* (Athens: Ohio University Press, 1983) is still valuable. See also W. McKane, *Selected Christian Hebraists* (Cambridge: Cambridge University Press, 1989). The Reformation era study of S.G. Burnett, *Christian Hebraism in the Reformation era (1500–1660): Authors, Books, and the Transmission of Jewish Learning* (Leiden: Brill, 2012), should also be consulted.

34. E. Schulz-Flügel, "The Latin Old Testament Tradition," in M. Sæbo (ed.), *Hebrew Bible/Old Testament: The History of Its Interpretation* I.1 (Göttingen: Vandenhoeck & Ruprecht, 1996), 659–660. A study on Augustine's language is C. Kirwan, "Augustine's Philosophy of Language," in E. Stump and N. Kretzmann (eds.), *The Cambridge Companion to Augustine* (Cambridge: Cambridge University Press, 2001), 186–204.

35. See *On Christian Doctrine* 2.7.

36. Augustine's *Letter* 72.2; Jerome's *Letter* 105.2.

37. *Letter* 28 is usually dated to 395 and *Letter* 71 to 403. Jerome's response comes in his *Letter* 112, which is usually given the number 75 in the collections of Augustine's. On the correspondence, see C. White, *The Correspondence (394–419) between Jerome and Augustine of Hippo* (Lewiston, NY: Edwin Mellen, 1990).

38. Augustine notes that Jerome had already done so in his translation of Job, apparently from the Hexaplaric text, and using the Hexaplaric signs. *Letters* 28.2.

39. *Epistle* 71 was the second letter. Augustine discusses the Septuagint in *On Christian Doctrine* 2.15.

40. The famous passage is in *Confessions* 1.14.23, but the question is how well his Greek developed from his self-portrait in the *Confessions*. D.T. Runia, *Philo in Early Christian Literature: A Survey* (Assen: Van Gorcum, 1993), 321–322, on the basis of other research, paints a more optimistic portrait. On his handling of Greek in the *Confessions*, see now P. Burton, *Language in the Confessions of Augustine* (Oxford: Oxford University Press, 2007).

41. Augustine, *Letter* 71.3.5.

42. A point Michael Graves suggested to me.

43. A. Kotzé, "Augustine, Jerome and the Septuagint," in J. Cook (ed.), *Septuagint and Reception: Essays Prepared for the Association for the Study of the Septuagint in South Africa* (Leiden: Brill, 2009), 260.

44. *City of God* 18.42.
45. C. Setzer, "The Jews in Carthage and Western North Africa, 66–235 CE," in S. Katz and R. Kalmin (eds.), *Cambridge History of Judaism*, vol. 4 (Cambridge: Cambridge University Press, 2006), 68–75; D. Efroymsen, "Tertullian's Anti-Jewish Rhetoric: Guilt by Association," *Union Seminary Quarterly Review* 36 (1980): 25–37.
46. *Apology* 19.2.
47. The *Adversus Judaeos* is not authentically Cyprian. See W. Horbury, "The Purpose of Pseudo-Cyprian, *Adversus Judaeos*," in W. Horbury (ed.), *Jews and Christians in Contact and Controversy* (Edinburgh: T&T Clark, 1998), 180–199. On these remarks, see Setzer, "Jews in Carthage and Western North Africa," 72–75.
48. Y. Le Bohec, "Inscriptions juives et judaisant de l'Afrique romaine," and "Juifs et Judaisants dans l'Afrique romaine: remarques Onomastique," *Antiquités africaines* 17 (1981): 165–207.
49. Schulz-Flügel, "Latin Old Testament Tradition," 657.

CHAPTER 14

1. *On Christian Doctrine* 2.17.
2. Ephrem, *Commentary on the Diatessaron* 1.18–19. David Taylor pointed this out to me.
3. See similar comments in E. Ulrich, "The Qumran Biblical Scrolls—The Scriptures of Late Second Temple Judaism," in T. Lim (ed.), *The Dead Sea Scrolls in Their Historical Context* (Edinburgh: T&T Clark, 2000), 71–72. My comments are similar to those made by him.
4. Some Protestant and Catholic scholars have made preliminary proposals, but the wider Christian theological community has yet to take these seriously. Readers interested in this question should see J.R. Wagner, "The Septuagint and the 'Search for the Christian Bible,'" in M. Bockmuehl and A.J. Torrance (eds.), *Scripture's Doctrine and Theology's Bible: How the New Testament Shapes Christian Dogmatics* (Grand Rapids, MI: Baker, 2008), 17–28, in which Wagner engages earlier arguments from Brevard Childs. H. Gese and H. Hübner, *Zur biblischen Theologie: alttestamentliche Vorträge* (Tübingen: Mohr Siebeck, 1983); Gese and Hübner, *Biblische Theologie des Neuen Testaments*, vol. 1 (Göttingen: Vandenhoeck & Ruprecht, 1990), argue from a German Protestant perspective; a Catholic perspective can be found in A. Schenker, "L'Ecriture Sainte subsiste en plusieurs formes canoniques simultanées," in *L'interpretatione della Bibbia nelle chiesas: Atti del Simposio promosso dalla Congregazione per la Dottrina della Fede* (Rome: Vatican, 2001), 178–186. Pope Benedict XVI quoted the German version of this article in a conference in Regensburg: Schenker, "Die Heilige Schrift subsistiert gleichzeitig in mehreren kanonischen Formen," in Schenker (ed.), *Studien zu Propheten und Religionsgeschichte* (Stuttgart: Verlag Katholisches Bibelwerk, 2003), 192–200.

5. J. Joosten, "Une théologie de la Septante? Réflexions méthodologiques sur l'intérpretation de la version grecque," *Revue de théologie et de philosophie* 132 (2000): 31–46; M. Rösel, "Towards a 'Theology of the Septuagint,'" in W. Kraus and R.G. Wooden (eds.), *Septuagint Research: Issues and Challenges in the Study of the Greek Jewish Scriptures* (Atlanta: Society of Biblical Literature, 2006), 242.
6. M. Rösel, "Translators as Interpreters," in M. Henze (ed.), *A Companion to Biblical Interpretation in Early Judaism* (Grand Rapids, MI: Eerdmans, 2012), 84; E. Tov, "Theologically Motivated Exegesis Embedded in the Septuagint," in Tov (ed.), *The Hebrew and Greek Bible: Collected Essays on the Septuagint* (Leiden: Brill, 1999), 257–269.
7. Rösel, "Translators as Interpreters," 86–87; Rösel, "The Reading and Translation of the Divine Name in the Masoretic Tradition and the Greek Pentateuch," *Journal for the Study of the Old Testament* 31 (2007): 411–428.

Further Reading

It is impossible to list every item of importance for the further study of the Septuagint, so the works that follow are only a selection of ones I consider important; my colleagues should not imagine that their omission means I think their work unimportant! I have also included only English titles, which is not to say I gladly left off the list the numerous important German, French, and Spanish titles. This is also why the items listed here are all relatively manageable for a next step beyond this book into the exciting world of Septuagint. One scholar has done more for the study of the Septuagint, the Hebrew Bible, and the Dead Sea Scrolls than any other in modern times, and it would be difficult to select a number from his more than five hundred publications. In addition to the meager few provided here, ambitious readers would do well to search for publications by Emanuel Tov.

GENERAL WORKS ON THE SEPTUAGINT
Introductions and Handbooks

Aitken, J.K. (ed.), *The T&T Clark Companion to the Septuagint* (London: Continuum, 2013).

Dines, J., *The Septuagint* (London: Continuum, 2004).

Fernandez Marcos, N., *The Septuagint in Context* (Leiden: Brill, 2000).

Jobes, K.H., and M. Silva, *Invitation to the Septuagint* (Grand Rapids, MI: Baker, 2000).

Law, T.M., and A. Salvesen, *The Oxford Handbook of the Septuagint* (Oxford: Oxford University Press, forthcoming).

Studies

Bons, E., and T.J. Kraus (eds.), *Et sapienter et eloquenter: Studies on Rhetorical and Stylistic Features of the Septuagint* (Göttingen: Vandenhoeck & Ruprecht, 2011).

Cook, J. (ed.), *Septuagint and Reception: Essays Prepared for the Association for the Study of the Septuagint in South Africa* (Leiden: Brill, 2009).

De Troyer, K. *Rewriting the Sacred Text: What the Old Greek Texts Tell Us about the Literary Development of the Bible* (Atlanta: Society of Biblical Literature, 2003).

Hengel, M., *The Septuagint as Christian Scripture* (Edinburgh: T&T Clark, 2002).

Hiebert, R.J.V. (ed.), *"Translation Is Required": The Septuagint in Retrospect and Prospect* (Atlanta: Society of Biblical Literature, 2010).

Kraus, W., and R.G. Wooden (eds.), *Septuagint Research: Issues and Challenges in the Study of the Greek Jewish Scriptures* (Atlanta: Society of Biblical Literature, 2006).

Law, T.M., and A. Salvesen (eds.), *Greek Scripture and the Rabbis* (Leuven: Peeters, 2012).

Law, T.M., M. Liljeström, and K. De Troyer (eds.), *On the Trail: Studies in Honour of Anneli Aejmelaeus* (CBET; Leuven: Peeters, 2013)

Müller, M., *The First Bible of the Church: A Plea for the Septuagint* (Sheffield: Sheffield Academic Press, 1996).

Rajak, T., *Translation and Survival: The Greek Bible of the Ancient Jewish Diaspora* (Oxford: Oxford University Press, 2009).

Voitila, A., and J. Jokiranta (eds.), *Scripture in Transition: Essays on Septuagint, Hebrew Bible, and Dead Sea Scrolls in Honour of Raija Sollamo* (Leiden: Brill, 2008).

Wasserstein, A., and D. Wasserstein, *The Legend of the Septuagint: From Classical Antiquity to Today* (Cambridge: Cambridge University Press, 2006).

GENERAL WORKS ON THE HEBREW BIBLE/OLD TESTAMENT

Carr, D.M., *The Formation of the Hebrew Bible* (New York: Oxford University Press, 2011).

Collins, J.J., *Introduction to the Hebrew Bible* (Minneapolis: Fortress Press, 2004).

Coogan, M.D., *The Old Testament: A Very Short Introduction* (Oxford: Oxford University Press, 2008).

Coogan, M.D., *A Brief Introduction to the Old Testament: The Hebrew Bible in Context*, 2d ed. (New York: Oxford University Press, 2012).

Hägg, T., "Canon Formation in Greek Literary Culture," in E. Thomassen (ed.), *Canon and Canonicity: The Formation and Use of Scripture* (Copenhagen: Museum Tusculanum Press, 2010), 109–128.

Law, T.M., "The Fanciful Portraits of Solomon: From the Deuteronomists to Josephus," *Annali di Storia dell'Esegesi* 30/1 (2013).

McDonald, L.M., *The Biblical Canon: Its Origin, Transmission, and Authority* (Peabody, MA: Hendrickson, 2007).

McDonald, L.M., and J.A. Sanders (eds.), *The Canon Debate* (Peabody, MA: Hendrickson, 2002).

Mulder, M.J. (ed.), *Mikra: Text, Translation, Reading & Interpretation of the Hebrew Bible in Ancient Judaism & Early Christianity* (Peabody, MA: Hendrickson, 2004).

Sæbo, M. (ed.), *Hebrew Bible/Old Testament: The History of its Interpretation*, 3 vols. (Göttingen: Vandenhoeck & Ruprecht, 1996–2008).

Tov, E., *Textual Criticism of the Hebrew Bible, 3d ed.* (Minneapolis: Fortress Press, 2012).

Yeivin, I., *Introduction to the Tiberian Masorah*, transl. and ed. E.J. Revell (Missoula, MT: Scholars Press, 1980), 61.

HISTORICAL CONTEXTS
The Greek World

Boardman, J., J. Griffin, and O. Murray (eds.), *The Oxford History of Greece and the Hellenistic World* (Oxford: Oxford University Press, 2001) (especially the essay by R. Lane Fox, "Hellenistic Culture and Literature," 338–364).

Errington, R.M., *The History of the Hellenistic World: 323–30 BC* (Oxford: Oxford University Press, 2008).

Green, P., *The Hellenistic Age: A Short History* (New York: Modern Library, 2008).

Green, P., *Alexander to Actium: The Historical Evolution of the Hellenistic Age* (Berkeley: University of California Press, 1993).

Moyer, I.S., *Egypt and the Limits of Hellenism* (Cambridge: Cambridge University Press, 2011).

Shipley, G., *The Greek World after Alexander 323–30 BC* (London: Routledge, 1999).

Ancient Israel and Early Judaism

Barclay, J.M., *Jews in the Mediterranean Diaspora: From Alexander to Trajan (323 BCE–117 CE)* (Berkeley: University of California Press, 1996).

Bickerman, E., *The Jews in the Greek Age* (Cambridge, MA: Harvard University Press, 1988).

Briant, P., *From Cyrus to Alexander: A History of the Persian Empire* (Winona Lake, IN: Eisenbrauns, 2002).

Cambridge History of Judaism, vols. 1–4 (Cambridge: Cambridge University Press, 1994–2006).

Cohen, S.J.D., *From the Maccabees to the Mishnah*, 2d ed. (Louisville, KY: Westminster John Knox Press, 2006).

Collins, J.J., *Between Athens and Jerusalem: Jewish Identity in the Hellenistic Diaspora*, 2d ed. (Grand Rapids, MI: Eerdmans, 1999).

Finkelstein, I., and N.A. Silberman, *The Bible Unearthed: Archaeology's New Vision of Ancient Israel and the Origin of Its Sacred Texts* (New York: Free Press, 2001).

Grabbe, L.L., *A History of Jews and Judaism in the Second Temple Period, vol. 1: Yehud: A History of the Persian Province of Judah* (London: T&T Clark, 2006).

Grabbe, L.L., *A History of Jews and Judaism in the Second Temple Period, vol. 2: The Coming of the Greeks—The Early Hellenistic Period (335–175 BCE)* (London: T&T Clark, 2008).

Grabbe, L.L., *Ancient Israel: What Do We Know and How Do We Know It?* (London: T&T Clark, 2007).

Gruen, E., *Heritage and Hellenism: The Reinvention of Jewish Traditon* (Berkeley: University of California Press, 2002).

Kovelman, A., *Between Alexandria and Jerusalem: The Dynamic of Jewish and Hellenistic Culture* (Leiden: Brill, 2005).

Modrzejewski, J., *The Jews of Egypt: from Rameses II to Emperor Hadrian* (Princeton, NJ: Princeton University Press, 1995).

Schürer, E., *A History of the Jewish People in the Age of Jesus Christ (175 B.C.–A.D. 135)*, 4 vols., ed. and rev. G. Vermes et al. (Edinburgh: T&T Clark, 1973–1987).

Schwartz, S., *Imperialism and Jewish Society: 200 BCE to 640 CE* (Princeton, NJ: Princeton University Press, 2001).

VanderKam, J.C., *An Introduction to Early Judaism* (Grand Rapids, MI: Eerdmans, 2001).

Wiesehöfer, J., *Ancient Persia*, 4th ed. (London: I.B. Tauris, 1996).

Roman World and Early Christianity

Cameron, A., *The Later Roman Empire, AD 284–430* (London: Fontana Press, 1993).

Cameron, A., *The Mediterranean World in Late Antiquity, AD 395–700*, 2d ed. (London: Routledge, 2012).

Green, B., *Christianity in Ancient Rome: The First Three Centuries* (London: T&T Clark, 2010).

Potter, D.S., *The Roman Empire at Bay, AD 180–395* (London: Routledge, 2004).

DEAD SEA SCROLLS AND THE SEPTUAGINT

Abegg, M.G., Jr., P.W. Flint, and E. Ulrich (eds.), *The Dead Sea Scrolls Bible: The Oldest Known Bible Translated for the First Time into English* (San Francisco: HarperCollins, 2002).

Dávid, N., A. Lang, K. De Troyer, and S. Tzoref (eds.), *The Hebrew Bible in Light of the Dead Sea Scrolls* (Göttingen: Vandenhoeck & Ruprecht, 2012).

García Martínez, F., and E.J.C. Tigchelaar (eds.), *The Dead Sea Scrolls Study Edition* (Leiden: Brill, 1997–1998).

Goodman, M.D., "The Qumran Sectarians and the Temple in Jerusalem," in C. Hempel (ed.), *The Dead Sea Scrolls: Texts and Context* (Leiden: Brill, 2010), 263–273.

Hempel, C. (ed.), *The Dead Sea Scrolls: Texts and Context* (Leiden: Brill, 2010).

Herbert, E.D., and E. Tov (eds.), *The Bible as Book: The Hebrew Bible and the Judean Desert Discoveries* (London: British Library, 2002).

Lange, A., E. Tov, and M. Weigold (eds.), *The Dead Sea Scrolls in Context: Integrating the Dead Sea Scrolls in the Study of Ancient Texts, Languages and Cultures* (Leiden: Brill, 2011).

Lim, T.H., and J.J. Collins (eds.), *The Oxford Handbook of the Dead Sea Scrolls* (Oxford: Oxford University Press, 2010).

Smelik, W., "The Languages of Roman Palestine," in C. Hezser (ed.), *The Oxford Handbook of Jewish Daily Life in Roman Palestine* (Oxford: Oxford University Press, 2010), 122–141.

Tov, E., *Textual Criticism of the Hebrew Bible*, 3d ed. (Minneapolis: Fortress Press, 2012).

Tov, E., "The Qumran Hebrew Texts and the Septuagint—an Overview," in
    S. Kreuzer et al. (eds.), *Die Septuaginta: Entstehung, Sprache, Geschichte* (Tübingen:
    Mohr Siebeck, 2012), 3–17.

Ulrich, E., "Pluriformity in the Biblical Text, Text Groups, and Questions of Canon,"
    in J. Trebolle Barrera and L. Vegas Montaner (eds.), *The Madrid Qumran Congress:
    Proceedings of the International Congress on the Dead Sea Scrolls, Madrid 18–21
    March, 1991, vol. 1* (Leiden: Brill, 1992), 23–42.

Ulrich, E., *The Dead Sea Scrolls and the Origins of the Bible* (Grand Rapids, MI:
    Eerdmans, 1999).

Ulrich, E., "The Qumran Biblical Scrolls—The Scriptures of Late Second Temple
    Judaism," in T. Lim (ed.), *The Dead Sea Scrolls in Their Historical Context*
    (Edinburgh: T&T Clark, 2000).

Ulrich, E., "The Absence of "Sectarian Variants" in the Jewish Scriptural Scrolls Found
    at Qumran," in E.D. Herbert and E. Tov (eds.), *The Bible as Book: The Hebrew Bible
    and the Judean Desert Discoveries* (London: British Library, 2002), 179–195.

Ulrich, E., "From Literature to Scripture: Reflections on the Growth of a Text's
    Authoritativeness," *Dead Sea Discoveries* 10.1 (2003): 3–25.

VanderKam, J., and P. Flint, *The Meaning of the Dead Sea Scrolls: Their Significance for
    Understanding the Bible, Judaism, Jesus, and Christianity* (London: T&T Clark, 2002).

Vermes, G., *The Complete Dead Sea Scrolls in English*, rev. ed. (London: Penguin, 2004).

Vermes, G., *The Story of the Scrolls: The Miraculous Discovery and True Significance of
    the Dead Sea Scrolls* (London: Penguin, 2010).

Zahn, M., *Rethinking Rewritten Scripture: Composition and Exegesis in the 4QReworked
    Pentateuch Manuscripts* (Leiden: Brill, 2011).

THE ORIGINS OF THE SEPTUAGINT
Translation and Multilingualism in the Ancient World

Adams, J.N., M. Janse, and S. Swain (eds.), *Bilingualism in Ancient Society: Language
    Contact and the Written Word* (Oxford: Oxford University Press, 2002).

Hallo, W.W., *The Ancient Near Eastern Background of Some Modern Western Institutions*
    (Leiden: Brill, 1996).

Hallo, W.W., *The World's Oldest Literature: Studies in Sumerian Belles-Lettres* (Leiden:
    Brill, 2010).

Papaconstantinou, A. (ed.), *The Multilingual Experience in Egypt, from the Ptolemies to
    the Abbasids* (Farnham, UK: Ashgate, 2010).

The Letter of Aristeas

Borchardt, F., "The LXX Myth and the Rise of Textual Fixity," *Journal of the Study of
    Judaism* 43 (2012): 1–21.

De Crom, D., "The Letter of Aristeas and the Authority of the Septuagint," *Journal for
    the Study of the Pseudepigrapha* 17.2 (2008): 141–160.

Honigman, S., *The Septuagint and Homeric Scholarship in Alexandria: A Study in the Narrative of the Letter of Aristeas* (London: Taylor & Francis, 2003).

Honigman, S., "The Narrative Function of the King and the Library in the *Letter of Aristeas*," in T. Rajak et al. (eds.), *Jewish Perspectives on Hellenistic Rulers* (Berkeley: University of California Press, 2007), 128–146.

Shutt, R.J.H., "Letter of Aristeas," in J.H. Charlesworth (ed.), *The Old Testament Pseudepigrapha, vol. 1* (Peabody, MA: Hendrickson Publishers, 2009), 7–34. (English translation)

Thackeray, H. St. J., "The *Letter of Aristeas*," in H.B. Swete, *An Introduction to the Old Testament in Greek* (Cambridge: Cambridge University Press, 1914), 531–606. (Greek text)

Wright, B., "The Letter of Aristeas and the Question of Septuagint Origins Redux," *Journal of Ancient Judaism* 2.3 (2011): 304–326 (and his other studies noted there).

The First Translation of the Septuagint

Aitken, J.K., "The Significance of Rhetoric in the Greek Pentateuch," in J.K. Aitken et al. (eds.), *On Stone and Scroll: Essays in Honour of Graham Ivor Davies* (Berlin: De Gruyter, 2012), 507–522.

Bons, E., and J. Joosten (eds.), *Septuagint Vocabulary. Pre-History, Usage, Reception* (Atlanta: Society of Biblical Literature, 2011).

Boyd-Taylor, C., "Robbers, Pirates and Licentious Women: Echoes of an Anti-Dionysiac Polemic in the Septuagint," in M. Karrer and W. Kraus (eds.), *Die Septuaginta—Texte, Kontexte, Lebenswelten* (Tübingen: Mohr Siebeck, 2008), 559–571.

Boyd-Taylor, C., *Reading Between the Lines: The Interlinear Paradigm for Septuagint Studies* (Leuven: Peeters, 2011).

Brooke, G.J., "The Temple Scroll and LXX Exodus 35–40," in G.J. Brooke and B. Lindars (eds.), *Septuagint, Scrolls and Cognate Writings* (Atlanta: Scholars Press, 1992), 81–106.

Evans, T., *Verbal Syntax in the Greek Pentateuch: Natural Greek Usage and Hebrew Interference* (Oxford: Oxford University Press, 2001).

Joosten, J., "'On the LXX Translators' Knowledge of Hebrew," in B.A. Taylor (ed.), *X Congress of the International Organization for Septuagint and Cognate Studies, Oslo, 1998* (Atlanta: Society of Biblical Literature, 2001), 165–179.

Joosten, J., "Language as Symptom: Linguistic Clues to the Social Background of the Seventy," *Textus* 23 (2007): 69–80.

Joosten, J., "To See God: Conflicting Exegetical Tendencies in the Septuagint," in M. Karrer and W. Kraus (eds.), *Die Septuaginta—Texte, Kontexte, Lebenswelten* (Tübingen: Mohr Siebeck, 2008), 287–299.

Joosten, J., "The Aramaic Background of the Seventy: Language, Culture and History," *Bulletin of the International Organization for Septuagint and Cognate Studies* 43 (2010): 53–72.

Joosten, J., "Rhetorical Ornamentation in the Septuagint: The Case of Grammatical Variation," in E. Bons and T.J. Kraus (eds.), *Et sapienter et eloquenter: Studies on Rhetorical and Stylistic Features of the Septuagint* (Göttingen: Vandenhoeck & Ruprecht, 2011), 11–22.

Lee, J.A., *A Lexical Study of the Septuagint Version of the Pentateuch* (Chico, CA: Scholars Press, 1983).

Pietersma, A., "A New Paradigm for Addressing Old Questions: The Relevance of the Interlinear Model for the Study of the Septuagint," in J. Cook (ed.), *Bible and Computer: Stellenbosch AIBI 6 Conference* (Leiden: Brill, 2002), 337–364.

Rösel, M., "Translators as Interpreters: Scriptural Interpretation in the Septuagint," in M. Henze (ed.), *A Companion to Biblical Interpretation in Early Judaism* (Grand Rapids, MI: Eerdmans, 2012), 85–86.

Salvesen, A., "Textual and Literary Criticism and the Book of Exodus: The Role of the Greek Versions," in T.M. Law, M. Liljeström, and K. De Troyer (eds.), *On the Trail: Studies in Honour of Anneli Aejmelaeus* (CBET; Leuven: Peeters, 2013).

THE SEPTUAGINT BOOKS

The research on the individual books (including the Apocrypha) is too abundant to list here, so readers should consult J.K. Aitken, *The T&T Clark Companion to the Septuagint* (London: Continuum, 2013) and the relevant introductions previously listed. In addition to the books in NETS, translations and introductions to the apocryphal and pseudepigraphal books are in J. Charlesworth (ed.), *The Old Testament Pseudepigrapha*, 2 vols. (Peabody, MA: Hendrickson Publishers, 2010). Readers should also consult the relevant articles on the apocryphal books in M.D. Coogan (ed.), *Oxford Encyclopedia of the Books of the Bible* (Oxford: Oxford University Press, 2012), which provided guidance for the discussion in Chapter 6 since (in most cases) they represent the latest overview of the books.

On the Apocrypha, some items of note are listed here.

DeSilva, D.A., *Introducing the Apocrypha: Message, Context, and Significance* (Grand Rapids, MI: Baker Academic, 2002).

Goodman, M.D. (ed.), *Oxford Bible Commentary: Apocrypha* (Oxford: Oxford University Press, 2012).

Harrington, D.J., *Invitation to the Apocrypha* (Grand Rapids, MI: Eerdmans, 1999).

Salvesen, A., "The Growth of the Apocrypha," in J. Rogerson and J. Lieu (eds.), *The Oxford Handbook of Biblical Studies* (Oxford: Oxford University Press, 2006), 489–517.

THE MOVE TO UNIFORMITY

The Septuagint revisions are treated in the standard introductions. Special studies on the formation of the Hebrew Bible and the revisions are listed here.

Alexander, P.S., "The Biblical Canon in Rabbinic Judaism," in P.S. Alexander and J.-D. Kaestli (eds.), *The Canon of Scripture in Jewish and Christian Tradition* (Lausanne: Éditions du Zèbre, 2007).

Carr, D.M., *The Formation of the Hebrew Bible* (Oxford: Oxford University Press, 2011).

Edrei, A., and D. Mendels, "A Split Jewish Diaspora: Its Dramatic Consequences," *Journal of the Study of the Pseudepigraph* 16.2 (2007): 91–137.

Khan, G., *A Short Introduction to the Tiberian Masoretic Bible and Its Reading Tradition* (Piscataway, NJ: Gorgias Press, 2012).

Law, T.M., "Kaige, Aquila, and Jewish Revision," in T.M. Law and A. Salvesen (eds.), *Greek Scripture and the Rabbis* (Leuven: Peeters, 2012), 39–64.

Lim, T.H., *The Formation of the Jewish Canon* (New Haven, CT: Yale University Press, 2013).

Tov, E., *Textual Criticism of the Hebrew Bible*, 3d ed. (Minneapolis: Fortress Press, 2012).

Salvesen, A., *Symmachus in the Pentateuch* (Manchester: Manchester University Press, 1991).

Salvesen, A., "Did Aquila and Symmachus Shelter under the Rabbinic Umbrella?" in T.M. Law and A. Salvesen (eds.), *Greek Scripture and the Rabbis* (Leuven: Peeters, 2012), 107–126.

THE SEPTUAGINT AND THE NEW TESTAMENT

DeSilva, D.A., *The Jewish Teachers of Jesus, James, and Jude: What Earliest Christianity Learned from the Apocrypha and Pseudepigrapha* (New York: Oxford University Press, 2012).

Evans, C.A., *Ancient Texts for New Testament Studies* (Peabody, MA: Hendrickson, 2005).

Hezser, C., *Jewish Literacy in Roman Palestine* (Tübingen: Mohr Siebeck, 2001).

Jobes, K., "The Septuagint Textual Tradition in 1 Peter," in W. Kraus and R.G. Wooden (eds.), *Septuagint Research: Issues and Challenges in the Study of the Greek Jewish Scriptures* (Atlanta: Society of Biblical Literature, 2006), 335–353.

Karrer, M., "The Epistle to the Hebrews and the Septuagint," in W. Kraus and G. Wooden (eds.), *Septuagint Research: Issues and Challenges in the Study of the Greek Jewish Scriptures* (Atlanta: Society of Biblical Literature, 2006), 335–353.

Lim, T.H., *Holy Scripture in the Qumran Commentaries and Pauline Letters* (Oxford: Oxford University Press, 1997).

Lincicum, D., *Paul and the Early Jewish Encounter with Deuteronomy* (Tübingen: Mohr Siebeck, 2011).

McLay, T., *The Use of the Septuagint in New Testament Research* (Grand Rapids, MI: Eerdmans, 2003).

Menken, M.J.J., *Old Testament Quotations in the Fourth Gospel: Studies in Textual Form* (Kampen: Kok Pharos, 1996).

Menken, M.J.J., *Matthew's Bible: The Old Testament Text of the Evangelist* (Leuven: Peeters, 2004).

Moyise, S., and M.J.J. Menken (eds.), *The Psalms in the New Testament* (London: Continuum, 2004)

Moyise, S., and M.J.J. Menken (eds.), *Isaiah in the New Testament* (London: Continuum, 2005).

Moyise, S., and M.J.J. Menken (eds.), *Deuteronomy in the New Testament* (London: Continuum, 2007).

Moyise, S., and M.J.J. Menken (eds.), *The Minor Prophets in the New Testament* (London: Continuum, 2009).

Norton, J., *Contours in the Text: Textual Variation in the Writings of Paul, Josephus, and the Yahad* (London: Continuum, 2011).

Steyn, G.J., *A Quest for the Assumed LXX Vorlage of the Explicit Citations in Hebrews* (Göttingen: Vandenhoeck & Ruprecht, 2011).

Wagner, J.R., *Heralds of the Good News: Isaiah and Paul in Concert in the Letter to the Romans* (Leiden: Brill, 2002).

Watson, F., "Mistranslation and the Death of Christ: Isaiah 53 LXX and Its Pauline Reception," in S.E. Porter and M.J. Boda (eds.), *Translating the New Testament: Text, Translation, Theology* (Grand Rapids, MI: Eerdmans), 215–250.

Watts, R., *Isaiah's New Exodus in Mark* (Tübingen: Mohr Siebeck, 1997).

Wilk, F., "The Letters of Paul as Witnesses to and for the Septuagint Text," in W. Kraus and R.G. Wooden (eds.), *Septuagint Research: Issues and Challenges in the Study of the Greek Jewish Scriptures* (Atlanta: Society of Biblical Literature, 2006), 253–272.

THE SEPTUAGINT IN EARLY CHRISTIANITY
Book Production and the Old Testament Canon in the Church

Bagnall, R.S., *Reading Papyri, Writing Ancient History* (London: Routledge, 1995).

Barton, J., *The Spirit and the Letter: Studies in the Biblical Canon* (London: SPCK, 1997).

Gallagher, E.L., *Hebrew Scripture in Patristic Biblical Theory* (Leiden: Brill, 2012).

Grafton, A., and M.H. Williams, *Christianity and the Transformation of the Book: Origen, Eusebius, and the Library of Caesarea* (Cambridge, MA: Harvard University Press, 2006).

Holmes, M.W., "The Biblical Canon," in S.A. Harvey and D. Hunter (eds.), *The Oxford Handbook of Early Christian Studies* (Oxford: Oxford University Press, 2008).

Hurtado, L., *The Earliest Christian Artifacts: Manuscripts and Christian Origins* (Grand Rapids, MI: Eerdmans, 2006).

Hurtado, L., and C. Keith, "Book Writing and Production in the Hellenistic and Roman Era," in J.C. Paget and J. Schaper (eds.), *The New Cambridge: Cambridge University Press, History of the Bible: From Beginnings to 600* (Cambridge: Cambridge University Press, 2013).

Johnson, W.A., "The Ancient Book," in R.S. Bagnall (ed.), *The Oxford Handbook of Papyrology* (Oxford: Oxford University Press, 2009).

Leuven Database of Ancient Books, http://www.trismegistos.org/ldab/.

McDonald, L.M., *Formation of the Bible: The Story of the Church's Canon* (Peabody, MA: Hendrickson, 2012).

Key Figures

Attridge, H.W., and G. Hata (eds.), *Eusebius, Christianity, and Judaism* (Leiden: Brill, 1992).

Barnes, T.D., *Constantine and Eusebius* (Cambridge: Cambridge University Press, 1981).

Burgess, R.W., "The Dates and Editions of Eusebius' *Chronici canones and Historia ecclesiastica*," *Journal of Theological Studies* 48 (1997): 471–504.

Cain, A., *The Letters of Jerome: Asceticism, Biblical Exegesis, and the Construction of Christian Authority in Late Antiquity* (Oxford: Oxford University Press, 2010).

Cain, A., and J. Lössl (eds.), *Jerome of Stridon: His Life, Writings and Legacy* (Farnham, UK: Ashgate, 2009).

Cameron, A., and S.G. Hall (eds.), *Eusebius: Life of Constantine* (Oxford: Oxford University Press, 1999).

Crouzel, H., *Origène* (Paris: Lethielleux, 1985). (English translation: Crouzel, *Origen*, trans. A.S. Worrall (Edinburgh: T&T Clark, 1989.)

De Lange, N.R.M., *Origen and the Jews* (Cambridge: Cambridge University Press, 1976).

Edwards, M.J., *Origen against Plato* (Aldershot, UK: Ashgate, 2002).

Grant, R.M., *Eusebius as Church Historian* (Oxford: Oxford University Press, 1980).

Graves, M., *Jerome's Hebrew Philology: A Study Based on His Commentary on Jeremiah* (Leiden: Brill, 2007).

Graves, M., *Jerome: Commentary on Jeremiah* (Downers Grove, IL: IVP, 2012).

Hanson, R.P.C., *Allegory and Event: A Study of the Sources and Significance of Origen's Interpretation of Scripture* (Louisville, KY: SCM, 2002).

Heine, R.E., *Origen: Scholarship in the Service of the Church* (Oxford: Oxford University Press, 2011).

Kamesar, A., *Jerome, Greek Scholarship and the Hebrew Bible: A Study of the Quaestiones Hebraicae in Genesim* (Oxford: Clarendon Press, 1993).

Kotzé, A., "Augustine, Jerome and the Septuagint," in J. Cook (ed.), *Septuagint and Reception: Essays Prepared for the Association for the Study of the Septuagint in South Africa* (Leiden: Brill, 2009), 245–260.

Law, T.M., "Origen's Parallel Bible: Textual Criticism, Apologetics, or Exegesis?" *Journal of Theological Studies* 59.1 (2008): 1–21.

Louth, A., "The Date of Eusebius' *Historia ecclesiastica*," *Journal of Theological Studies* 41 (1990): 111–123.

Martens, P.W., *Origen and Scripture: The Contours of the Exegetical Life* (Oxford: Oxford University Press, 2012).

Romeny, B. ter Haar, *A Syrian in Greek Dress: The Use of Greek, Hebrew, and Syriac Biblical Texts in Eusebius of Emesa's Commentary on Genesis* (Leuven: Peeters, 1997).

Salvesen, A., "A Convergence of the Ways? The Judaizing of Christian Scripture by Origen and Jerome," in A.H. Becker and A. Yoshiko Reed (eds.), *The Ways that Never Parted: Jews and Christians in Late Antiquity and the Early Middle Ages* (Tübingen: Mohr Siebeck, 2003), 233–258.

Trigg, J.W., *Origen* (London: Routledge, 1998).

Williams, M.H., *The Monk and the Book: Jerome and the Making of Christian Scholarship* (Chicago: University of Chicago Press, 2006).

Winn, R.E., *Eusebius of Emessa: Church and Theology in the Mid-Fourth Century* (Washington, DC: Catholic University of America Press, 2011).

White, C., *The Correspondence (394–419) between Jerome and Augustine of Hippo* (Lewiston: Edwin Mellen, 1990).

Bible and Liturgy

Bogaert, P.-M., "The Bible in Latin c. 600–c. 900," in R. Marsden and E.A. Matter (eds.), *The New Cambridge History of the Bible: From 600 to 1450* (Cambridge: Cambridge University Press, 2012), 69–92.

Caulley, T.S., and H. Lichtenberger (eds.), *Die Septuaginta und das frühe Christentum/ The Septuagint and Christian Origins* (Tübingen: Mohr Siebeck, 2011).

Ceulemans, R., "Greek Christian Access to 'The Three,' 250–600 CE," in T.M. Law and A. Salvesen (eds.), *Greek Scripture and the Rabbis* (Leuven: Peeters, 2012), 165–192.

de Wet, C.L., "The Reception of the Susanna Narrative (Dan. XIII; LXX) in Early Christianity," in J. Cook (ed.), *Septuagint and Reception: Essays Prepared for the Association for the Study of the Septuagint in South Africa* (Leiden: Brill, 2009), 229–244.

Horbury, W., "Old Testament Interpretation in the Writings of the Church Fathers," in M.J. Mulder (ed.), *Mikra: Text, Translation, Reading & Interpretation of the Hebrew Bible in Ancient Judaism & Early Christianity* (Peabody, MA: Hendrickson Publishers, 2004), 727–787.

Johnson, M.E., "The Apostolic Tradition," in G. Wainwright and K.B. Westerfield Tucker (eds.), *The Oxford History of Christian Worship* (Oxford: Oxford University Press, 2006), 32–75.

Kannengiesser, C., *Handbook of Patristic Exegesis: The Bible in Ancient Christianity* (Leiden: Brill, 2006).

Law, T.M., and A. Salvesen (eds.), *Greek Scripture and the Rabbis* (Leuven: Peeters, 2012).

Rouwhorst, G., "Continuity and Discontinuity between Jewish and Christian Liturgy," *Bijdragen* 54 (1993): 72–83.

Rouwhorst, G., "The Reception of the Jewish Sabbath in Early Christianity," in P. Post et al. (eds.), *Christian Feast and Festival* (Leuven: Peeters, 2001), 223–266.

Rouwhorst, G., "The Reading of Scripture in Early Christian Liturgy," in L.V. Rutgers (ed.), *What Athens Has to Do with Jerusalem* (Leuven: Peeters, 2002), 305–331.

Schulz-Flügel, E., "The Latin Old Testament Tradition," in M. Sæbo (ed.), *Hebrew Bible/Old Testament: The History of Its Interpretation* I.1 (Göttingen: Vandenhoeck & Ruprecht, 1996), 642–662.

Taft, R.F., "The Interpolation of the Sanctus into the Anaphora: When and Where? A Review of the Dossier," *Orientalia Christiana Periodica* 57 (1991): 281–308; 58 (1992) 83–121.

Index

Index